JUSTVIRTUAL.COM

Author

Dan Hawes

Illustrator

Christian Nelson

Editor

Madeline J. Renshaw

External Reviewers

Jim Anderson
Dr. Ali Arya
John Boquist
Regis Brown
Chris Hawes
Doris Litke
Nathalie Malette
Dr. Richard Smith

To Sky,

Once my precious baby girl, you're blossoming into a spectacular Aerospace Engineer with the audacity to envisage galaxies as your playground.

You constantly inspire me to reach beyond.

I love you more than the entire Universe, including Jupiter.

Acknowledgments

There are many people that made this book possible. Firstly, to my Toonrush colleagues and co-workers who share my vision of creating disruptive technology solutions that will take education and commerce to the next level. Edin Ibric, thanks for your amazing designs, great ideas, and passion for excellence. Jonathan Jackson, I can't believe how proficient you are with new technology and how committed you are to the user experience. Madeline Renshaw, you brilliantly and fearlessly edited each draft with a commitment to making it so much better. Alf Marcelissen, you're incredible; no problem is beyond your grasp. Christian Nelson, so creative; you bring ideas to life visually like no other. Barb Tudino and Hayley Anderson, thanks for being so persistent and taking care of the details and the finances that keep us moving. To the rest of the Toonrush team who are so committed to creating positive user experiences (Barry, Michelle, Sara, Amin, Adam, Michael, Leanne, Doug, Nancy, Shelby, Jay, and Sophie).

Dr. Richard Smith (SFU), a key technology advisor, reviewer, and friend. Your insights are always prescient. Regis Brown, Entertainment mogul, thanks for the great feedback. Doris Litke, our first external editorial reviewer, thank you for such great insight and feedback. To George Fowlie, a trusted advisor and Michael Atkins, a mentor and personal inspiration.

Thank you to all those who took the time to don a VR headset regularly and helped us improve our VR software. John Boquist, Alf Marcelissen, Leanne Benner, Grant Colby, Karl Bermel, Sandra Sukstorf, Doug Sinclair, Sophie Cortez, Jim, Kate, and Kiera Woodside, Richard Smith, Christian Nelson, Blaede Court-Suzuki, Cheryl Hawes, Gabriela Hawes, Sharon Hawes, Chris Hawes, Cristin Tierney, Justin Pelley. Further to John Boquist,

Rohan MacLean, Kevin Waldbillig, and Dave Lowenstein whose idiosyncrasies inspired some of our fictional characteristics.

Don Gray, Givex CEO, mentor and technology visionary, Debra Demeza, and all of my wonderfully talented colleagues at Givex Corp, a global financial IT company committed to using AI and advanced technology to transform the customer experience and the digital transaction marketplace. You are innovators. Thanks for the opportunity to work on such inspiring projects.

To Carleton University, Faculty of Engineering and Design, School of Information Technology, global leaders in the immersive VR research space. Their team of researchers have been exploring this technology domain for many years, long before it became popular. They are technologists and teachers who truly care about teaching innovation and the student experience. Thank you to all the wonderful professors and colleagues that contributed to my doctoral journey and informed our VR research, much of which is referenced in this book. Thanks to Dr. Rob Teather, Dr. Jim Davies, Dr. Karen Collins, Dr. Derek Reilly, Dr. Audrey Girouard, Dr. Rob Biddle, Dr. Ashraf Matrawy, Dr. Omair Shafiq, Dr. Omar Bani-Taha, and Dr. Gerry Chan.

In particular, Dr. Ali Arya whose vision and passion for teaching innovation with VR will transform the learning experience for students and teachers. Designing learning technology to make people better; there is no more venerable a goal. I am proud to be part of this team.

To my partner, Nathalie Malette who has been with me the whole way and is a bedrock of support and love. She is always a source of great ideas and editing. To my siblings who are always incredibly supportive and helpful, Sandra, Cheryl, Sharon,

Chris, and Jeff. To Grace and Max. And to my daughter, Sky. You are always my inspiration!

Preface

This book is targeted at professionals, students, and curious people who want to learn about virtual reality (VR) and the Metaverse in a fun and memorable way. Whether you are starting a business, considering an investment, or preparing your company for the next big technology wave, this book will demystify these concepts and help answer three critical questions.

- What is the Metaverse?
- What are the technologies that make it all work?
- What are the disruptive innovation opportunities?

Designed as a story-based teaching tool, the reading or listening experience will help you understand VR and the Metaverse in the context of a real-world, albeit fictional, scenario. So why do we mix these technology concepts within a story framework? Because creating a story context makes learning more enjoyable and memorable. According to eminent psychologist Jerome Bruner, stories help us retain twenty two times more facts than those acquired without story context. As such, it is my hope that you will gain a contextual understanding of these ideas in a way that is more relevant and relatable to your situation.

The book is academically referenced but to make the story more readable, we have moved the references to the end of the book, sorted by page number. There is also a glossary of acronyms and a glossary of terms included to make technical concepts more accessible.

Finally, VR and the Metaverse are technologies that most people should try to understand as they will impact all of us significantly in the years to come. Unfortunately, the media frenzy of the early 2020s constantly confused and complicated these critical concepts and they are often presented with such aplomb by people who have little experience with the technology. Hopefully, this book can serve as an antidote to this confusion and simplify your understanding so that you can be informed and join the conversation. I hope you enjoy this experience.

Sincerely, Dan

Contents

CHAPTER ONE

Here are the Winners

As she walked to the center of the stage to announce the winner of the Billion Dollar Metaverse Challenge, all eyes were on her. She walked with poise and a confidence that could only be granted through years of adversity, both sought and conquered.

Naomi Grace was a serious badass. As an Asian immigrant who could not speak a word of English when she arrived here at ten years old, what she had accomplished was impressive. She did not come from money; in fact, her parents struggled just to keep her in school. She had to work for everything she had achieved. From fast food restaurant service to cosmetics retail to book-keeping for a local gaming establishment, Naomi had done it all. Her relentless work ethic and keen mind guided her to increasingly larger challenges. While her post-secondary education was primarily focused on math and data science, she also had a keen affinity for money and rose from a junior fund coordinator to the lead money manager for a trillion-dollar high-tech innovation fund in less than a decade. And now, she had just set the world on fire.

As she addressed the crowd, all went silent.

"Friends, entrepreneurs, and incredibly excited media colleagues, this is the moment that we've all been waiting for. Six months ago, we announced the Billion Dollar Metaverse Challenge. We've been convinced for some time that the world of Virtual Reality and the Metaverse is on the brink of revolution, a disruption so fundamental that it could change the nature of how we educate, entertain, and do business.

"As you know, the Just Virtual Innovation Fund (**JVIF**) does not focus on bricks and mortar. We focus exclusively on disruptive virtual enterprises. As such, we are offering one billion dollars of funding over a five-year period for the top three new metaverse businesses: five hundred million dollars for first place, three hundred million for second place, and two hundred million for third place. We identified five categories that we feel have the potential to change the world: Education, Entertainment, Commerce, Environment, and Social/Community Building. We've been asked, why such a significant prize? The answer: we're looking for big thinkers and partners who think on a global scale and are committed to that journey.

"Truthfully, we did not expect the response that we received. The media coverage has been unexpectedly magnificent, and the quality of applications spectacular. In fact, more than six hundred and ninety thousand submissions were received and assessed by a panel of judges and a specialized Artificial Intelligence (AI) application software."

Ahh's of incredulity rose from the crowd, then subsided. When she first announced the JV challenge, news of the contest spread like wildfire as entrepreneurs, students, developers, and investors from all over the world joined the challenge, arguably the most exciting thing that had happened to the business sector in decades. They were there to compete for the grand prize but also to showcase their ideas. The media frenzy was Super Bowl-like with several networks dedicating twenty-four-seven channel coverage for the final weeks. The competition had been fierce but now it was all over. Thousands gathered in the ballroom, while hundreds of millions watched on TV, the Internet, or the Metaverse. The anticipation was palpable. Naomi continued.

"From those submissions, we selected one hundred participants for the next round, and after an intense round of questions, reduced further to the ten finalist teams."

A round of applause. The next five minutes would make mega-millionaires of some, while others would be sent back to square one, so close but with nothing to show.

"And here are the winners."

The room grew silent.

CHAPTER TWO

The Hurting and the Sharing

Only six months ago, I was unemployed, looking for any gig, and wondering if I could even survive. Unlike my big business and government friends, I had chosen the path of an independent creative producer. No pension, no security, just the right to create and be passionate about what you do every day. And while I had no regrets, at a certain point, passion doesn't pay the bills.

I loved games, animation, movies, and TV. I also enjoyed being part of the creative process. I'd studied computers and technology in school to complement my creative drive and even had some success in the early days. I thought I'd done everything right. But then the world changed; it seemed like the grounds were constantly shifting, and every good idea I ever had, fell just short. Sometimes life just doesn't turn out as we plan. As it turned out, I wasn't the only one.

Jon Isaacson was one of the gang but always his own person. He was a free spirit, a gifted artist, a nature explorer, and loved to be alone. He had the disposition and thoughtfulness of Henry David Thoreau, a similarly motivated artist, writer, and naturalist but with a heap of visual artistic talent on top. He was loved by all, which made his gruesome death particularly hard to take. He had just moved to the Yukon territory to paint and get closer to nature. In an ironic twist, Jon got much closer to nature than even he'd hoped as he was brutally mauled and consumed by one of the hungrier polar bears in the area. That was it. It was over.

The Super Six (now the Fab Five) were getting together to mourn and console each other on Jon's recent passing. We were all best friends in university, where we partied and studied and then partied some more, but we hadn't spent any meaningful time together in almost twenty years.

I was ambivalent about the meet-up. On the one hand, I missed my old friends and was incredibly excited about spending time. On the other hand, I was embarrassed as life wasn't nearly as glorious as my Facebook posts might have suggested. In fact, after a failed marriage and a financial settlement that took all but the kitchen sink, I was on the verge of desperation. But as it turned out, the rest of the Fab Five had challenges of their own.

We agreed to meet at a local pub restaurant a few blocks from the university. The menu was "pubby," ranging from steak and shepherd's pie to cheeseburgers, with several salad bowls and even gluten-free options for the most conscientious eaters. Mostly though, this place was about the beer. They had the widest selection of craft beers of any restaurant in the city, and I had a sense that we'd be consuming our fair share that evening.

I got to the restaurant early to make sure we could secure enough seats and a good position within the pub. As I arrived at the restaurant, I noticed that Jag was already there and seated at a table. As I walked over to meet him, we exchanged a hearty "handsome man hug" made popular by SNL in the late 1990s. It involved holding one hand in a handshake position and wrapping the other around the back, all while looking incredibly handsome. We both performed it flawlessly.

Jag Babar was perhaps my closest friend, and we had maintained contact over the years. On the surface, he was a success. Jag was a financial wiz and stock trader with prescient insights on business and investments, but he'd just been laid off by a ruthless bank that felt that AI algorithms could replace his insights. What was more, he couldn't keep a date. Jag was particularly enamored with a beautiful young lady who now wouldn't return his calls. As it turned out, his "all hockey, all the time" lifestyle was not going over big with the dating community. Nonetheless, as a rabid Montreal Canadiens hockey fan who rarely missed a game on TV, he seemed to get along okay.

As we settled and ordered our first beer, the rest of the group slowly filtered in. First Dania, then RoMac, and finally, fabulous Frances Johnson. The whole gang was here now, except, of course, Jon Isaacson, our recently deceased friend. He would weigh heavy on us that evening as we recounted several classic stories about his fun-loving nature and silly party antics.

As the night progressed and one beer became two, then three, our inhibitions dropped, and we started to share the real stories about what was happening to us. Perhaps because I had a head start with the beer, I suddenly felt compelled to share my challenges, and how life really had not shaped up as I had expected. I talked about my failed marriage, my fledgling career, financial duress, and my complete lack of self-confidence and direction. The masks were off, and it felt good to admit it. It was cathartic and emotional, but I felt safe for the first time in many years. The caring and love shared within the group was unconditional.

Dania, inspired by my honesty and after downing a fourth beer of pure liquid courage, started to share her stories and misadventures. Dania Loeven was a real character and was usually at the center of any controversies or conflicts that seemed to arise in our younger, wilder times. Her original last name was McLoeven, but she quickly tired of the constant references to the Superbad movie character, hence the rename. Ironically, she was super badass. She was very attractive and knew how to flaunt it but did not suffer fools well. She could sell a man his own shirt while he was still wearing it. After a short tenure as an actress, she moved through various businesses in sales and eventually ended up with a once-hot, new marijuana company.

The fact was, she hated her job, and her dating life allowed her to meet the soft underbelly of society. Dania was not happy, but she was still in a better state than RoMac. I think his situation was the worst of all.

As far back as I can remember, Rohan MacDuff was steady as she goes. He always wanted to be a teacher, and we all knew he would be great at it. He loved kids of all ages, and he was always explaining things and challenging us to think beyond our current norms. It was annoying at the time, but we understood it for what it was: his future. But RoMac, as we called him, had his own challenges. While he could spell pedagogy frontwards, backward, or sideways, he was perpetually "unlucky" at love, and his private school that espoused the merits of life-long learning had just gone bankrupt. But then his fortunes got even worse. He was recently diagnosed with Syncope Euphoria, a rare disease that caused him to faint whenever he got excited. Suffice it to say; it had serious consequences on his sex life.

One by one, we went around the table and toasted heartily after each story. RoMac and Jag shared their stories next. The dinner was shaping up to be more of a group therapy session but with copious alcohol consumption. I wasn't sure how we would feel tomorrow morning, but tonight, it felt great. For the first time in a long time, I didn't feel lonely.

The last, but definitely not the least of the Fab Five, was Frances Johnson. Frances always had her shit together. She was smart, funny, and a brilliant programmer. She was also an activist for racial equality because she wasn't busy enough. She could disassemble a computer, reprogram the EPROM, and have it back together before you could say, "What's an EPROM?" By the way, EPROM stands for Erasable Programmable Read Only Memory. Frances had worked with all the hot new tech ventures over the past two decades in capacities ranging from database analyst, C++, and Python programmer, and most recently, AI architect. While her career was on fire, her marriage was not, or you might argue that it was, but in burning down the house kind of way. We all remembered her boyfriend Jimbo from school. He was a super nice guy, and you couldn't help but like him. They seemed like a match made in heaven, and after a wedding for the ages, what could possibly have gone wrong? As it turned out, Jimbo was even nicer to the ladies at work and maintained regular carnal relationships with not one but several. So, with three children, and a full slate at work, Frances kicked his sorry ass out the door. You go, girl! And he went!

As the night wore on, we realized that we had not ordered food yet. No wonder we were so "open and sharing." Prompted by our waiter, Wally Billings, we scoured the menus looking for nutrients to absorb all this alcohol.

As we ate our meals, the drinks of choice changed from beer to coffee or tea, and the tone of the conversation sounded less like an empathy party and more like a brainstorming session.

Dania, always the one to call it out, posited, "So, what's next? We're sitting here lamenting about how horrible our lives have become, but what are we doing about it?"

"Well, what can we do about it?" quipped RoMac. "It is what it is."

"Is it? While our 'come to Jesus' today was fantastic, if we do nothing to change our situations, we're just sadasses. We might as well just find our own polar bear nemeses and join Jon, wherever the hell he is." She caught herself. "God love ya, Jon. Wherever you are."

We all toasted, "To Jon!"

As uncomfortable as it felt to hear this, it did make sense. Dania always made sense and said out loud what most people were thinking.

She continued, "What we need to think about is

how to get from sadass to badass. We should do something together. Join a club, take a course, become a sommelier. Or what about starting a business together? Look at all the talent we have here. Frances, you're one of the smartest people I know, and you're as close to a human AI as it gets. Jag, you're a finance wiz, and you've done everything anyone can do in finance. And Joe?"

That was me. Joe Colby occasionally called JC, but after being teased about my initials representing a more prominent deity, I shut that down. "What about me?" I asked.

"You're super creative, and you know everything about technology. You have your head in the clouds half the time, but if you ever got your shit together, it would be scary," she said, "And RoMac, you are an amazing teacher. You understand all that stuff about what makes us smarter and how to motivate people to be better. That's a rare skill.

"And look at me. I'm just a blowhard, but I'll tell you this. I can sell. I can sell anything, and after hearing our stories tonight, my first job is to sell us on yourselves."

I had to admit; it was working. Less than two hours ago, I was feeling apathetic and completely unmotivated, but now I was starting to feel my energy slowly starting to build. Maybe an ass-kicking was what we needed.

"So, what do you suggest?" asked Frances.

"We need something! A challenge. Something big to work together on, an opportunity to make a difference," said Dania. We all agreed.

At that moment, Wally Billings, the waiter, walked by and politely cut in.

"I couldn't help but overhear what you were talking about. You want to do something big, different, and meaningful, right?"

Yes, we all agreed. By this time, Dania had us convinced that if we didn't do something, we'd be wasting our lives away.

"What did you have in mind?" I asked.

"It may be just a coincidence, but there's this venture capital contest that just came across the tech and finance news today that seemed interesting. It's all over TNN. It's called 'The Billion Dollar Metaverse Challenge.' They are investing a billion dollars in funding the three winning teams."

As Wally continued to recount the details, it was becoming increasingly apparent that this could be the opportunity that Dania was talking about.

CHAPTER THREE

The Reluctant Heroes

Most of us had heard about the Metaverse. It was all the rage, the new buzzword for the next layer of the Internet. We'd all been through the Internet revolution, dubbed at the time the "information superhighway," so we were somewhat skeptical of these media monikers. And while the media was enamored with this "next big thing," and there were lots of strong opinions, most had never even donned a virtual reality (VR) headset.

I knew a bit more than most, as I'd already been involved with projects that used virtual reality technology, and I was certain that Frances had also worked on web-based implementations, but everything seemed very speculative at this stage.

But a billion dollars? Crazy! Someone knew something because that was serious coin.

Dania spoke up, "I don't know a ton about the Metaverse, but I think between us, this would be a great project to work on together. It might be just what we need. And what the hell do we have to lose?"

"Seriously?" asked RoMac, "We have tons to lose. A contest like this will be all-consuming of both time and money for the next six months. I have commitments and bills to pay. Who's going to pay my son's college tuition or for my daughter's braces? How do you propose we manage that?"

"He's right," said Jag, "this contest will be all over every news channel and tech website on the planet by tomorrow. Who knows how many people will be competing? Millions, probably; it's like entering a lottery with odds that are stacked against you beyond just the numbers. Most of these contestants will be younger, smarter, better educated, and with fewer bills to pay. It is a bit of a fool's errand if you ask me."

Dania looked down in discouragement. Always the optimist, she just had the air seriously let out of her balloon, but RoMac and Jag were right. Something like this might be too much to take on and probably didn't make sense. On the other hand, Dania made a good point; we did need "something," and we weren't total losers.

I thought for a moment.

"RoMac, Jag, you may be right. Given the size of the investment prize and the crazy competition that is imminent, it would be a huge sacrifice and a very, very long shot. And, yes, the younger, brighter, and more educated teams would put us at a disadvantage. By that same measure, however, our collective experiences may serve as an advantage for us, arguably offsetting the advantages of youth." The group remained sullen and unaffected as I worked towards my point.

"We also have an additional advantage that may not be that obvious. We need this badly, or something like this. Let's be honest. As we spoke tonight, not one of us felt that we were on the right path, nor had things worked out remotely close to how we had dreamed our lives would be. And maybe that's life, and we should just settle. Or maybe not. Personally, it feels like everything I've ever done was logical and made sense. And look where that has gotten me."

"Ditto," smiled Frances, "I have three kids and no time for anything, but something about this feels right."

Okay, I thought, then shared, "What if we took some time to find out a bit more about this? Call it an exploratory stage or a fact-finding mission. That'll give us all a bit more time to digest the idea and get a better sense of what is possible."

Even though Jag and RoMac remained reluctant, we all agreed to this baby step.

"But where do we start?" asked Jag, "Don't we need an expert to help us understand this technology?"

"You're right," said Wally, as he cleaned up the glasses and plates from the table, "and I know just the guy. His name is Elias, and he's a VR and Innovation Professor from the local university. In fact, I'm a graduate student, and I'm working for him right now. If you want to know anything about VR, the Metaverse, or business innovation, he's your man."

"Cool, can we meet this, Elias?" I asked.

"Absolutely," said Wally, "He works at the Faculty of Engineering and Design, and he's only about six blocks from here. I'll set up a meeting for you guys next Tuesday afternoon if you'd like. He's always around on Tuesdays."

"Thanks, Wally. That would be great," I responded as we nodded our acceptance.

I knew there was a lot more to Wally when we first met him. It almost seemed like he was acting out a role in a game as some sort of beacon or guide. This whole contest thing seemed a bit "convenient," but I've heard sometimes that's how the universe worked. When the student is ready, the master will appear. Or something like that. In this case, it was a student(s), plural. In any case, it would be a fun learning experience. Wally got a big tip that evening.

As we left the restaurant, even though RoMac and Jag were still on the fence, we all agreed to take next Tuesday afternoon off and meet at the coffee shop next to the university about an hour before the meeting with Elias. After saying goodbye with the requisite kisses and handsome man hugs, I felt something different; a strong sense that something was about to change.

Knowing we had about five days before the meeting, I dug into my research. Using Google Scholar, ChatGPT, and a few other recently popularized AI tools, I explored every bit of current research about Virtual Reality, the Metaverse, and how it might be applied. Suffice it to say; I was still confused. I also researched what I could find about Elias. He was an interesting guy.

Firstly, he was mononymous (one name), like Madonna, Cher, or Drake, which suggested something eclectic and independent in his thought process. A definite polymath, he was an engineer, dancer, artist, and a nationally ranked ping pong player. What was more, as we would soon learn, he was incredibly people-skilled and one of the finest teachers we'd ever met. In fact, if we were going to have an expert to mentor us through this contest, I could not have imagined a better person.

We met at 1 pm at the coffee shop to prepare our questions for the 2 pm meeting with Elias. Jag and RoMac seemed a bit more open to the idea than they were the previous week and were now willing to commit time to learn more. While we were excited about meeting this guy, a sense of urgency was building, and the clock was also ticking on the contest where the media coverage had reached a frenzied state.

No doubt Elias would be aware of the contest and what was at stake. After a forty-minute team discussion, we had a million questions. We agreed, though, to focus on the basics to first understand what we could about virtual reality and the Metaverse. We would need to truly understand what the Metaverse was and why it was such a big deal. Building on the basics, we would also need to gain an understanding of how it all worked and the technologies that were used to create such a compelling experience.

While this approach seemed logical, there was a great deal of information and understanding that had to be assimilated and reflected upon within a group context. It occurred to me that we would need a framework or paradigm to gather and make sense of this complexity. As we would eventually discover, Elias understood this need far better than we did.

CHAPTER FOUR

Meeting the Mentor

We finished our coffee, sufficiently javanated, and made our way over to the university to meet Elias. His office was humble and nondescript, with a few pieces of art and a pile of books.

Noticing that the full team was in attendance, he suggested we move into the boardroom to give us some extra space.

We recounted our back story and how we ended up here. We told Elias about our friend Jon Isaacson, his untimely and brutal death, and how our renewed sense of our own mortalities was a powerful force of motivation. We also told him how Wally Billings had overheard our conversation at the local restaurant suggesting that his advisor, Elias, was the VR, Metaverse, and innovation guru that could help us with our quest in the Billion Dollar Metaverse Challenge. We also disclosed our reluctance and concern about getting in over our heads and wasting everybody's time and money.

Elias smiled.

"Wally is way too kind, and the challenge sounds exciting. But yes, I do think a contest like this will be an all-consuming endeavor. Only you can decide whether it is worth your time and mental energy, so I'm sorry I can't help you with that decision.

"I do have some experience within the domain of VR and the Metaverse. You should know, however, that opinions are quite divided on this subject. While academia can be a fertile ground for spirited debate, the real marketplace outside our doors is also still figuring things out.

"Now, I do have one problem. There has been a great deal of excitement about this metaverse challenge, as you know, and three student groups from this university have already contacted me asking for training and support."

I could feel my heart sink. This was too good to be true. Our chances had just dropped considerably. We needed this knowledge and insight, and this guy was the Buddha.

I think he sensed our initial disappointment, so he persisted.

"In fairness to my students, I must remain neutral, but here is what I've decided to do, and I'm hoping this will work for everyone. I will offer three classes over the next month to these teams from the university, and you can also attend. It is my understanding that you are alumni of this school. Is that correct?"

Yes, we nodded in unison, looking at each other

reassuringly and realizing that we'd just survived a key milestone. It would have been great to have Elias to ourselves, our very own Mr. Myagi, but this would help us learn what we needed to know, and it was fair. Also, while the other student groups would be competitors, perhaps a larger group could help us all learn more.

Elias continued.

"The first session will focus on your understanding of the basics. What is VR, and what is the Metaverse? Where did it come from, and where is it going? Once you understand the basics, you will also need to touch, feel, and fully experience the technology. I highly recommend you become equipped for this with a consumer VR headset so you can play and experiment on your own time, but we can also provide access for anyone to our VR lab equipment.

"The second class will be a deep dive into the technology. It will be intense, but there is a great deal of technology that is required to make these experiences happen, and many of these technologies are constantly changing, moving targets, you might say, that can affect the overall experience quite profoundly.

"We'll learn about stereoscopy (how the headset works), the computer network topology: how the information arrives at the headset, the software and servers that work together to create the experience, and the types of artificial intelligence and Internet of Things (IoT) devices that are often used to solve problems.

"The third class will focus on the business challenges and innovation opportunities in the emerging Metaverse. We'll look at my experience innovation questions and identify the types of applications that offer disruptive opportunities that you might want to consider for your competition. From what I understand, there are five categories, so we'll look at potential applications in each of these categories; Education, Entertainment, Commerce, Environment, and Social/Community Building."

This sounded amazing. He inspired such confidence. Within three weeks, we would have as good an understanding as anyone of the technology, applications, and business possibilities. The rest would be up to us.

After leaving the university, we stood outside the front doors to discuss the final verdict. Dania, Frances, and I were already committed, but Jag and RoMac had not yet given the full thumbs up.

"Well, guys," I said, "What's it going to be?" RoMac and Jag looked at each other and nodded.

"The more I thought about this, the more I felt that if we didn't at least try, we might regret this. So yeah, I'm in," said Jag. We all looked at RoMac.

"You guys are crazy; ya know that," he smiled, "But what the hell? I'm not sure how I'll get through this, but better to be part of team crazy than lose touch with you guys again. I must admit that I'm feeling excited about learning all this new stuff, and I can already see applications that could make education much better. Yeah, I'm in. Dammit!"

We closed with a group hug.

CHAPTER FIVE

Understanding Virtual Reality and Presence

When we arrived at the first session three days later, we were expecting to enter a modern classroom with all sorts of tech gadgetry. It was anything but that. Instead, the room was set up as more of an academic lobby with comfortable chairs dispersed all around the space, roughly ten feet apart. Elias motioned to several Meta Quest virtual reality headsets sitting on the table near the front. Many of the students were already seated and wearing their headsets.

"If you're going to learn about VR and the Metaverse, what better place to learn? Pick up a headset and grab a seat anywhere. We'll be starting in five minutes," Elias said.

This was a bit of a surprise, but it made total sense.

I'd played around with VR headsets a few years back with games like Arizona Sunshine, where I spent a few hours shooting zombies, but it was nothing like this. Those systems were tethered via cables and were awkward. They were connected to mega-expensive gaming PCs and equally expensive RTX graphics cards. This solution was mobile, slick, and easy to use.

We took our places and donned our virtual reality headsets. As I pressed the power button, after a few seconds of transition screen, I was placed in a gorgeously high-resolution virtual space. I think I had my "aha" moment as I looked around at an incredibly beautiful university campus located on the side of a rock cliff and next to a gorgeous lake with all sorts of trees and foliage. It was awe-inspiring. I held my hands up to see two controllers, presenting as my hands, responding to my hand movements that were also augmented with visual controls on the buttons.

The **B** Button toggled a large digital menu that looked like a gaming heads-up display (HUD). It presented me with an array of options, like seating, rooms, presentations, avatars, and chat. The **A** button, when held down, created a beam that could teleport the avatar to any destination within range of the beam. Very cool!

A thumb wheel allowed me to click left or right, changing my directional view incrementally by about twenty degrees, and a concave button that, when pressed, would bring up additional menu features or reorient me if I held it down for one cycle. Two additional trigger buttons on the back of the handset allowed me to "shoot" a selected item or select and move items or menus within the virtual space. After playing around for about five minutes, the interface felt comfortable and intuitive. I was ready, just in time for class.

As I lifted the headset slightly to see my group members dispersed in chairs around me, I could see they all appeared to be comfortable and ready to go as well.

I surveyed the virtual expanse, observing several avatars exploring, and getting familiar with their surroundings. Then I heard a voice in the virtual space. It was unmistakably Elias.

"Let's meet in the lecture hall," he said.

As I hit the B key, the menu appeared; I pointed at and hit the trigger for the "rooms" button, which brought up a dozen room options, including Cottages, Podcast Domes, Beaches, Breakout Spaces, Coffee Shops, and various lecture spaces. I hit the trigger on the lecture hall and, within seconds, was standing in one of the neatest lecture spaces I'd ever seen, with a large screen, a sunroof, pop culture posters, and the kind of seats you would see in an executive movie theatre.

I selected a seat and sat with my team, along with fifteen other students. There was Elias at the front, looking as Zen and "in the moment" as could be. He wore a beige T-shirt and faded jeans. His hair was cut short, but his mustache and goatee betrayed his intelligence and thoughtfulness. He looked like a high priest of something, which of course, he was.

As I brought up the menu, I hit the avatar button to realize that I was embodied in the default robot option. I liked robots but thought I'd like something a bit more personal. I scrolled through the various avatar options and chose an avatar that looked "sort of" like me, but not really. I'd say my avatar was aspirational. He was about twenty pounds lighter, with better hair and a much more youthful look. In fact, he was way better looking than I ever was, even in my prime. But, what the hell, this was my experience.

As I glanced around the classroom, I chuckled to myself. I was not the only one encumbered by my own narcissism. Except for the shepherd and goat avatars in the back of the room, this might have been the finest looking group of students I've ever seen. Metaverse one, humility zero.

Elias began.

"Virtual Reality. What is it?"

After a few feeble responses from the crowd, Elias took over.

"Virtual reality (VR) is a computer-generated simulation of a three-dimensional (3D) environment using various technologies to create a user experience that feels real. It's that simple. The goal of a virtual reality experience is to make it feel so real that your brain interprets the virtual reality as your current reality and will treat all environment cues as if they are real.

"For example, as you look around the room, it likely feels like a typical university lecture hall. As such, all the environmental stimuli should also create a response no different than how you would interpret this in real life. If this room is designed properly, your senses become familiar and comfortable with the environment, and the perceived virtual space 'goes away' as you become engaged in the learning discussion we are having now. But what happens to your senses if I present a new visual stimulus?" Elias conjures up a long hose and nozzle.

"What if I sprayed Jag with this hose? What would he do?"

"Nothing. It's not real," said Dania.

"Really? Let's see," said Elias. In one motion, he turned the hose directly on Jag, who quickly ducked to avoid the flow of water.

"Wow!" Jag chuckled nervously.

Elias continued, "The water obviously wasn't real, and consciously Jag was aware of this, but his subconscious mind was not.

"Anyone not afraid of snakes here?"

A burly avatar named Nate, sitting in the front row, proudly raised his hand to assert his fearlessness. Elias conjured and tossed a sixteen-foot boa constrictor snake toward his feet, causing Nate to dive out of the chair. We all laughed. Nate did too, but awkwardly, with a mix of embarrassment and, Holy Sh—, amazement.

"That, my friends, is called **Presence**," he continued, "Presence is the subjective feeling of 'being there.' It causes the user to suspend disbelief, believing they are in the real world and reacting to stimuli as if they were."

I am here.

"Why does our brain interpret reality in this way?" asked Dania, nicely outfitted in mid-seventeenth century regal attire, suitable for an afternoon stroll in Versailles gardens.

"We're not one hundred percent sure," Elias responded, "We do know it involves processing from multiple areas of the brain. For example, the parietal lobe, located near the top of our heads, helps us maintain a sense of spatial awareness relative to objects in the real or virtual world. The prefrontal cortex, located in the front of the brain, helps us manage attention and make critical decisions. The cingulate cortex, part of the limbic system located near the inner part of the brain, helps us to remember, navigate, and maintain self-awareness. Finally, another important region in the limbic system is the amygdala, an almond-sized structure that was responsible for managing the fight/flight response that told Nate to get away from the boa constrictor. So, while neuroscience is quite complex, the effects are quite predictable, and most of us would have responded in a similar manner. Sorry, Nate." Elias smiled.

"The other concept that is critical to understanding

VR is **Immersion.** Anyone?" Elias gestured.

RoMac raised his hand, and Elias nodded.

"Isn't immersion something about how deeply you are engrossed in the world, like when you get lost in a movie or a good book? You're immersed, right?"

"That would seem to make sense, would it not?" asked Elias rhetorically, "And immersion as a general concept refers to a subjective feeling, but in a different context, like how we define presence."

As Elias scanned the group, he noticed a lot of confused expressions. He continued.

"Confused? Understandably. Unfortunately, as is sometimes the case in academia, definitions are very specific and not necessarily sensitive to the real-world vernacular. Nonetheless, the scientific literature refers to Immersion as a non-subjective and quantifiable measure of technology fidelity.

"Specifically, immersion is the objective fidelity of sensory stimuli produced by a technology system. It is measurable and controllable, allowing different systems to be compared. Further, these quantifiable aspects of immersion relate to multiple modes of sensory perception, including visual, auditory, haptic, kinesthetic, vestibular, and even olfactory/gustatory, as you can see on the chart behind me." Elias motioned to the large screen.

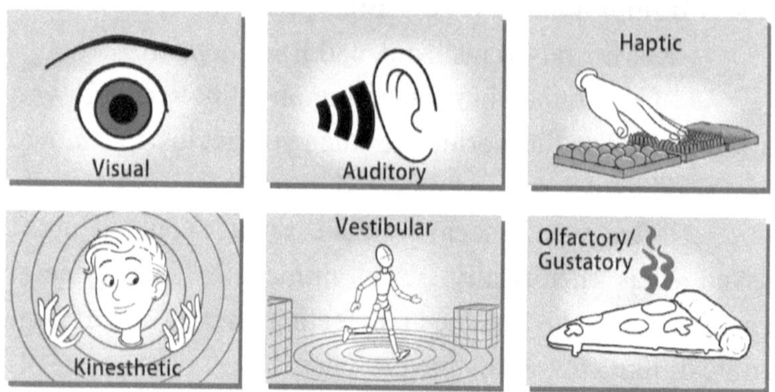

Multiple Modes of Sensory Perception

"For example, the **Field of View (FoV)** is a critical variable that defines the width of the visual field. It is how much of the world you can see without moving your head. The leading consumer VR headsets have an FoV ranging from eighty-nine to 106 degrees, whereas higher-end tethered (connected to a computer) headsets may have 120-to-130-degree FoVs allowing you to see more of the world at once. They are also far more expensive and a bit more cumbersome with PC cables and extra sensors compared to the four hundred dollar untethered (no cable) consumer VR units.

Example Fields of View (FoV)

"If the technology trends continue, high-end features will soon be available on mobile untethered consumer headsets. Even the features of the leading commercial untethered products would have been tens of thousands of dollars in academia less than a decade ago.

"**Frame rates**, or the number of times the screen refreshes per second, is also a critical metric that can seriously affect the user experience. Frame rates that are too low and not refreshed frequently enough can cause motion sickness. The human brain expects consistent visual information flow, but when the images are choppy or jumpy, it can cause disorientation, nausea, dizziness, or even eye strain. Low frame refresh rates can also cause visual artifacts, such as flickering, and can reduce feelings of presence. In general, most VR developers strive for frame refresh rates of at least sixty or more frames per second (fps) but, ideally, 120 fps if there is sufficient processing power available.

"**The resolution** or the number of pixels that make up the images displayed on the headsets is another factor that contributes to the visual experience. The granularity and sharpness of the images in the VR environment make the environments feel more or less real. Higher resolutions feel more realistic, whereas lower resolutions can appear cartoony and non-real. The latest Oculus Quest Pro (2023) offers a resolution of 2160 x 2160 pixels per eye.

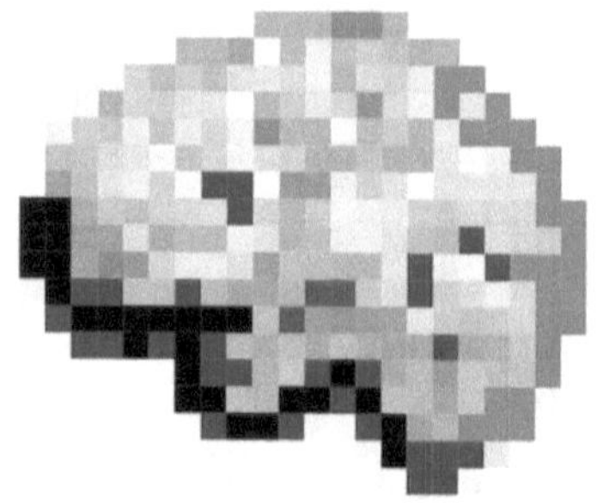
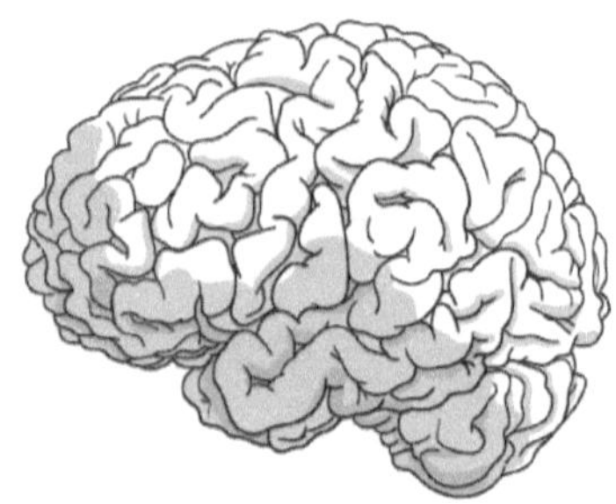

Low Resolution   **High Resolution**

Comparing Resolution of Images

"As you'll notice, on the screen above, the object on the right has much higher render quality so it is much easier to look at. Higher render quality may not always be a good thing. If you are processing or 'rendering' in real-time in a VR headset, too many triangles, higher resolution, or specialized lighting may simply not work or may take way too long to process, ruining the user experience and their sense of presence. Hence the designer must consider the capabilities and limitations of the computing environment that they are designing for."

"What about render quality?" I asked, "I hear a great deal about that, but not sure what it entails."

"Ahh, yes, render quality! Good question," responded Elias, "The render quality is the overall visual experience affected by the number of textures and geometric structures (triangles or polygons) and the lighting/shading techniques used to create the images that constitute the 3D virtual space."

"I know I learned this many years ago, but I forget. What is a polygon?" asked RoMac.

"A polygon is a two-dimensional (2D) shape with four sides," Elias answered, "It could take the form of a square, rectangle, or quadrilateral. And, of course, most of you remember that triangles are simply three-sided geometric structures. These 2D shapes connect to create the surface of the objects within a 3D space." He points to the screen.

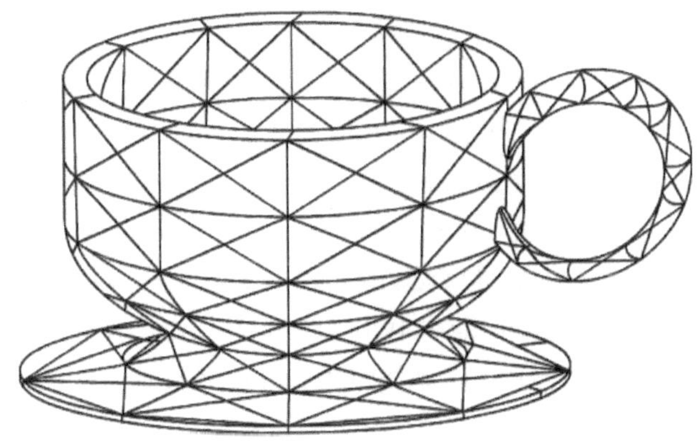

Surface of Cup with Triangles and Polygons

"Triangles and polygons are used in computer graphics and 3D modeling because they are shapes that computers can process easily. The computer's GPU combines these shapes to make images look detailed and realistic. The more triangles or polygons, the better the image quality.

"In VR and gaming, triangles are most commonly used because they are simple and flexible. Triangles are easy for the graphics processor to handle, but they can also form complex shapes. For 3D modeling, designers often prefer polygons or 'quads,' as they work better when a surface is divided. The use of quads affords modelers more control of the fine texturing and lighting outcomes. During rendering, these quads are then turned back into triangles, a process known as triangulation.

"Now, resolution, frame rates, and FoV are critical aspects of the overall experience, but the speed with which images are presented is equally important.

"**Latency** is the time it takes for a user's actions to show up in a virtual environment. It's important for immersion and feeling present. Latency over twenty milliseconds (ms) is noticeable, and over forty ms can cause discomfort or motion sickness. There are two types of latency: Motion to photon latency is the delay in showing physical movements (like head or hand), whereas input latency is the delay in input devices affecting the virtual environment. For example, if pressing a button takes two seconds to respond, it can be very frustrating. Good VR systems aim to keep both types of latency below ten ms."

I was amazed to discover that our senses are highly sensitive to timing. Most visual processing under fifty ms is considered subconscious, which is the range for VR image processing. At 120 frames per second, an image appears every eight to nine ms. Our subconscious mind is like a supercomputer, processing information we're not aware of, shaping our experiences. It's incredible that we're not consciously aware of such influential factors.

As Elias continued, I returned from imagination

mode.

"Okay, we could talk all day about the wonders of our visual processing, but we also need to consider how auditory sensations affect us.

"The **quality of the sound** contributes significantly to the overall user experience.

"Spatial audio refers to an immersive sound experience where audio is localized and perceived as coming from a specific direction. For example, if I can identify where you are in the space with sound, and it corresponds visually, it will contribute to a more authentic experience and increase the feeling of presence."

Modes of Audio Sensation

Elias then transported himself to the far-right corner of the room.

"Like when I'm over here, you can sense my location and the direction of my voice, or when I'm over here."

Elias then appeared in the bottom left corner of the room, then back to his central teaching position.

"There are many other variables that can affect the sound experience. For example, **frequency response** or the range of frequencies supported by the VR system and **dynamic range**, the difference between the loudest and softest sounds, both contribute to the perceived quality of sound that we hear in VR.

"**Interaural time and level differences** refer to the latency and level differences between the left and right ear. A properly designed spatial audio solution will minimize the latency or time difference between audio changes to the left or right ear and maintain consistency in sound levels between the left and right ears.

"This task of creating high-quality audio becomes significantly more manageable when working with pre-recorded content, as it allows sound designers to execute a thorough mix, as commonly heard in TV and film. Unfortunately, real-time VR experiences do not offer this luxury. Nonetheless, game platforms such as Unreal Engine and Unity offer robust spatial audio tools that alleviate much of the burden for VR experience designers.

"While visual and auditory sensory modes contribute most to the current VR experience, there are several other sensory modes that also affect the VR user experience. I'll do a high-level run-through of these other secondary yet important sensory modes.

"**Haptics** is a technology that provides a sense of touch feedback to the user. Typically, handheld controllers or wearable devices like gloves, vests, or even full-body suits provide physical stimulation. These devices can use electric currents to stimulate nerves or motors to resist movement, creating a sense of touch. The use of haptics can be very effective in creating higher feelings of presence where it is important to truly 'feel' the interaction and manipulation of objects.

"VR Haptic technology is used within many different applications commercially today. It is used in VR gaming to allow gamers to feel vibrations and other sensations as they interact with the virtual environment, enhancing their sense of presence in the game. Training and simulation scenarios, such as medical training, military training, and flight simulations, enable users to practice tasks and procedures with realistic tactile feedback, improving the effectiveness of the training. Designers can create virtual prototypes to simulate the tactile properties of objects and materials, enabling designers and engineers to test and evaluate their designs before physical prototyping. These are just a few of the current applications, but the possibilities are limitless."

"Speaking about limitless possibilities, what about using these suits and devices for virtual sex?" asked Dania, verbalizing, as always, what many of the students were already thinking.

Elias chuckled softly, acknowledging that he'd expected this question. He'd likely encountered it many times before while teaching this material.

"I have no doubt that these devices and many other similar devices are already being used by many people. In fact, from my understanding, it is a flourishing industry. I will leave the rest of the story to your imaginations as fortunately, or unfortunately, depending on your perspective, the contest does not include this domain."

The crowd laughed. Elias continued.

"Okay, Kinesthetics.

"Kinesthetics relates to our sense of body movement and position in 3D space. Motion trackers, accelerometers, gyroscopes, cameras, and other sensors in hands and headsets monitor our body positions. Full-body suits can provide more detailed data. This information is sent to the headset/computer in real-time to sync the physical and virtual bodies.

For low latency, data should be sampled at least a hundred times per second to reduce delays between our body and the VR visuals. Quick response and synchronization are crucial for presence. If your hands update their position even one-tenth of a second after the physical movement, it will reduce your sense of presence, become incredibly distracting, and may even contribute to cybersickness.

"Another potential source of cybersickness is the vestibular system. The vestibular system is a complex network of organs and nerves in the inner ear that contributes to our sense of balance and spatial orientation. Much like the computer sensors that provide kinesthetic feedback to the VR system, the vestibular system provides information to our brain about our position and movement in three-dimensional space. This helps us maintain our balance and stability.

"Related to both the vestibular system and kinesthetic systems is **Proprioception**, the sense that allows us to perceive the position, movement, and orientation of our body parts without relying on visual input. It enables us to have spatial awareness and control over our limbs, helping with balance, coordination, and motor skills. The kinesthetic system provides information about the position and movement of our limbs and joints, while the vestibular system contributes to our sense of balance and spatial orientation. Proprioception integrates inputs from these systems to give us a comprehensive perception of our body's position and movement in space.

"Finally, let's consider two final senses that are currently not deployed in any commercial context but are worth noting. Our **gustatory sense** (taste) and our **olfactory sense** (smell) could contribute significantly to feelings of presence and even memory recall in future VR systems but are currently not an option for current VR design consideration."

Elias pointed to the image on the large screen behind him.

"The first VR movie system (The Heilig Sensorama, 1956-62), far from a mobile experience, included stereo video and audio, tilt sensation, wind, and even scent. Unfortunately, virtual olfactory and gustatory sensation technology, like flying cars, failed to make the jump to our current technology landscape.

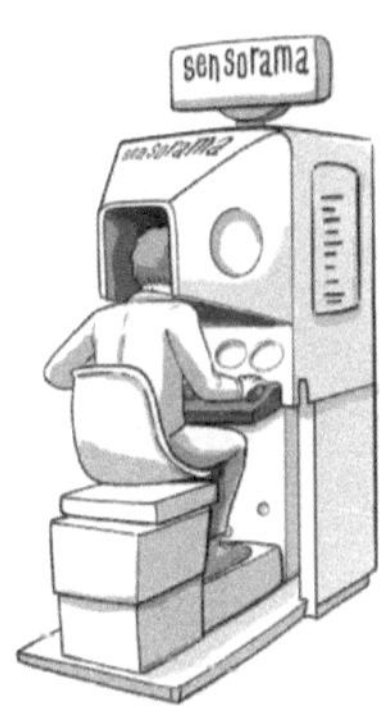

Concept Sketch of Heilig Sensorama

"Connecting odor dispensers that are triggered by entering specific environments, like the smell of fresh bread while entering a bakery or café, could greatly enhance the user experience and the authentic feeling of 'being there.' Similarly, using oral haptic technology that stimulates taste buds could prove viable at some future point. Today, however, both virtual senses remain novel and not viable with our current VR solutions."

Elias looked out at the group.

"So based on what we've learned, we can say that presence is directly affected by immersion, and the degree of immersion is determined by multiple sensory modalities. These modes of perception include visual, auditory, haptic, kinesthetic, vestibular, and someday perhaps, olfactory, and gustatory. And the overall immersive experience, the aggregate of all these elements, contributes to the feeling of presence."

"Now, while the empirical aspects of immersion provide a quantifiable, measurable set of variables to optimize, an equally significant qualitative component is the overall design of the VR user experience. Good design serves to amplify the sense of authenticity and suspension of disbelief, while poor design, even with highly immersive specifications, may diminish the sense of existence within a virtual environment."

VR User Experience (UX) Design

"Key among these elements is the design of the spatial environment, along with its inhabitants - both player characters and non-player characters (NPCs). The space needs to be effective and engaging, and the characters ought to be compelling and consistent with the reality the experience aims to portray. It is these intricacies of design that go a long way to engendering an authentic atmosphere and believable interactions within the virtual world.

"Further contributing to the design equation are the **embodiment** options granted to players. This empowers them not only to assume avatars that mirror their preferences but also to fine-tune these digital personas to their liking, thus enhancing the feeling of belongingness within the immersive virtual world.

"**Interactivity** is also critical, both in terms of degree and intuitiveness. Seamless interaction, thoughtfully woven into the VR experience can amplify the sense of authenticity and immersion.

"A **robust narrative arc** is a cornerstone of any storytelling experience, as it provides structure, purpose, and emotional resonance. In combination with social interaction, it strengthens the connective tissue between participants and the world they inhabit.

"**Environmental cues** serve as subtle anchors, grounding participants in the virtual world. These cues, by reflecting the logic and consistency of the real world, reduce cognitive dissonance and enhance feelings of presence.

"Equally critical is the deployment of **haptic feedback** from gloves, suits, or even controllers, enabling a tangible, tactile connection with the digital world. When well implemented, it blurs the line between the physical and the digital, intensifying the feeling of 'being there.'

"Lastly, investing in the design of **high-quality spatial audio** may elevate the overall immersive quality. By providing a more holistic, encompassing auditory environment, it can make the experience feel more real, complete, and immersive.

"So, by combining the critical elements of immersion with good design, we can elevate the overall experience and subjective feelings of presence. But are there other factors that might affect how present we feel within a virtual space? Does anyone know what other factors we may want to consider?"

"Don't we all have different sensory capabilities?" queried Jag. "For example, RoMac is a bit hard of hearing, whereas I can hear a pin drop two rooms away. So wouldn't we all be experiencing something different depending on how well our senses work?"

"Excellent point, Jag," Elias said, "Yes, absolutely. In fact, you might also argue that a VR system, like the real world, is inherently biased as we all experience the world in a unique way.

"So, while immersion within a technology system contributes significantly to the subjective feeling of presence, it also combines with people's baseline experiences, expectations, and the quality of their perceptual skills. This is what makes the feeling of presence a subjective experience.

"For example, if you are a seasoned art collector, you might look at a piece of digital art and consider it inauthentic and of poor quality, whereas a person with little or no art experience might be unaffected and consider the art and the overall experience awe-inspiring. Same virtual experience but different expectations, hence a different feeling of authenticity and presence."

"And if my sense of balance or hand-eye coordination was different, so also would my experience be, would it not?" asked Jag.

"Exactly," said Elias. "Imagine five variables.

D = Design – the quality of the many factors of UX design
I = Immersion – the measure of technology fidelity
C = Capability – the quality of our perceptual abilities
E = Experience – your past experiences and expectations
P = Presence – the subjective feeling of 'being there'

"So, we define presence in an equation where Presence equals Design plus Immersion plus Capability plus Experience. $P = D + I + C + E$. Any difference in D, I, C, or E will change the value of P."

Elias pointed to the projected image. "For those of you who like to play board games or visit Las Vegas, this pneumonic should be easy to remember. If you want to optimize the feeling of presence, it's simply a roll of the D-I-C-E and P = D+I+C+E."

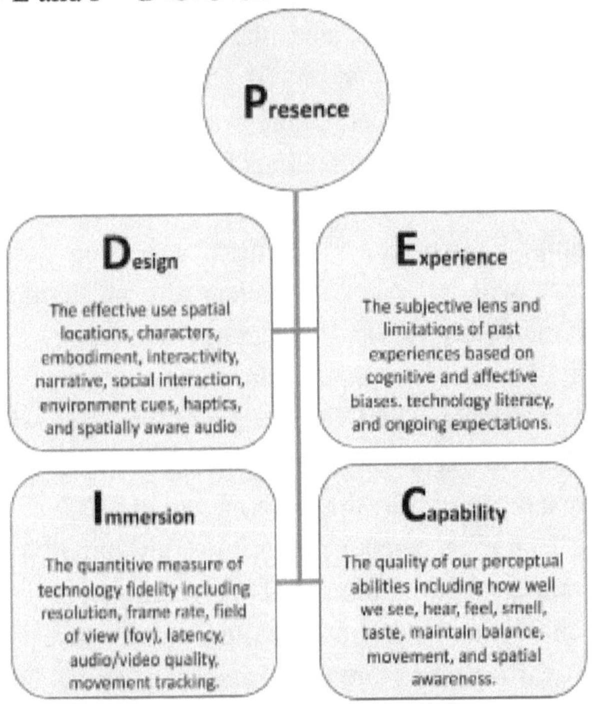

Presence = Design + Immersion + Capability + Experience

Elias looked around the room.

"Okay, unless anyone has any other questions, I suggest we take a break and come back in fifteen minutes, where we'll discuss the history of VR and just what makes it so special."

As we took off our headsets and looked around at each other, there was a collective sense of awe. Wow, we'd just experienced a VR classroom for the first time, and it was incredible. Why were we just learning about this now?

If attaining a feeling of presence and engagement was the intent of this training exercise, Elias had just scored a perfect ten out of ten with our five judges. This might have been the best ninety-minute lecture that I'd ever experienced.

We made our way to the coffee nook on the floor below, where we chatted and marveled at how simple the process was and how we could attend courses from our homes in our underwear. Then, we started to think more about all the possible applications for our contest.

"I can't help but think how this technology changes everything," said JB, "The next generation of retail commerce will be able to simulate almost anything and make it incredibly fun and engaging. Want to buy shoes or an outfit? No problem. Dress your avatar up based on your exact measurements and get a sense of what you will look like. What's more, with one of those haptic suits, you could even get a sense of how the clothing would fit."

"I know, the retail possibilities are mind-blowing," said Frances. "I'm thinking about refurnishing my new place, and I simply do not have the time to take my kids traipsing through furniture stores across the city to find what I want. And even then, I may not even like it once I see it at home. I'm very particular.

"Imagine, we could create software tools to allow people to create a simulated model of their house, then let the virtual AI retail agent, with the intelligence of a world-class interior designer, suggest how to furnish it based on their budget and design preferences. Within seconds, a customer could walk through their newly furnished home with all of the finishing touches, including art. Then the buyer could modify their selections or simply purchase. There would be a much greater selection as you would not be limited by physical space. That would work for me." Frances smiled proudly like she'd just solved a complex math problem.

I don't think I'd seen Frances this excited in a while. She was pretty lowkey, but now she was enthusiastically connecting the dots on what could be possible with the technology but also how it could help solve a problem that she'd been dealing with. Isn't that how most great things are invented? I thought. What is the expression? Necessity is the mother of invention. You have a problem or need, so you figure out how to solve it. It felt like this VR technology was like the new Lego but for grown-ups.

We mused further about how we could use the haptic suits to create environmental scenarios to allow people to feel what it would be like to live in a world of global warming or to swim and explore the oceans and reefs as if wearing scuba gear. Then we realized that our break time was almost up. After some gentle jabs at each other's avatars, we excitedly scurried back up the stairs for the next session.

CHAPTER SIX

What's the Big Deal about Virtual Reality?

When we arrived back in the classroom, we quickly re-donned our headsets, chose our seats, and were ready to go. Elias began but was immediately interrupted.

Suddenly, the screen flickered, and a mysterious figure appeared at the front of the classroom, wearing a skin-tight superhero suit and an obnoxious grin. He addressed the class.

The Disruptor

"Hello, mortals, I am the Disruptor, ruler of the virtual domain. I am here to ensure that you never come back here again. You thought your class would proceed without a hitch? You thought you'd learn in peace? Well, think again!"

With a snap of his fingers, the screen resolution on our digital menus was pixelated beyond recognition.

"Bid farewell to crystal-clear video and hello to glorious, vintage pixelation! Now, embrace the chaos of the lag leash as your interactions slow to a crawl! Muahaha!" he gleefully pronounced like an old-time comic supervillain.

And with that, everything appeared to be out of sync, like we'd lost hand-eye coordination and the world was moving in slow motion. The audio began to lag as well, causing all communication to stutter and slow. We could hardly hear what he was saying. Yet he continued to torment us.

With another wave of his hand, the lights started dimming, making it very hard to see.

All the while, Elias was shaking his head in disgust

but then appeared to leave.

The Disruptor continued, "And now, my pièce de résistance: Behold as your once-tidy theatre descends into disarray! How can you focus on your studies amidst such disorder?"

With that, the seats in the theatre rose to the ceiling and began flying around while the Disruptor cackled with glee, watching the chaos unfold before him, followed by yet another annoying Muahaha!

But then, a calming presence seemed to fill the virtual classroom. As the visibility improved, we could see a well-dressed lady in a dark suit and dark shades manifesting in the center of the stage. She exuded an aura of authority and control as she smiled reassuringly at the students before addressing them.

Ms. Presence

"Worry not, dear students. I am Ms. Presence; you can call me Ms. P. I have come to rid you of the dreadful Disruptor. His irritating ways have gone unchecked for far too long. Did you hear that Disruptor?" but the Disruptor appeared to be frozen, at least momentarily.

"With the power of my Illumination Invocation, I will now restore your ability to see clearly."

Ms. P took a deep breath and began to channel her powers. Suddenly, the lights on our control screens returned to their normal brightness. She waved her hand again, and the pixelated video fields were replaced with high-definition clarity.

"Your visual spaces and screens are crystal clear once more!"

Then she snapped her fingers, and the lagging audio instantly smoothed out, allowing for seamless communication between all of us. It felt like the pop when your ears cleared after a long flight.

Ms. P continued.

"Now, with my Tempo Tamer, I banish the lag that plagued your interactions. Timing will no longer be a problem in this virtual space."

Everything seemed to return to normal speed, and our hand-eye coordination appeared to be functioning once again. When I touched my screen, it responded.

Finally, she extended her arms, causing all the seats to return to their proper places, but then, the Disruptor suddenly appeared to come alive, enraged by the undoing of his mischief.

"How dare you undo my glorious chaos, Ms. P! You may have countered my antics for now, but I'll be back!" yelled the Disruptor.

"And so will I," Ms. P responded. "Disruptor, your reign of annoyance ends today. I will not allow your irritating ways to disturb the lives of these students any longer. No matter where you go or what you do, I will always be there to restore presence."

As the Disruptor attempted to launch another attack, Ms. P effortlessly deflected it with her powers, much to the Disruptor's frustration.

"This isn't the last you'll see of me, Ms. P!" said the Disruptor as he looked for a door to complete his dramatic exit but could find nothing. He just stood there frothing angrily. Ms. P had taken away all of his powers.

Then with a warm smile and a nod, Ms. P and the Disruptor faded from the room like the ending of a good play.

The message was clear. Low immersion was caused by bad visuals, poor audio, low latency, no interactivity, and general disarray. This served to reduce the feelings of presence and the overall experience.

In our brief discussion afterward, we all seemed to experience the event a bit differently. Frances could see alright but hear almost nothing at all, while Dania could still hear the audio. RoMac actually took off the headset to avoid fainting. He didn't deal well with these types of changing sensory experiences, no doubt due to his Syncope Euphoria affliction.

As we reflected, it became clear. Immersion, different capabilities, and previous experiences yielded unique subjective experiences and feelings of presence for all of us. Elias had just personified and dramatized the P = D + I + C + E (Presence = Design + Immersion + Capability + Experience) formula in such a memorable way. We would all likely remember these critical points forever.

As Elias returned to center stage, we all rose and gave him a standing ovation. He was off to a strong start.

He bowed politely.

"Now, where were we?" he asked.

"The History of Virtual Reality. Does anyone know when the first true virtual reality technology was conceived? Hint, the answer is NOT the Heilig Sensorama that we talked about earlier. The original technology far preceded this application."

Several avatar hands shot up and attempted to answer, but none of the answers were even close. Most had little or no historical perspective and associated the initial concept of VR with popular culture or the Hollywood perspective. The Matrix, Thirteenth Floor, Star Trek TNG, Total Recall, and a host of other movies or TV shows played with these concepts in their storytelling, but these were all long after even the original Sensorama and were all science fiction, at the time at least.

No one could identify the origin of the actual technology. As Elias triggered the next chart on the IMAX-like screen, we were in awe. The history of VR technology dates back to 1838 when Sir Charles Wheatstone created the stereoscope, the technology upon which all virtual reality is based. I remembered a little toy called the View-Master that was apparently introduced at the 1939 World's Fair and became a popular kids Christmas toy in the late 1970 and 80s. By the early 2010s, the view-master was usurped by a similar headset or cardboard structure with a space to place one's mobile phone.

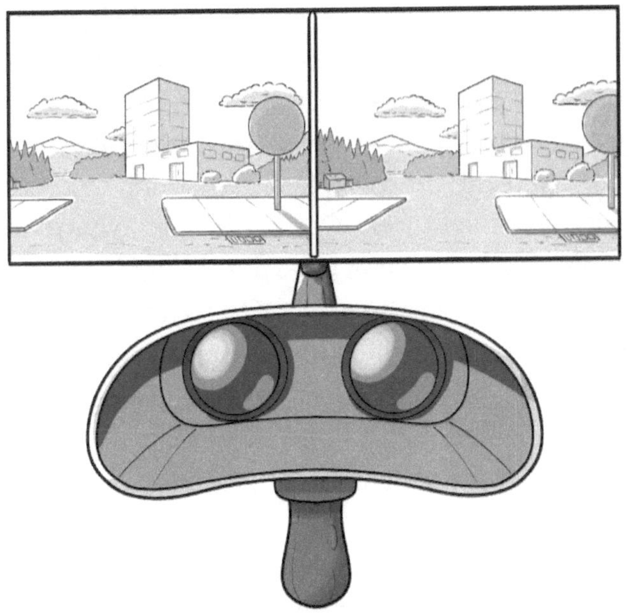

**The Stereoscopic View
invented by Sir Charles Wheatstone, 1838**

"Stereoscopy was based on a simple idea," said Elias, "The human brain can combine two slightly different images into a single 3D image. When we look at these images that are slightly offset through the stereoscope, they are combined into one 3D image that creates depth perception. Hence, we see a picture of this world in three dimensions.

"Wheatstone's original stereoscope consisted of two mirrors placed at a forty-five-degree angle with a small hole in the center. The user would then look through the hole with one eye, then the other, seeing slightly offset perspectives. The brain would then combine these images in a single 3D image, creating the illusion of 3D and depth perception. This was a pivotal invention and paved the way for future technologies like augmented and virtual reality.

"Stereoscopy uses the technique called parallax to create this illusion. The parallax is the relative difference in the apparent position of an object when viewed from two different positions. This is the same technology that our eyes use to determine depth perception. By seeing objects from different perspectives (left eye versus right eye), it allows our brain to see the world in three dimensions."

"In a VR headset, the parallax effect plays a critical role in creating a sense of depth and immersion. To achieve this, the headset displays slightly different images to each eye, mimicking the natural 'parallax' that occurs due to the separation between our eyes. VR headsets use motion tracking and precise rendering to continuously update the images presented to each eye, maintaining the parallax effect and adjusting it based on the user's movements and head position.

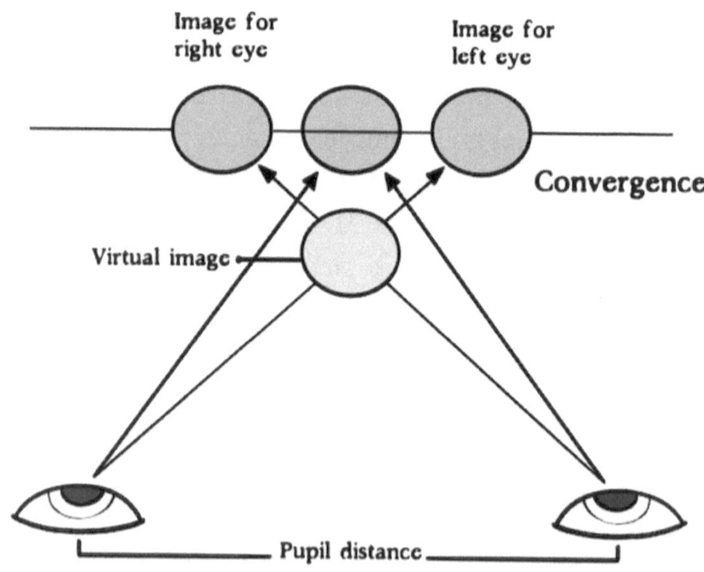

The Parallax Effect

One of the students, Shane, in the second row wearing a medieval jouster outfit, interjected.

"Does that mean that the Cyclops cannot see the world in 3D?"

"That's correct, Shane. The Cyclops would not see the world in 3D as we do. It is likely, however, that the Cyclops' brain would use other visual clues, like the relative size of objects, shadows, and even motion parallax, where objects in the foreground will appear to move more quickly than objects in the background to make sense of the world. So, fear not for the Cyclops."

VR and the Metaverse

"Before we delve into the metaverse idea, it will be important to fully understand the range of VR applications and the building blocks of the Metaverse.

"I'd like to clarify a few terms that are used in academia to define various degrees of virtual reality and elements within. Has anyone heard of the idea of augmented reality or AR?"

Elias surveyed the crowd and nodded to the skier avatar in the second row.

"That's when images are overlaid into the real world for a game like Pokémon Go, is it not?"

"Exactly," said Elias, "Many of you may have played these sorts of games where characters are superimposed or augmented in the real environment. Other examples of AR would be those Snapchat filters that overlay on your face or perhaps IKEA allowing you to view a potential furniture layout overlaid in your own space. Most often, your mobile phone is used to see these images, but AR glasses can also be used.

"In fact, both Microsoft and Apple have AR products that overlay virtual objects into real environments. The Microsoft HoloLens has been around since 2015 with various iterations. The HoloLens has been used for many applications, including training where students interact with and manipulate 3D objects, design and engineering tasks that allow designers to previsualize new products, medical applications where the glasses are used to assist in surgical procedures, and many other business processes.

"And, most recently, Apple has released their foray into the spatial computing market. The Apple Vision Pro glasses appear to be targeting similar applications.

"There are also many other companies, like Vuzix, Magic Leap, and Snap, that have released AR glasses. But none of these companies have managed to gain traction in the consumer marketplace, a critical milestone for any product hoping to survive and thrive. These companies have chosen to redefine the product category as 'spatial computing', a more progressive term that elucidates that idea of computation within virtual spaces.

"They will all be challenged with the inherent limitations of current AR technology. Some of the limitations include:

"**Hardware**: Current AR glasses/headsets can be bulky, and battery life can be a limiting factor for portable devices. Processing power is another constraint, affecting the complexity and detail of the virtual elements that can be rendered.

"**Field of View (FoV)**: The FoV in most current AR devices is quite limited, which restricts the area in which virtual objects can be displayed. An ideal AR device would have an FoV comparable to human vision. While most of the consumer VR devices regularly boast FoVs in the range of one hundred to 130 degrees, most AR devices rarely exceed sixty degrees.

"**Tracking and Latency**: Tracking the position and orientation of the user's head and accurately aligning virtual objects with the real world are challenging tasks. Any latency in these systems can make the virtual objects seem to 'float' or 'drift', breaking the illusion of reality.

"While these AR products can be useful for high-end business applications and limitations like FoV, tracking/latency, and clunky hardware will eventually be ameliorated, these products are very expensive. The Vision Pro and HoloLens are both priced above $3,500 + and, as such, are unlikely to capture interest within the consumer market.

"Most of these glasses, including the Microsoft HoloLens and the Apple Vision Pro glasses, are also referred to as Mixed Reality (MR) glasses.

"Is anyone familiar with that term?" Elias asked.

"Isn't that a mix of augmented and virtual reality?" asked Dania.

"Partially right, Dania. It does reside on the continuum between augmented reality which is typically objects superimposed on the real world, and virtual reality, where everything is simulated. MR does overlay digital objects over the real world like AR, but may use sensors and dynamic calibration to create more of a sense of presence. It's more comprehensive than AR but not fully immersive like VR. Mixed reality applications lend themselves to more interactivity and are often used as training tools, whereas augmented reality applications tend to be more informational and are generally used in entertainment and commercial scenarios," said Elias.

"Can you give us some examples?" asked Jag.

"Sure," said Elias.

"An airplane manufacturer, for example, can use MR technology to train mechanics and technicians to perform maintenance tasks on its aircraft. They could use spatial mapping to create a realistic and immersive training environment where trainees can practice complex tasks in a more natural and intuitive way on a simulated model airplane. That could drastically reduce the cost of their trainees working on real aircraft.

"Or a warehousing company could use MR technology to optimize operations to reduce errors in picking and packing orders. They could use spatial mapping to guide workers through the warehouse and provide real-time information on order locations and inventory levels, creating a more efficient workflow.

"There are also anatomy learning applications that use 3D models of the human body and spatial mapping to create a more natural and immersive learning experience, allowing students to interact like interacting with real-world objects. The student doctors could be in a real operating room, overlaid with a virtual body, working together as a team to perform virtual surgery."

"And with virtual reality, everything is virtual, correct? There is no real world, just a virtual one?" I asked.

"Yes," Elias confirmed.

"But could I have augmented reality or mixed reality within virtual reality?" I asked. "Like a virtual scoreboard or even a spatial map for my virtual space?"

"Yes, you can. Academia uses an umbrella term called XR or Extended Reality to describe varying degrees of virtualization. AR, MR, and VR are really subsets of XR, but it can get confusing. For simplicity, I refer to the technology as virtual reality.

"Academics might argue with this approach, but the real-world vernacular tends to recognize the technology term more generally as virtual reality or VR. So, I am going to propose that we use the term virtual reality in a more general sense that includes both augmented and mixed realities."

"What about the idea of digital twinning? We've heard about that idea in the media, but I was never quite sure what they meant. Is that still VR?" asked RoMac.

"Yes," said Elias, "It is still VR, but it also combines with other technologies like remote sensors and AI to solve larger-scale challenges.

"Digital twinning is a VR technology that creates a digital replica or simulation of a physical system or environment, allowing for real-time monitoring, analysis, and control. It can also be used to simulate different scenarios and test changes without affecting the real-world system or to effect change on a real system remotely when it might be too dangerous or impractical to do with people.

"Smart Cities, for example, can use digital twinning technology where sensors and other data sources are used to create a real-time digital replica of the city's infrastructure, and can then be used to monitor and optimize city operations, such as traffic flow, energy usage, and public safety.

"The aerospace industry uses digital twinning to simulate and test aircraft designs and performance. By creating a digital twin of an aircraft, engineers can test different design configurations and optimize performance before manufacturing and testing in the physical world. Flight simulator programs are also examples of digital twinning. These aircraft environments used to train pilots are often one hundred percent accurate, allowing student pilots to try and fail more at zero cost in a twinned environment. The knowledge and experience acquired by the students are also transferrable to real airplane models. Similar virtual technology can also be used to remotely control drones or more advanced systems for surveillance or military applications.

"One of the more compelling opportunities for digital twinning is within dangerous or hard-to-access environments. In the nuclear power industry, for example, digital twinning is used to create a virtual replica of the nuclear power plant. This allows operators to simulate various scenarios and test changes in the virtual environment before implementing them in the real-world environment. In the event of an emergency, such as a nuclear meltdown, operators can use the digital twin to remotely monitor and control the plant, including shutting down equipment and regulating cooling systems. This allows operators to control the dangerous environment from a safe location, potentially saving lives."

"Wow, that's a very exciting technology," said RoMac. "Is that really being used today?"

"Absolutely," said Elias, "These larger industrial applications can more easily justify large investments in this type of technology because the scale of potential savings in both cost and human lives is immense.

"Are we all good with our VR concepts so far?" he asked.

As Elias scanned the audience, the avatars collectively nodded to proceed. "Okay, we have a few more concepts to cover.

"You may also see the acronyms IVR and DVR. IVR is referred to as immersive virtual reality and is experienced within a VR Head Mounted Device (HMD), while DVR or desktop virtual reality is viewed or experienced on a computer desktop, much like the experience of watching a 3D movie or playing a 3D game on a large screen. The world exists in 3D within the screen, so it is like looking through a window. IVR and DVR are both considered 'Virtual Reality,' and both offer varying degrees of immersion, but when people refer to immersive virtual reality, they generally mean VR experienced from within a head-mounted device."

Elias continued.

"Finally, in academia, there is a concept called affordances created by a researcher named James Gibson. Put simply; an affordance is the objective property of a given environment or an object that lets the individual perform an action upon it. For example, what kind of action could we perform on a chair?" Elias queried the audience. Jag responded first.

"You can sit in it," said Jag.

"Or stand on it if you are at a concert," bellowed a hipster-clad avatar in the second row.

Elias smiled.

"That is correct. It is simply an action afforded by the objects or environments to the individual. And based on those affordances, what could you do with virtual reality technology?"

Several hands went up. Elias pointed to RoMac,

who had transitioned from skeptic to keener in less than a week.

"You can immerse yourself in the world," said RoMac.

"Exactly," responded Elias, "What else?"

"Interact in the environment?" came a voice from the front.

"Bingo," responded Elias.

"You can design and create things. Worlds that people can enter," said Jag.

Elias nodded and motioned the students for more ideas.

"You can become an avatar and dress up however you want," said the punk rocker at the back of the class.

"That's called embodiment," responded Elias, "And that is a very important affordance, as we'll see later.

"Anyone else?" Elias surveyed the crowd. No hands, so he continued.

"What the technology allows one to do, defines the nature of the experience. But we can also build upon these basic capabilities and create something much greater. For example, an iPhone has many technologies that have affordances of their own. Screens afford us to see and touch, processors can compute and present graphics and imagery, and memory can store relevant information. An operating system affords us a base for other programs or applications. It's endless. Even Apple's famous 'There's an app for that' campaign clearly identifies the myriad opportunities with these underlying technology affordances.

"To keep things simple, however, I'm going to use the term capability rather than affordance. The terms are related, but 'capabilities' is a more practical word, and we're most interested in the VR business applications, not the theory.

"I'd also like to point out that VR applications, like any software experience, will change and improve over time, incorporating new innovations and new technologies.

Elias paced back and forth across the front of the stage, gathering his thoughts.

"So, let's get to the heart of the matter. Why all the fuss? Why are people so excited about virtual reality and the concept of the Metaverse?"

Immersion

"As discussed earlier, immersion is the ability to be immersed in a virtual world. The experience of immersion is both objective and measurable but also enables other capabilities. For example, if you recall our P = DICE formula (Presence = Design + Immersion + Capability + Experience), immersion contributes to the feeling of presence, which is also affected by your sensory capability and your previous life experiences. Let's focus first on immersion.

"Immersion allows us to experience sensory stimuli (visual, auditory, haptic, kinesthetic, and vestibular) within the virtual world, increasing engagement and, in some cases, creating a sense of awe and wonder. This is not always the case, however, and the highest quality specifications may not necessarily lead to a better experience, as they are subject to the quality of design, as discussed earlier. Have you ever been to an animated movie that is incredibly well animated, with ultra-high resolution and amazing special effects (SFX), but with a horrible story and characters that simply do not work? I've been to a few and because other aspects of the creative process are weak, then the overall experience is not good. Even so, all other things being equal, the higher the quality of the immersive experience, the more likely it is to increase the feeling of presence and authenticity.

"There is also clear evidence that memory recall and specific situational learning environments also improve with immersion. A situated learning effect is something you learn in an environment that is aligned or related to the task at hand. For example, you are more likely to learn about animation and storytelling within a virtual animation studio environment compared to, say, a simple classroom or a gymnasium. In fact, recent studies were able to demonstrate these positive immersive effects."

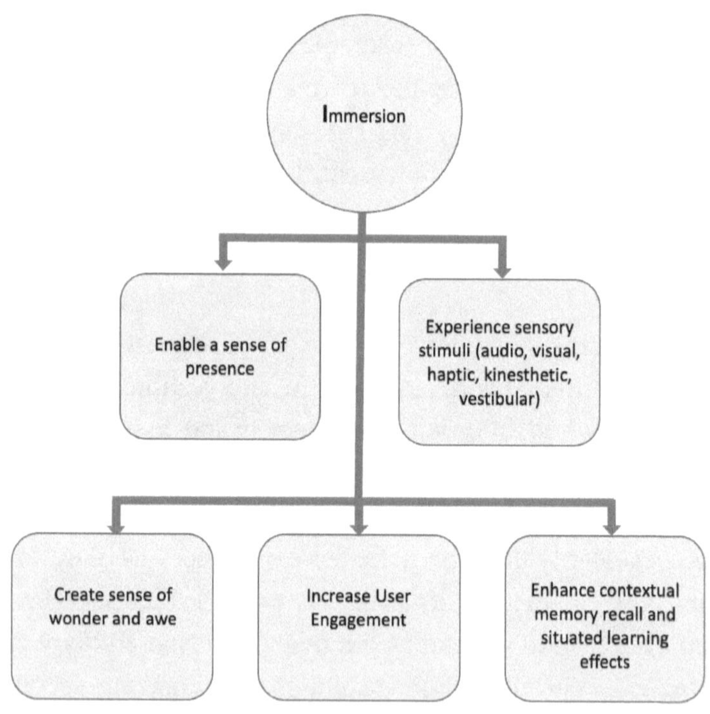

Benefits of Immersion

Embodiment

"The Proteus Effect posits that as we change our digital self-representations, these self-perceptions can change our behavior. When immersed in a virtual environment, you can embody or inhabit an avatar and experience the world through their first-person perspective. Whether you are embodied as a pirate, a teacher, a musician, or even Albert Einstein, there is plenty of research evidence to suggest that you will identify with that persona, so much so that you can inhabit that real persona and take on some of those capabilities. A 2018 study performed at the University of Barcelona called 'Being Einstein' found that participants showed improved cognitive performance on tasks related to spatial reasoning and problem-solving skills when embodied in the Einstein avatar compared to participants who did not embody that persona.

"Another research study performed by the same group from Barcelona showed that the virtual embodiment of white people as black avatars reduced implicit racial bias. In the same study, the data suggested that the number of exposures to these avatars also led to greater overall implicit bias reduction suggesting that the idea of mere exposure would also contribute to a reduction of racism. However, a follow-up study in 2020 related to this study cautioned about the blanket application of these embodiment theories, suggesting, with supporting data, that having negative experiences during the embodiment process can actually increase implicit racial bias.

"These studies used a testing process called the Harvard Implicit Association Test (IAT). The test assumes that people have unconscious, implicit biases that may affect behavior and decision-making. The testing process measures the timed response to pairs of stimuli (words and images) when asked to categorize these stimuli, for example, as black vs. white or good vs. bad. From this test, participants are given a 'Bias Score' that may be compared to previous baseline tests taken prior to these embodiment exposures.

"The results of these studies are very promising. From the above research, one can conclude that multiple embodiment exposures to non-negative experiences could be a useful approach to positively affect people's perceptions of others that may differ in relation to race, sexual orientation, or gender identity. It may also be suggestive of a VR-based educational approach that could help us overcome many social and racial barriers across the world.

"The embodiment of these different people, personas, or groups are subjective experiences that could not be achieved without this type of technology. Finally, as with immersion, the embodiment process also contributes to elevating the feeling of presence within the virtual world."

Frances, a passionate human rights advocate, raised her hand, and Elias acknowledged it.

"Are you trying to tell me that if we inhabit the avatars of other races, racial biases will be reduced? In other words, it can help reduce racism? If that is the case, why aren't we working with our kids to expose them to other races and cultures in this way when they are young? This could change the world."

Elias nodded in agreement and expanded.

"You are absolutely right. This is the reason I choose to work in the field. It is exciting. Immersive VR technology can connect us all, building bridges that were not previously possible. We could create classes, seminars, and regular weekly activities with our youth around the corner, around the country, or around the world. This technology takes the idea of a pen pal to a whole new level.

"So, why hasn't it happened yet? The technology experience is still relatively new, and as it becomes more accessible, it will proliferate and change the nature of the educational experiences that we create for our youth. I'm very optimistic."

Frances was shaking her head.

"This is amazing."

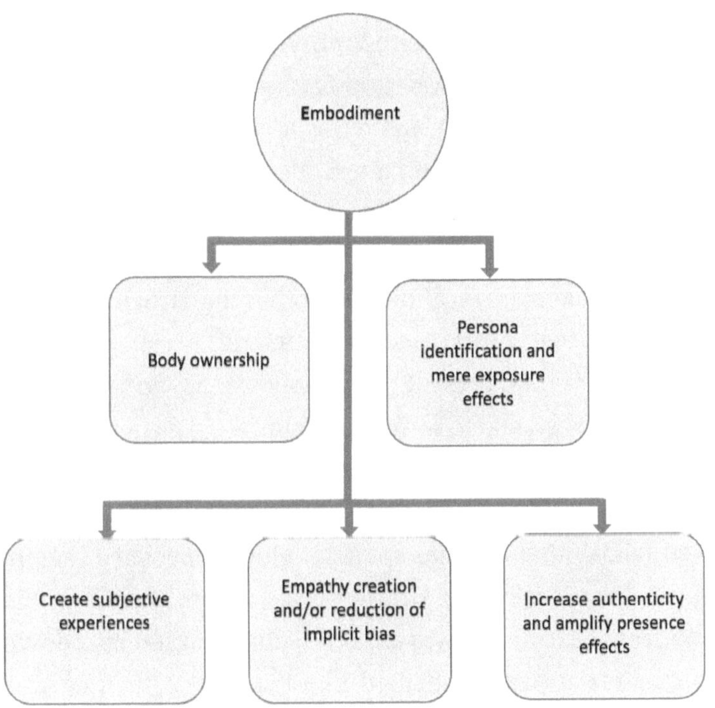

Benefits of Embodiment

Interactivity

"VR technology allows us to interact within the environment. We can travel or move from place to place within a virtual world or between worlds. This can be achieved in several ways. The concept of teleporting allows us to direct a light beam and, upon a trigger, immediately be located at the end of that beam. The same process may be achieved more gradually by walking to that same location to experience the journey. Other methods of finding your way around a virtual space, or 'wayfinding,' may involve maps, signs, or audio support providing directional input. There is a wonderful VR application called Wander that uses the entire Google Maps repository to visit pretty much anywhere in the world with a text, voice, or map selection. I highly recommend you try this out.

"We can also manipulate objects within a world and interact with avatars (real or not) within the virtual world."

With that, Elias issued a command.

"Computer, present me a globe of the world." And a large globe was created in front of him.

"Where would you like to visit?" inquired Elias.

"Take us to a beautiful beach in the Caribbean!" yelled Jag. With that, Elias spun the globe, selected a region, and presto, we were all sitting on a beautiful beach in the Caribbean, hearing the waves, and feeling the sun beat down upon us. Or at least it seemed like the sun. Wow, that was impressive.

"Machu Picchu," I suggested, and within a few moments, Elias had the entire class standing on one of the highest elevations of the fifteenth Century Inca Citadel in the Andes mountains. We were literally looking down over the

Urubamba River and the Cusco regions of Peru.

"The possibilities are unlimited, and we can travel to an infinite number of worlds based on fact or fiction," said Elias.

Moments later, we were flying in a bus headed towards Hogwarts, the set of the Harry Potter books and films. A collective "Wow" was heard from the students. To say we were impressed was an understatement. And with a large gust of wind, we were literally blown away. And now we were back in the classroom.

Move over, Merlin. There is a new wizard in town, I thought.

"If you think about this," mused Elias, "This is a complete game changer for education. We've barely begun to wrap our minds around what is possible and just how much we can do to improve our learning experiences.

"We can interact with other players to play all sorts of games, both single and multiuser, or to learn how to perform various tasks or processes."

In front of our eyes, we watched Elias change into a burger chef as he flipped burgers and added various condiments to the final product, presenting us with one of the most delicious-looking burgers that I'd ever seen. Yup, and now I'm hungry, I thought.

"Making burgers is a very simple process," Elias added, "but one that many of us had to learn at one time. This is a much better way to learn than, say, facing a lineup of several dozen hungry customers."

Another great point. Interestingly, like many young people, that was actually something I had to do back in high school. To date, it's still the toughest and lowest-paying job I have ever had. It could have been so much less stressful had I properly learned how to do it outside the line of fire.

"Burger flipping is neat," said RoMac, "but what about more complicated stuff?"

"Like what?" asked Elias.

"Like firefighting. That's a very complicated process and much riskier," RoMac responded.

"Okay," said Elias, "How about this?"

It was such a perfect segue it almost seemed planned. In seconds, Elias had conjured a raging fire at the front of the room and clad in classic firefighting garb, including hat and mask, was actually fighting a fire. He provided a short demonstration of how to manage an "out-of-control fire" and then offered the hose to RoMac, who politely refused. The wizard continued.

"While this might appear impressive, with a full body haptic suit, you would also be able to feel heat and pressure like you would experience with a real fire, creating a super realistic simulation. So, whether you are flipping burgers, fighting fires, flying F18 fighter jets, or practicing your public speaking in front of a simulated audience, the ability to create and interact with different worlds and processes is limited by one's own imagination. We'll learn more about the creation of worlds in the next section."

Elias concluded with thoughts on interactivity.

"Finally, as with immersion and embodiment, the ability to interact with an authentic situation and have control over that virtual world further contributes to our feelings of presence."

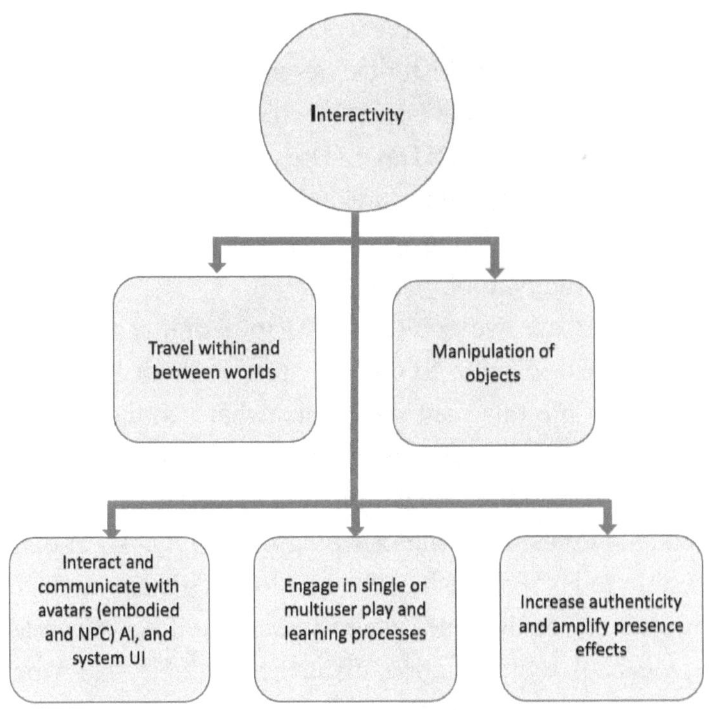

Benefits of Interactivity

A Creative Canvas and a Computational Platform

Elias began.,"One of the most exciting elements of VR is that it provides a creative canvas to make any type of world, character, or digital asset that you could possibly imagine. If a designer wants to start with an existing frame of reference from the 'real world,' they can simply recreate or change the current reality. In this way, you could previsualize how an existing world could change for the better, amplifying the positive aspects, minimizing or diminishing the negative aspects, and adding entirely new elements.

"This revised virtual world, with past and present

iterations, could serve as a wonderful tool for non-fiction storytelling or even historical re-enactments. What if we could give students that visceral feeling of what it was like to experience the famous 'I Have a Dream' speech by Dr. Martin Luther King in 1963 alongside 250,000 people marching on the Lincoln Memorial in Washington, DC? What a powerful empathy-building tool.

"Perhaps we could go live to a digital re-creation of any world location to cover a story without leaving the studio? While this may seem somewhat inauthentic, real-time camera feeds and sensors from these remote locations could sample and update a digitally twinned environment in a manner almost indistinguishable from reality. All of this is possible today. Expensive, but possible. This could change how journalism is done, where the storytelling is overlaid on a digital representation of an action zone that would otherwise not be accessible.

"If your preference is fiction storytelling, we can create entirely new worlds like the Harry Potter example (past, present, and future). While the cost of building high-quality worlds is still considerable, with improved software and better AI tools, world-building will soon be a commodity and available to all the world's artists and set designers. And when we compare the cost of filmmaking in the 'real world' by creating expensive physical sets and modifying cities to accommodate the process of shooting a film, the digital alternative will soon become the more economical option.

"In fact, many movies and TV shows are leaning toward the use of these tools, such as Unreal Engine or Unity, to create entire worlds for characters to inhabit. The recent Avatar 2 movie, 'The Way of Water,' is almost an entire digital recreation of a fictitious world that simply could not be achieved in a real-world setting. Ready Player One, a futuristic movie about virtual reality, uses advanced gaming and VR tools to create and interact with the ultimate online universe called the Oasis."

To demonstrate the diverse worlds created in Ready Player One, Elias triggered a video trailer of the Ready Player One movie and motioned to the large screen. We all watched in amazement as high-action scenes with dozens of characters in imaginary worlds enacted seamlessly, like a next-generation video game.

He continued, "What was originally conceived as a virtual world based in the year 2045 is now looking more like what will be the current state of technology in 2030. Underpinning these virtual worlds is a globally scalable computational platform bringing together many technologies that operate together to create powerful digital experiences. By combining cloud-based software services (security, game engines, personalized databases, preference engines, etc.), artificial intelligence (AI), biometrics, Internet of Things (IoT) sensor technologies, and powerful game engine tools, we can now simulate any process or world activity.

"Would you like to experience what it would be like to be the mayor of New York? There is no reason why we could not simulate the existing city and the scenarios that one might face in that role. Further, an analysis of your decisions relative to historical data might allow you to measure your effectiveness against others that may have occupied that role, against other AI-generated alternatives, or against an entire population of gamers.

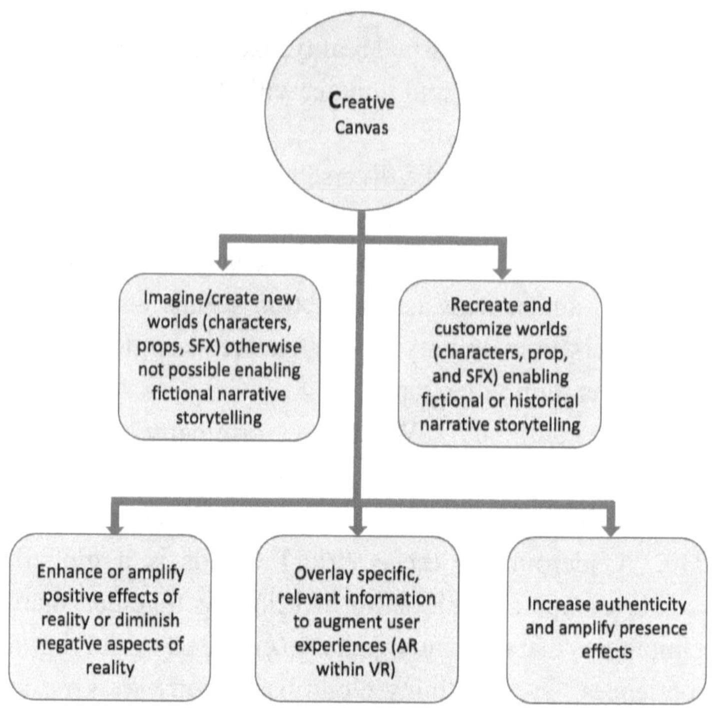

Benefits of the Creative Canvas

"While software packages like Microsoft Flight Simulator, SimCity, The Sims, and a host of other similar games popularized the idea of learning via simulation, the quality of graphics, the levels of immersion, and the sophistication of the algorithms pale in comparison to what is now possible and what is to come.

"Current consumer flight simulation technology (2023), for example, uses high-end Graphics Processing Units (GPUs) like NVIDIA's new RTX 40 series to offer full real-time ray tracing (advanced lighting simulations) and to render up to 5K pixels (5120x1440). Most humans cannot process visual imagery beyond 5K. So, for many, these high-end simulations will be as good as it gets and difficult to distinguish from reality. Advanced motion systems like electric actuators and hydraulic systems can simulate the sensation of motion and vibrations of an aircraft in flight. Even consumer flight simulators can provide full physics engines, simulate weather effects, and provide real-time machine learning analysis and guidance from data generated by these user experiences. And all for less than $120. In some cases, these systems are being used to train private pilots and other aviation professionals.

"More advanced military or industrial simulators utilize advanced motion platforms and centrifuges to simulate feelings of gravitational forces (G-forces) to train pilots on high-speed maneuvers and more dangerous training scenarios, saving billions of dollars and many lives that could have been lost without the capabilities learned in these advanced training simulators."

"I must admit, this is a bit overwhelming. It seems that everything is possible; like being a mosquito at a nudist colony, where do you bite?" asked Jag.

Elias chuckled.

"That's right, Jag, it can be overwhelming. The challenge is how we stay focused on creating experiences that are thoughtful, well-architected, and meaningful without getting too focused on the next shiny new technology. Companies and people will have to pick their spots. Acknowledging that change will be constant, even with what we think will last forever.

"We're at an inflection point in history where technology and innovation are accelerating, and with enough time and money, yes, anything IS possible. Ray Kurzweil refers to the singularity, a time when AI technology begins to exceed the capability of humans. And we, in this room, may face that reality in our time, some say in the next several years."

"So, how do we deal with that?" asked Dania, "Is AI technology going to obsolete us all?"

"It is a real concern and the subject of much debate in both academia and geopolitics. The recently released ChatGPT by the Open AI group at MIT has created even more media buzz than The Billion Dollar Metaverse Challenge (BDMC). Lots of people are scared," said Elias, "They are afraid that AI will replace people and take their jobs. And yes, as has been the case before, that will happen. But new jobs and opportunities will be created.

"There have been many cases in history when disruptive technology has threatened to change the way humans live. The automobile obsoleted the horse and buggy and allowed us to connect with people physically that may not have been accessible via horse and buggy. Airplanes supplanted boats and trains for transcontinental and intercontinental travel, and computers have automated much of the tedious office tasks, freeing us up to focus on higher-value activities.

"So, my advice would be lean into the technology, embrace it and figure out how we can use it to add value to a process, create new experiences, and connect more with people. We have major challenges ahead, and having smart AI to help us solve problems faster and communicate better isn't the biggest issue. We will figure it out."

"Thank you, Elias. It makes sense," said Dania.

"You're welcome, Dania. Now this next section is one of the most interesting and offers great possibilities for all of us. This is where many of the VR capabilities come together to enable positive change. We'll also gain a better understanding of how much we are affected by our immediate environment. Why don't we take a five-minute break before we delve into the world of priming?" Elias suggested.

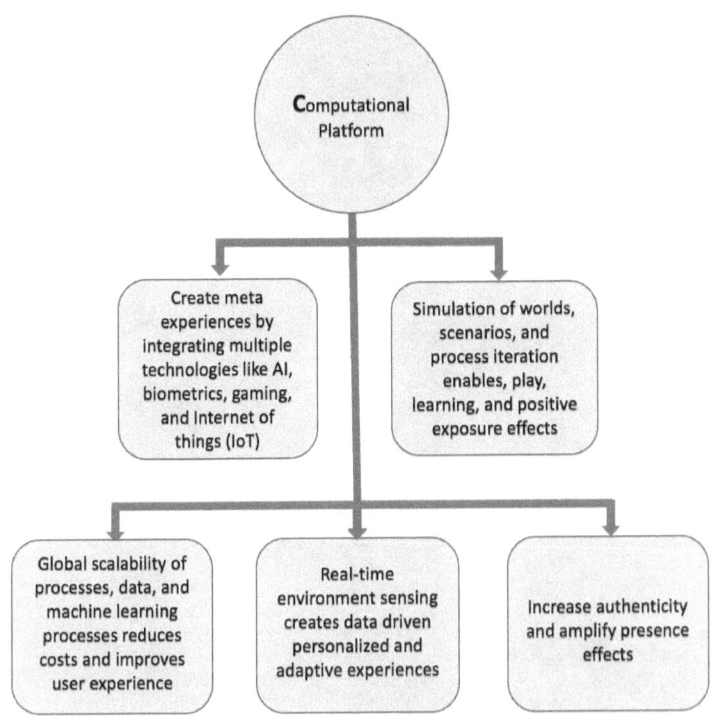

Benefits of the Computational Platform

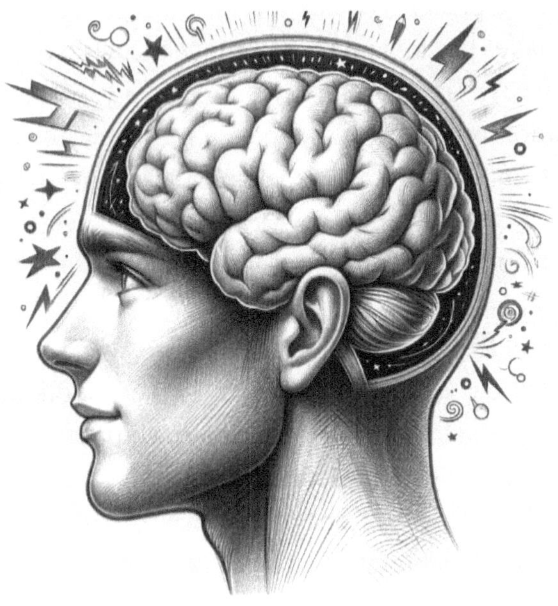

CHAPTER SEVEN

Prime Time

A Priming Substrate

"Creating simulated worlds would not be complete without those subtle influences that nudge us to act, think, or perceive in a certain way. Like the real world, these influences can be as simple as where we place signs, the color of things, lighting, sound, or messaging that occurs within our periphery. Suffice it to say virtual worlds will offer many opportunities to advertise and influence our embodied avatars to buy both virtual and real goods, services, and experiences.

"This process is called priming, and it can be used for both positive and/or exploitive intent. In traditional psychology, priming occurs because the prime stimulus or action makes the content and subsequent cognitive processes more accessible, potentially influencing all stages of information processing: attention, comprehension, memory retrieval, inference, and response generation. The priming stimulus can be subliminal: brief and not detectable to the individual who is exposed, or supraliminal: detectable by the individual but not obvious."

Suddenly, the room went dark. Then as the lights came back on, we found ourselves in the middle of a busy laundromat, watching people filling and emptying washing machines, folding clothes, and socializing.

Elias stood in front of the group. "Good afternoon, contestants. Welcome to Choose That Word. Please fill in the blank to complete the following word."

With that, the letters S O _ P appeared in the digital squares above the stacked washing machines.

No problem, I thought. I aimed my beam towards the blank spot, at which point, a small keypad appeared below the word. I selected the letter 'A' to complete the word. It was obviously SOAP.

"Is everybody done?" Elias queried to a chorus of nods.

"Okay, round two," he exclaimed.

With that, the room went dark again as we appeared to travel through a wormhole, landing in a small food court somewhere in the Metaverse. As we looked around, we saw various concession stands offering food choices ranging from Greek cuisine, burgers, and cinnamon buns to Asian stir-fry and even coffee shops.

"Contestants, this round has three words. You have five seconds for each word. Begin now," he said.

One after another, the words were presented in front of us.

S P O O _

That one was easy, SPOON.

P L A T _

I was torn between PLATO and PLATE. I chose PLATE. It seemed to make the most sense.

Finally, S O _ P.

Hmm, I smiled knowingly.

It was S O U P.

Done, and with a total time of ten seconds. Oh, yeah. I killed it, or so I thought.

A few seconds later, we were transported back to our classroom environment. As we reviewed the results, it became obvious just how vulnerable our thought processes were to previous stimuli and the environment around us. Every one of us chose the word SOAP when we were in the laundromat, and less than sixty seconds later, chose SOUP when in the context of a food-oriented environment.

We could have easily chosen SPOOL or SPOOK for the second word. But instead, we all chose SPOON. Why? As Elias explained, we were in a food-related environment, so that was the first word that popped into our consciousness. We were primed, or "pre-sueded", subconsciously to select that word. Similarly, even with our previous exposure to the word SOAP, we instinctively chose SOUP as the situational context of food suggested. Primed again.

Interestingly, most of us struggled with PLATO versus PLATE, with half choosing PLATO and half choosing PLATE. While PLATE was consistent with the food environment, PLATO was consistent with Greek, which was prominently presented as one of the food choices.

Elias continued. "While this was a small local experiment, there is a canon of research related to priming effects of words, behaviors, motivations, and emotions where such stimuli can subtly, yet profoundly affect our thought processes.

"Daniel Kahneman, a prominent cognitive scientist and Nobel Laureate, describes priming as a process that affects our associative machine, a vast network of memories in which each idea is linked to many others. Priming one idea or concept will activate many others, all happening concurrently and mostly at a subconscious level, like a ripple of waves on a pond, initiated by one idea that will activate through a small part of the network of associative memory.

"These priming influences are used extensively in the real world to influence us. Every billboard, street or business sign, logo, and city park is meant to influence us. The billboards might be there to remind us of a brand that we will recall the next time we need cosmetics or sporting apparel. A street sign may direct our transport to keep us safe, while the business signs present an invitation to come in and do business. The park invites a respite to help you relax or take a break in nature. In fact, everything about the design of the environment around us sends a message that affects how we feel, think, and behave.

"While we like to believe that we are one hundred percent in control of our thoughts and behaviors, many studies suggest the opposite; that we can be profoundly influenced with little or no awareness. There was a classic 1996 experiment performed by Dr. John Bargh and colleagues dubbed 'The Florida Effect'. In this study, one group of students was primed to create sentences with words related to the elderly. Words like Florida, balding, forgetful, gray, or wrinkle were used to prime the concept of old age. The second group was exposed to neutral words. The study participants were then asked to leave the laboratory. The actual experiment was a deception. The intent of the study was to compare the walking speeds of the primed participants as they left the laboratory compared to the groups not primed by the elderly concepts. As predicted, the elderly primed groups walked much slower, exhibiting a significant behavioral priming effect.

"A post-test questionnaire asked students if they suspected that test activities influenced their thoughts or actions in any way. Participants unanimously concluded that the study had no impact on their subsequent thoughts or actions, even though the slower walking results of the primed participants were significant. These priming effects can also go both ways. In a reverse study of the elderly cognitive priming concepts, a German researcher performed the opposite sequences of actions where participants were asked to walk around the room at roughly one-third of their normal walking pace. As predicted, the concept of the elderly stereotypic words was more readily recognized in a subsequent task, indicating that stereotypes can be activated simply by stereotypical movements.

"A similar reciprocal priming study compared the effect of various facial configurations on affective (emotional) responses. The study determined that simulating a smile by placing a pencil sideways in the mouth made Far Side cartoons seem funnier. Conversely, facial configurations of a frown, achieved by placing a pencil in the mouth pointing outwards, reduced the affective response. In short, the cartoons were seen as funnier while in a smiling position. This finding lends great credence to the concept that acting in a specific manner can invoke a corresponding emotion and to age-old wisdom that suggests we smile if we wish to be happy."

A hand shot up in the first row. Elias turned to acknowledge the avatar dressed in an elegant dinner suit worthy of the Great Gatsby.

"So basically, what you are saying here is 'fake it till you make it?'"

Elias laughed but also acknowledged that the feelings, sometimes induced by physical actions prior to a specific outcome, can be instrumental in helping that outcome to be realized. He noted that these subconscious priming processes could be so subtle that they can be powerful tools to affect positive changes in unobtrusive ways. He continued.

"Here is another great example. A 1997 study tested in-store music effects of specific musical pieces related to countries of origin and purchases of wine. Four different types of French and German wine were displayed equally prominently in a supermarket drink area over a two-week period, changing location occasionally but maintaining equal positioning. The wines were similar in price and degree of dryness. Over the two-week period, French accordion and German Bierkeller music played intermittently. Interestingly, when French music played, 76.9% of the bottles of wine sold in the area were French wine. When German music played, 73.3% of the bottles of wine sold in the area were of German origin. When respondents were asked whether they thought the music influenced their choice of wine, most felt that there was little or no effect.

"Daily nature walks have also been shown to prime happiness and positive affect. In fact, the power of simple natural views was illustrated in a 1984 study based on recovery records from a suburban Pennsylvania hospital. In this study, patients with a view of a hospital window of outside natural environments saw considerably faster rates of recovery than those with no window view.

"Nature exposure has been shown to improve physical and psychological well-being, but its impact on social behavior has also become increasingly important, particularly within collaborative, team-oriented learning environments. In a 2016 study, participants were tested on their social behavior prior to entering a large urban park compared to participants in the after condition. To test the nature impact, researchers purposely, though meant to appear accidental, dropped a glove from their tote bags as participants were either entering or leaving the park. The 'helping rate' for those leaving the park was far greater than for those who were entering the park, suggesting a positive prosocial effect created by this nature exposure.

"What if we could use our technology solutions to improve mental states? Feelings of positive affect (elevated mood) have been shown to have a positive impact on information organization and creativity. In a 1987 study, positive affect was induced in study participants by viewing a few minutes of a comedy film or by receiving a small bag of candy. Another group received neutral stimuli, while two more groups engaged in a physical exercise meant to represent affective arousal. In performing two tasks that required creative ingenuity, the positive-affect groups, primed with candy or funny movies, saw improved performance, while the control groups and exercise groups saw no performance increase. So, if we can elevate mood, we may also be able to improve cognitive performance."

"But how does this relate to virtual reality again?"

asked Jag.

"Good question. Thanks for bearing with me. I was just returning to that," said Elias.

"While these priming influences are used extensively in the real world to influence us, it can be very expensive to create beautiful spaces with positive influence, as well as inaccessible to most people. But what if we could create these spaces digitally and make them universally accessible? There is plenty of empirical evidence to support the transferability of these priming 'effects' to virtual environments. In fact, the more we feel 'present' in our virtual environment, the more we will be affected by these priming influences because our subconscious mind perceives the virtual world as reality. Like the boa constrictor snake that Nate managed to escape from earlier, or the feeling you get when walking on a virtual plank from a high-rise building one hundred stories up, the emotions and responses are just as real.

"A 2013 study of virtual environments showed that virtual spaces, designed to induce creativity, do make people and teams more creative, and spaces that are more related to the function being performed, like animation within a virtual animation studio, can improve academic performance in that domain. Think of it like an actor that is 'in a role.' They will perform much better in that 'pretend state' … because isn't that what actors do?

"So, we can create our spaces in very specific ways that are meant to induce creativity, improve cognition, or even reduce anxiety. These are challenges that are very difficult to do in the real world. As mentioned earlier, the cost of designing physical spaces is incredibly expensive, takes years, and in the final analysis, creates a subjective experience loved by some but possibly disliked by others.

Have you ever looked at a piece of art in the park and thought, 'Is that really art?' or walked across a university campus thinking that this design represents something out of the Middle Ages? Some cultures might perceive historic North American and European university campuses as artifacts and stark reminders of European Colonialism. The truth is: reality is subjective. And an outdated infrastructure that primes thoughts of global hegemony for some might just as easily conjure feelings of oppression, violence, and insecurity for others. In other cases, compromise designs may be intended to appeal to the lowest common denominator.

"Virtual reality can change all of that. Worlds and environments custom suited to very specific tastes can be created and altered at a tiny fraction of what it might cost in the real world. What is more, these designs may be personalized to accommodate varying tastes, cultures, and preferences. You may prefer beautiful gardens amidst deep old-growth forests with magnificent deciduous trees like Maples and Grand Oaks. Whereas I may prefer to be close to water with plenty of shoreline and conifer trees in the distance. You may prefer historic structures and cathedrals; I may prefer futuristic designs with a minimalist philosophy.

"Even more compelling, we can be coincident within the same virtual spaces, meeting, discussing, or working but experiencing completely different environments and ambient effects. In fact, using personalization and adaptive artificial intelligence, combined with sensors to detect biological signs like heart rate, blood pressure, or galvanic skin response (GSR), we can analyze and predict your preferences and create those environments in real time, allowing you to regulate your emotional state.

"Here is an example. Perhaps you are a student in a large lecture hall with screens on the side walls for aesthetic or ambient effect. If you've chosen to allow the system to automatically reduce anxiety levels, you might see beautiful waterfalls or nature scenes on those screens with soft classical music playing. Whereas another student attempting to 'stay awake' may prefer more kinetic scenes, like action sports or fast camera cinematography. Neither is right or wrong but rather a subjective experience.

"As a professor, what if I am teaching students about the concepts of filmmaking and animation? I could populate those peripheral screens with Hollywood movie posters or iconic animation characters that conjure positive feelings and strong associations related to the subject matter. As discussed earlier, this type of peripheral imagery has been shown to improve academic performance by creating a positive situated learning effect. And yet, while this may work wonderfully for native North Americans, what if you grew up in Eastern Europe, Northern Asia, or the Middle East, perhaps? You may prefer a cultural localization option that will populate those same screens with icons and visuals related to Chinese, Persian, or Slavic cultures, achieving the same intended positive feelings and situated learning effect. This is all possible within VR."

"But isn't that weird? It's like we would all be living in a different world," asked Dania, as always, articulating what many of us were thinking.

Elias responded, "Good point Dania. It is arguable that everyone is now living in a different world, and the shared experience is diminished somewhat as students may not have a common experience. In this case, I would argue that they do remain in synchrony with the specific subject matter content, which is most important. It moves us positively in the direction of cultural diversity, inclusiveness, and fairness. So, if each of you can have those personalized experiences, with the same core content, at no consequence to the other students, why not?

"Now, Dania, visualize for a few moments those posters populated with pictures of Bulgarian film icons and animated characters that you've never heard of. How do you feel?"

He paused for a few moments.

"I'm curious, but I have no positive feeling. I'm indifferent, I guess," said Dania.

"Okay, now visualize those posters populated with pictures of Mickey Mouse, the Frozen characters, Toy Story, and Walt Disney. How does that make you feel?" asked Elias.

Dania smiled, "Okay, I get it. I feel happy. I have great memories of watching those movies and laughing with my family."

Elias continued, "We are affected by more than just the environments we create, however. The people within that environment, how they present culturally, and the effects in the environment also impact how we feel and perceive.

"Earlier in this lecture, we talked about the positive cognitive effects of embodying the Albert Einstein avatar. Empirical research has shown that we do this by inhabiting the stereotypical effects of that avatar. Earlier studies from the 1990s generally concluded that priming a stereotype or trait leads to overt behavioral changes in adherence to that stereotype. This is a well-known concept called 'stereotype threat' that can have a positive or negative impact.

"Stereotype threat is a psychological state where apprehension about a negative stereotype may disrupt or diminish cognitive and academic performance within that group. A 1995 study showed that African American minority groups were vulnerable to negative stereotypes related to scholastic ability, and the mere salience of the negative stereotype could impair performance. Further research also suggests that by priming positive stereotypes or eliminating the saliency of potentially negative stereotype cues, threats could be reduced, and cognitive performance improved.

"VR solutions allow us to design and control environmental variables that may help mitigate these stereotype threats but also offer further positive priming effects. While avatar embodiment effects are profound, we are also affected by the people or avatars in our general vicinity. They create the context that we become familiar with. Avatars that over-represent one group may cause other minority groups to feel less represented and less secure as a result. As in the real world, this is a negative stereotype cue.

"In VR, we can directly address this issue by using system-generated avatars to create more diverse, representative characters and by creating a baseline context that is both fair and more truly representative. This may also apply to teachers, leaders, or business colleagues. Studies have also clearly shown that in real life, girls perform better at math with a female math teacher at the helm. This represents a positive stereotype cue that may help ameliorate possible negative and erroneous stereotypes that girls may not be as good as boys at math. So, particularly with asynchronous (not live) content, the teacher avatar could be a personalization option chosen at the time of the presentation.

"We can also design the assets and structures within

the environment to be less representative of specific cultures, genders, or sexual preferences, effectively leveling the playing field for all participants. Or, as discussed, create different environments to accommodate varying preferences in any of these domains.

"In this way, VR worlds can represent diegetic prototypes of ideal future worlds that we could never attain otherwise. The idea of diegetic prototypes (a fictional object that is part of the narrative) can help suspend disbelief by normalizing visualizations of a more diverse, equitable future, enabling positive social change over the longer term.

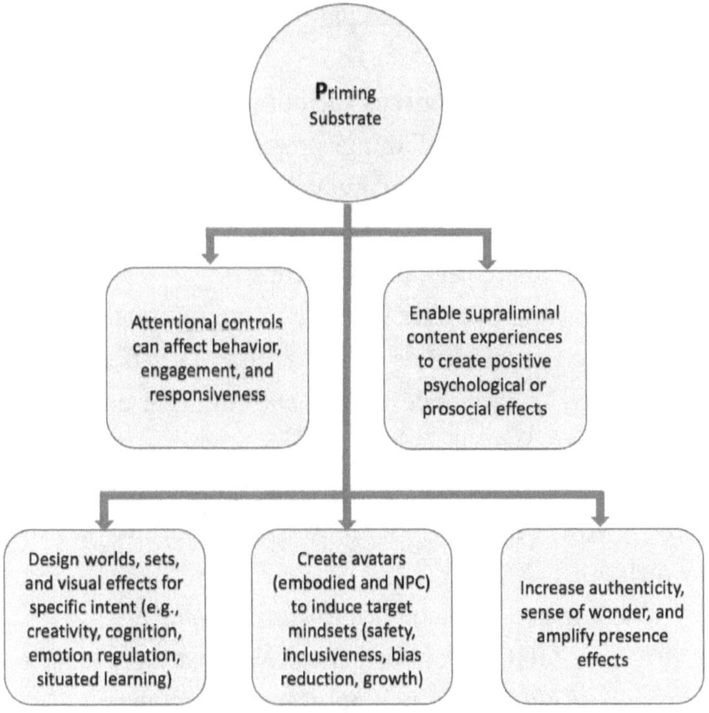

Benefits of the Priming Substrate

"In summary, we talked about six main VR

capabilities: Immersion, Embodiment, Interactivity, Creative Canvas, Computational Platform, and Priming Substrate.

"**Immersion** allows us to have a multisensory experience with our eyes, ears, hands, bodies, and internal guidance systems that manage our hand-eye coordination, spatial orientation, and balance.

"**Embodiment** gives us the feeling of body ownership and even allows us to identify with the avatar personas, the same way an actor would if they were playing a specific role and they were dressed up for the performance.

"**Interactivity** allows us to travel, navigate, interact with characters or system resources, and manipulate the virtual world, allowing us to play, learn, or experience how things work.

"The **creative canvas** and **computational platforms** work together to make all things possible. We can create any simulated real, fictional, or hybrid world and any iterative experiences that we can imagine. We can create a film set for linear or interactive digital storytelling.

"Working together with our computational platform, within these virtual worlds lies a **priming substrate**, giving us the ability to influence, affect, and improve our feelings and behaviors. We can reduce anxiety, improve creativity or cognition, and increase diversity in an unobtrusive manner.

"Now, before we wrap up today's lecture, are there any questions?"

Jag raised his hand briefly and began.

"You talked about presence. Why isn't presence one of these core elements? Is it not important enough?"

"That's an interesting question," remarked Elias.

"Yes, presence is extremely important. In fact, achieving that feeling of being fully present in the virtual world is the first objective of VR. This makes everything else possible and much more effective. So, while the other core capabilities are 'things that you can do,' presence is a feeling or result that you can achieve *because* of the 'things that you can do.'

"But it is not a guaranteed feeling. For example, if the quantified levels of immersion are poor with low resolution and high latency, or the virtual world is poorly designed, the feelings of presence will be diminished considerably, possibly to nothing, and the experience becomes more of a distraction. Hence, presence is not a given but most often resides on a continuum from "no presence' to 'fully present.'"

One last question, I thought. Elias acknowledged my raised hand.

"At the beginning of the lecture, you mentioned that you would explain the difference between VR and 'The Metaverse.' Can you explain?" I asked.

Elias smiled widely, "I was waiting for that question. If you're going to compete in a Billion Dollar Metaverse Challenge, it would be good to know what a Metaverse is, would it not?"

"Absolutely," signaled the crowd with nodding heads.

"The Metaverse," Elias began, "became a big thing in business culture only recently. The term Metaverse was first used in a 1992 science fiction novel called 'Snow Crash' by Neal Stephenson, where he describes a futuristic immersive world accessible via headset or computer. In fact, he described much of what we've been discussing and what constitutes VR today. While the Metaverse term is newly coined in popular culture, similar references to virtual reality worlds existed, as we noted in academia in the 1950s and 60s, and were referenced in a slew of movies and books from the 1980s, including Neuromancer, Tron, and Lawn Mower Man. A more advanced form of virtual reality was presented in Star Trek: The Next Generation (the late 1980s) as the Holodeck, a fully immersive VR user interface (UI) that surpassed the need for even a headset.

"All these historic media references are great, but they can also be confusing. The media talks about this futuristic world that will someday be the Metaverse. I tend to think of it more simply as many connected virtual reality experiences. Why? Because that is what it is.

"Most of you understand the Internet, a global network of computers connected with an Internet protocol (IP) that we can interact with to read, view, watch videos, learn, or transact. Most of you use it every day. In fact, you are using it right now, as VR uses the Internet as the underlying medium of communication. After today, you should understand VR: an immersive 3D experience accessible via the Internet like almost every other website in the world.

"The Metaverse is a network of these VR experiences accessible via the Internet. So really, the Metaverse is made up of 'The Internet' and many connected VR experiences.

"And for the next question, I'm sure you are asking yourselves, 'Does the Metaverse exist?' The answer is unequivocal. **YES.** In the same way Paris existed in the sixteenth century, New York in the eighteenth century, and Beijing in the fourteenth century, the Metaverse, as a network of VR sites, exists today. Paris, Beijing, and New York are far grander today than they were back then, obviously, but they existed, and much of the original architecture remains today.

"There are thousands of connected VR experiences out there already. In fact, from your Meta Quest VR headset, you can jump to dozens of these VR application sites from the main landing world. The Campus VR Network (www.campusvr.net) that we are using now is one of those connected VR applications. So, while the Metaverse, as we've come to define it, is very much in the early stages, it is here and now. A great quote that encapsulated the concept was published in The Economist in 2004 by William Gibson, the author of Neuromancer.

'The future is already here – it's just not evenly distributed.'
-- William Gibson.

"So, while I describe the Metaverse as a network of VR-based building blocks, it is not intended to diminish the concept. Rather, to understand the underpinnings and structure that provide the resources and digital components that make it real. Over time, we'll understand the impact less by what the Metaverse is and more by what it enables in very much the same way that Marshall McLuhan contextualized other disruptive communication technologies.

"McLuhan posited that *'the medium is the message'* and theorized that the medium is any innovation or enhancement that extends human capability. The lightbulb brings light to an environment providing new visual insights and allowing many new activities during periods of darkness. Similarly, VR and the Metaverse will enable many new possibilities, including the design of high-fidelity learning spaces and custom-designed scenarios in business, education, and commerce to realistically simulate specifically desired contexts.

"To relate this to the earlier examples, while these extensions of our visual/spatial capability provide a tangible, observable result manifesting as the Metaverse, McLuhan's theory suggests that the message is the overall impact of the medium. For example, providing customized VR learning environments will create feelings of presence and authenticity but may also improve academic performance, induce positive affect, and improve creativity.

"By connecting people and cultures from around the world within authentic and culturally diverse environments for gaming, learning, or simply hanging out, it will become a conduit of tolerance, reduced racism, and global empathy building. All of this can be achieved while reducing carbon emissions on the planet as humans choose digital alternatives that are far less toxic than automobiles. And, in many cases, better options than profligate international travel just because we can."

Elias scanned the environment.

No hands, so he concluded, "In closing, I will leave you with this. There are so many aspects of virtual reality and the Metaverse that excite me. The technology applications are limited by our own imaginations and our budgets, obviously. To encapsulate the 'best of' VR, I've created a top ten list for your reference to consider when thinking about the next steps for your contest submissions. I will see you next week."

Top Ten Benefits of
Virtual Reality and the Metaverse

1. VR can create experiences and simulations that are otherwise just not possible.

2. VR is globally scalable and can link the entire world with near-reality-like experiences. This makes the world very small and connects us all in ways we never thought possible.

3. VR allows us to bring global communities together in shared spaces that are designed with specific intent.

4. We can connect experts and teachers to learners in real time anytime, anywhere in the world.

5. Cloud-based personalization technology and AI can enable personalized adaptive learning experiences that are suited to everyone's unique needs and pace.

6. VR affords the design of spaces and avatars to improve creativity, cognition, and academic performance.

7. VR experiences may also facilitate the design of culturally diverse worlds and characters to improve inclusiveness, reducing stereotype threats and implicit racial biases.

8. VR-based gamification and data analytics tools make the process of learning fun and engaging.

9. As a result of network efficiency and the use of localized/ edge computing applications, there is efficiency inherent with VR technology that will reduce overall Internet traffic.

10. Eco Solutions. As we move a portion of our interactions to virtual, this reduces carbon emissions and pollution.

CHAPTER EIGHT

In Digestion and Reflection

As we took off our headsets and looked at each other, there was a collective sense of, "Wow, this stuff is amazing," mitigated somewhat by a feeling of, "What have we gotten ourselves into?"

We exited the building together and agreed to meet up the next day after work to start putting together our pitches for our initial submission. Within three weeks, for the first elimination round, along with tens of thousands of other teams, we would submit a one-page pitch of our metaverse business concept.

There was so much to think about. For one, I was surprised by the current state of technology. Even though tech was a big part of my life, I could not believe the VR class that we had just experienced. Elias was right, and the quote from that Neuromancer dude was also dead on. The technology, more than sufficient as an alternative to online learning and a damn site better than Zoom-like technology, was here NOW. This would be a game changer once people had a chance to fully experience it. So how do we participate? I thought. And this was just one domain. There were five submission categories that needed to be considered.

The next day after work, we met at the local pub, where we first decided to embark on this metaverse challenge. Three weeks ago, these same five forlorn souls met here in the same place to mourn the death of our friend. Three weeks later, the same five people were meeting but now with a renewed sense of purpose, possibly induced by a sense of our own mortality brought on by JI's passing but also with an excitement about our new sense of hope and possibility. I was no business genius, but based on everything I'd seen so far, I was convinced that this VR/metaverse technology was going to change the world for the better.

But where to start? There was a great deal of work to do. Firstly, we had to explore the various categories to determine what would give us the best chance of winning. Then we had to research each domain and come up with a viable pitch. Would we choose one category or place submissions in all five categories?

I arrived first, and when I saw our good waiter friend Wally Billings over behind the bar, I motioned for him to come over. He smiled, acknowledged me, and said he'd be right over. As I waited, I noticed a large screen in the center of the bar area was doing a news update on the Metaverse Challenge. Interestingly, normally these screens are filled with sporting events like baseball, football, or hockey combined with a million highlights featuring "best of" sporting moments. Today, we watched Technology News Network (TNN). All tech, all the time!

The lead anchor, Bunk Thursday, was giving an update on the Metaverse Challenge.

"Well, it's less than three weeks from the first submission to The Billion Dollar Metaverse Challenge, and it has taken the world by storm. Perhaps people are bored with the ongoing soap opera that sporting events have become, but we're seeing burgeoning viewership on all things tech. People seem to be excited. To discuss this, we have our lead tech correspondent, Katherine Hong, in the studio with us today. Good afternoon, Katherine."

"Good afternoon to you, Bunk. It's nice to be here," she replied.

"So, Katherine, what's all the fuss about with this Metaverse Challenge? Why has it become such a big thing? It seems like that's all anybody is talking about," asked Bunk.

"Good question. There are a few reasons for this Bunk. Firstly, I think we've hit a point of confluence where the technology experience and the economic viability curve are meeting. For example, the latest VR headset technology, retailing for about four hundred dollars, offers the capabilities of what would have cost researcher groups tens of thousands of dollars for equivalent functionality less than twenty years ago. And four hundred dollars is a fraction of the cost of the latest smartphones. Today, with a VR headset and a twenty-dollar software package, you can visit any landmark in the world, exercise, play games, meditate, or even attend classes.

"Secondly, it also brings people together in a way that was never possible before. Because these applications are underpinned by the Internet, it has all the inherent advantages and recent innovations of the Web, but with a next-generation 3D visual experience. It really is the next layer of the Internet, or Web 3.0, if you prefer. I can connect to friends, family, and different social or cultural groups anywhere in the world. And not just on a web page or chat forum, but in a room, café, or cottage where real people are present and embodied. This offers a truly social experience for the over fifty million estimated users with these VR Headsets currently.

"Thirdly, I think people are frustrated with rising inflation, pandemics, lockdowns, and the general feeling that governments around the world are always a step behind. A contest like this offers an escape, hope, and a sense of control where you can imagine a future world and possibly, create it.

"Finally, Bunk, there is just plain excitement about the competition. A billion dollars is a lot of cash, and people are genuinely excited by that. Who doesn't want a billion dollars?" Katherine smiles.

"Thanks for the wonderful insight, Katherine," offered Bunk, "But there appears to be a lot of negative rhetoric and opinion about VR and the whole metaverse idea. For example, here is a recent quote from Olivia West, an investigative journalist and human rights advocate.

"'This Metaverse is a hoax and a fraud. People are not going to live in a virtual world, wearing a VR headset all day and disconnecting from people. People are going to lose a lot of money from this technology, and what is worse, most people can't afford it. It's time that we stood up against this craziness and put public policies in place the prevent this from happening.'

"So, what do you say to the Naysayers?"

"Well, the great thing about this topic is it does elicit lots of different opinions, and that spirited discussion is good. I will say this, however.

"Many media folks with strong negative opinions, like Olivia, have never actually taken the time to try a VR headset for any reasonable amount of time or to learn how the technology works. They make spurious claims and spew ideology that challenges all that is good about technological innovation.

"I do not think people will spend all day, every day, in a VR headset either, but questioning whether this market will happen makes no sense at all. That ship has already sailed. VR is already being used for all sorts of applications, and the technology is growing faster than any other technology today at this point. Depending on what your sources are, the annual growth rate of the VR industry is expected to exceed fifteen percent, with a tenfold increase in market size over the next five years.

"Personally, I view VR as a spatial computing device, a compliment to my computer and smartphone. I use my headset for teaching about six hours per week, for short meetings, and, yes, for some lifestyle and entertainment applications," Katherine smiles radiantly, "I'm a bit of a gamer. Overall, I spend less than three hours per day in VR. This may seem like a lot of time, but the average person spends more daily time than this banging away on their smartphone.

"I also think there will be lots of winners and losers, and much of that discourse is playing itself out in the media right now. For example, let's say that thirty percent of our business and education meetings move to the Metaverse, which reduces consumption considerably in many different areas. It means fewer cars on the road, less gas or electricity consumption, less clothing, and less fast-food consumption. It also means that we will require fewer new schools or business buildings. If your livelihood is linked to any of these industries, you will experience a decline. On the other hand, there will be lots of new opportunities created for those involved in building the Metaverse, writing software, designing virtual spaces and digital clothing, or other asset designs. Admittedly, all technology tools can have both positive and negative effects. A knife can carve beautiful art but also kill people. TVs can be used to educate, inform, and entertain people in positive ways but can also be used to spew negative propaganda and can become an addictive device for many people. We make choices and create public policies on how to apply technologies safely. Burying our heads in the sand only empowers the negative use of technology. This is something we should all embrace.

"To Olivia, I can only suggest that she take the time to learn more about how this technology can make the world better and join us in this technology revolution. With less consumption and reduced carbon emission, this IS the type of solution that will help solve many of the challenges we are currently facing. It is part of the solution.

"And finally, the market is here. It is growing fast, so for all our viewers, the question is not if this is going to happen but what role you choose to play in this new digital world."

"Thank you, Katherine," Bunk answers. "It's always wonderful to get your technology insights for our viewers. You are so direct, and you speak from the heart."

"You're welcome. My pleasure," says Katherine.

Bunk closes, "Don't forget, if you want more of Katherine's technology acumen, visit her podcast, 'Tech me? Tech you!' dropping monthly on our TNN website.

"Coming up next, 'Is this just a game? Are we living in a virtual reality already, simply avatars that are connected to consciousness in a higher dimension?' Our next guest, an MIT graduate and researcher, has some interesting theories to share. Stay tuned."

A gentle tap on my shoulder caught me by surprise. Wally smiled.

"Hi, Wally," I said, "I got caught up in the interview. They have some interesting guests on TNN."

He agreed and asked me if we were staying for dinner or just for drinks. I suggested that we would likely prefer a high-top table for drinks, as we could only stay for an hour or so.

Just as I was being seated, Frances and Dania walked in and joined me at the table. We exchanged hugs.

"Are the other guys coming?" I asked. Frances shrugged, and Dania gave an equally non-informative expression. But just then, my cellphone vibrated. It was a text from RoMac. He and Jag were caught in traffic and would be there in five. "All good," I responded, "See you soon."

Wally took our drink orders while Frances and Dania got comfortable.

"So, how do you guys feel today after that lecture yesterday?" I asked.

"Honestly?" queried Frances, rarely the first to respond, especially in the presence of Dania, the quickest wit in the West, "I had a difficult time sleeping last night.

My mind was racing about the possibilities."

"Wow, me too," added Dania, "I kept thinking about all the things we could do. It's a bit like playing God and having the opportunity to create your own reality."

We chuckled at the thought, but Dania was right. This technology offered a sense of agency and a feeling of renewed possibility, like the feeling you get with a do-over, a blank canvas, or when a deck of cards is redealt. God knows we all needed one of those.

At that point, RoMac and Jag came in and joined us at the table. After exchanging pleasantries and making a toast to our new endeavor, we got down to work. In the next three weeks, we had to come up with a business idea that was going to change the world and ameliorate every financial worry we ever had and then some.

"Here's the first question then," I said, "There are five categories. Have you thought about what we should focus on? What categories do you prefer?"

"I'm pretty keen about the educational space," said RoMac, "I know that I'm biased, as teaching has been my life, but I was blown away by what Elias was demonstrating and how we could totally transform the teaching experience, for both the student and the teacher."

"I dunno," responded Jag, "At the end of the day, I think it's all about selling stuff and doing it in more innovative ways. I think we should consider something in Commerce, something that could change the nature of the whole buying experience."

"Okay, what about you, Frances?" I asked, "With all that mental cycling last night, was there anything that really kept you up?"

"Ya know, I've always dreamed of doing something

big, building a global community focused on a just cause. I've been heavily involved with lots of causes, women's rights, diversity, inclusiveness, and gender rights, but my sense is we'd need to pick one thing and build with a global scale in mind. I'm just not sure what that 'just cause' is at this point. I need to think about it."

"Okay, Dania, how about you?" I asked.

"I'm a bit like Frances. I have an idea, but I'm not quite sure specifically. I've spent my life selling 'shit,' most recently marijuana franchises, and while that's fine, this is a chance to create something unique that solves big problems. What were all the categories again?" she asked.

"There were five categories that we could choose. Education, Entertainment, Commerce, Environment, Social/Community Building," I responded.

"So, I think I'd like to do something with the environment," said Dania, "I learned a lot about marijuana, what it takes to properly grow, and the impact that even a subtle weather change can have on entire crops."

"Okay, so we have four of the five categories covered. No one interested in the entertainment space?" I asked.

I had some major concerns myself about the entertainment marketplace. Based on the current state of gaming on Xbox, PlayStation, Nintendo, and PC games, the likely transition of all these games, which were already designed as 3D experiences, seemed imminent, an inevitable tidal wave of activity from companies with deep pockets, strong franchises, and existing gamers. This would be a difficult area to compete within. Nonetheless, someone had to cover this space.

"Okay, then perhaps I can work up an idea or

concept in that domain. That way, we could have some initial research in all five categories. And given that each pitch is only one page, it might not be a bad idea to submit one for each category if each entry is treated independently," I offered.

"Agreed," said Dania, "But before we go, let's decide on a template that can be used for our research summary. That way, we'll have some consistency for our ideas and a basis for the comparison."

"Great idea!" said Jag, "I think we should keep it simple. Perhaps an overview of the business, the target market audience, and what it is that is special or unique about the business you are proposing."

"Like a unique selling proposition?" said Dania.

"Yeah, exactly," responded Jag.

"What about the money? And how are we going to get that money?" said Frances.

"Good point," I said, "Got to have that 'SHOW ME THE MONEY' section. We need to identify the business model, how we make money, and how we intend to market that business."

"What about the money needed to invest? Should we not indicate how much money it will take?" asked RoMac.

"I'm assuming that all these details would be taken care of at a later stage. We only have one page to sell our idea, and besides, whatever business we pitch will need to deploy hundreds of millions of dollars. That's the whole idea, right? So, THINK BIG," implored Frances.

A general nod of agreement from all.

"So, each of us will come up with the best concept we can think of for one of the five categories containing the following sections.

- Overview/Executive Summary of the Business
- Target Market/Market Analysis
- Business Model and/or Revenue Streams
- Unique Selling Proposition
- Marketing Strategy

"Then we can dig into each area to flesh out these sections in more detail. Are we all on the same page?" I said.

"Yes," said Jag, "But that's a lot to cram into one page. It better be rock solid and succinct."

"Absolutely," I agreed, "But that's the challenge, I guess."

We hugged and agreed to meet later that week at the coffee shop near the university to discuss our progress and prep for Elias' next lecture.

CHAPTER NINE

Visualizing the Metaverse

As I started working through my research that week, I kept trying to visualize what a day in the Metaverse would be like. I appreciated the exciting VR applications, many already here, and how they would form the building blocks of the Metaverse. Still, we needed to understand these components' overall effects. How would it change life as we know it? If I could visualize that, it would help me understand the business opportunity to serve that new reality.

So, I started to imagine what it would be like in the year 2044, on a day like any other, with all the technology predictions about the Metaverse and what we had learned from Elias fully realized. What would it be like to wake up, prepare for the day, go to school, shop, and have some fun? I closed my eyes and continued to imagine and visualize my future experience and transported myself into the year 2044.

2044, A Day Like Any Other

I woke up to my personalized AI alarm playing "Stayin' Alive" by the Bee Gees at the exact moment I was dreaming about dancing like John Travolta in Saturday Night Fever. Talk about perfect timing! I couldn't help but laugh and do a little dance while getting out of bed.

I put on my glasses and checked my calendar while sipping my morning coffee. Today was going to be a busy one, with three classes at Metaversity One (M1), some shopping, and social activities later that evening. But first, I readied for my yoga class. It was my morning ritual and always seemed to make the rest of my day go much better.

"Good morning!" a cheerful voice greeted me. It was Skylar. She was going to join me for yoga today. Skylar was my Koyaboki.

The phrase "Koya aboki", shortened to Koyaboki, is translated directly as "learned friend" in the African Hausa language. Koyabokis were a type of artificial intelligence called Pedagogical Agents of Learning or PALs. M1 created their own brand of PALs called Koyabokis, and the students absolutely loved them. Ever since I started at M1, I had the use of my Koyaboki, which I called Skylar. You could use them as much as you wanted in your learning or personal life, and once you graduated, the Koyaboki was yours to keep.

Skylar was incredible, and I'm not sure how I would

have gotten by without her. The more we got to know each other, the closer we became. That might have seemed weird, but I could ask Skylar anything, and she would provide a thoughtful, considerate, and sometimes funny answer. She was also very curious and asked me many questions, which was good because it forced me to think about and recall things that were important.

Today's yoga session took place on a breathtaking mountainside meadow with lush green grass and vibrant wildflowers. The snow-capped peaks in the distance and the soothing sound of a nearby waterfall created the perfect atmosphere for relaxation and mindfulness.

When we arrived, we were greeted by our yoga instructor, an AI-driven holographic avatar with the calming presence and expertise of a seasoned yogi. Participants from all around the world joined in, each with their unique avatars. It was amazing to see people of different ages, genders, cultures, and skill levels come together for this shared experience.

As the class began, our instructor guided us through a series of asanas, or yoga postures, while providing clear and detailed instructions. Skylar was there to offer personalized adjustments and modifications based on my flexibility and fitness level. The haptic feedback from my suit allowed me to "feel" Skylar's gentle guidance as I moved through the postures.

As we transitioned into a balancing pose, a soft breeze rustled through the virtual trees, and I could "feel" the sensation of the grass beneath my feet. It was amazing how easily I was able to lose myself in the moment and fully engage with the practice.

During the relaxation phase at the end of the class,

our instructor led us through a guided meditation. As we lay in savasana, the sound of the waterfall and the gentle chirping of birds enveloped us, transporting our minds to a place of tranquility and peace.

The class concluded with a heartfelt "Namaste" from our instructor and a virtual group hug among the participants. It was incredible to see how this class could bring people together, transcending geographical boundaries and fostering a sense of community and connection.

As we left the virtual yoga class, I couldn't help but feel revitalized and rejuvenated.

But now it was time for school. While I didn't have a specific requirement, I had committed to myself that I would complete three classes every weekday. At this rate, it would allow me to level up every four months and complete my annual requirements. If I continued at this pace, I would complete my degree in sixteen months, but since I was considering a two-month break after my second-year level-up, I would be done in eighteen months.

This was an amazingly flexible system because some of my friends were still taking four years to complete their degrees at the local university. This new program that M1 offered saved me over two years of time and a whole lot of money. At five thousand dollars annually, I could get my degree for less than $7,500 and be available to work full-time within eighteen months.

Even though M1 was growing exponentially and with user satisfaction ratings through the roof, there were still some traditionalists that scoffed at the idea of a Metaversity. I was convinced, however, and anyone who had been open-minded enough to experience M1 was blown away. Each and every class was a compelling digital experience that left you wanting more. What was more, it was presented as a game journey which made the whole process incredibly fun. The local university tuition was fifteen thousand dollars annually, and most degree programs took four years to complete. Further, their course content usually consisted of badly designed slideshow presentations, many internet videos, and unmotivated professors that seemed disconnected from what was really happening in the marketplace.

Today, it was Archeology 101, Advanced Math, and Early English Literature. Well, I chose English Literature; the course could be simultaneously offered in 126 languages. My friend Amin took his section in Persian Literature, while Kabushiko, another classmate, took hers in Japanese Lit.

When I first stepped into the virtual archeology classroom at M1, I found myself standing in the middle of an ancient city, so realistic that I could almost feel the breeze rustling through the leaves of the virtual trees.

"Hey, Joey!" a cheerful voice greeted me. It was Skylar. Today, we were exploring the ruins of Machu Picchu, and I was excited to dive into the lesson. As the AI-driven holographic professor began their lecture, Skylar and I examined 3D models and high-resolution images of the artifacts. Skylar's vast knowledge of archeology and the ability to answer my questions in real-time made the learning process feel engaging and personal.

When it was time for the hands-on activity, I put on my haptic suit and gloves, which allowed me to "touch" and "feel" the virtual artifacts. I marveled at the intricate carvings and weathered textures as Skylar guided me through the proper handling techniques and provided context on each object's historical significance.

We then joined a small group of students for a virtual excavation, where we started unearthing buried treasures. With Skylar's help, I operated an AI-driven drone that could virtually dig without disturbing the physical environment. The ground-penetrating radar, or LIDAR technology we used, allowed us to identify and map the hidden structures beneath the surface.

One of the most thrilling moments was when we discovered a piece of pottery with ancient inscriptions. Skylar assisted me with her AI-powered language model to decipher the text, revealing a fascinating story about the people who once lived there. Years ago, the AI language module was called ChatGPT, an AI that showed a fraction of the promise of today's bots but scared people with how knowledgeable it seemed to be. Everyone was afraid of losing their jobs. As it turned out, though, this technology created way more jobs than were lost and really helped to democratize education for the masses. Today, all M1's Koyaboki models had these new language features, and they are a hundred times smarter than those early dinosaurs like ChatGPT.

As the class progressed, we had the opportunity to travel back in time and walk through the fully restored ancient city, referred to as "The Lost City of the Incas." Interacting with AI-driven NPCs (non-player characters) and hearing their first-hand accounts of daily life was like stepping into a living history book. Skylar helped me analyze the information, deepening my understanding of the customs and events of the past.

At the end of the class, the professor reminded us about our final course project and asked if we had any questions or concerns. We were good. For our final project, Skylar and I decided to investigate a real archeological site.

By combining all the techniques we'd have learned, we would put together a comprehensive analysis of the site, and our findings would be showcased in M1s virtual museum, complete with interactive exhibits and a holographic guided tour. That is, if it was good enough.

But now, it was time for math class.

I took a brief bio break, then teleported into the main math classroom at M1. I was awed by the vibrant environment surrounding me. It was as if I had entered a living, breathing world made of numbers and geometric shapes.

Skylar greeted me again with a warm smile. Today she would guide me through the complexities of the math curriculum and ensure that I had a personalized learning experience tailored to my needs.

Today's class was focused on exploring fractals, and the virtual environment was filled with mesmerizing 3D patterns and infinite sequences. We started by examining the famous Mandelbrot set, and I couldn't believe how intricate and beautiful the patterns were as I zoomed in closer and closer.

The AI-driven professor began the lesson with an interactive lecture on the principles of fractals, including their properties and how they could be generated. Skylar was always there to provide additional context, examples, and even fun facts about fractals' applications in nature and art.

As the lecture progressed, the virtual environment dynamically adjusted to reflect the concepts being discussed. With Skylar's guidance, I was able to manipulate the virtual fractals, changing their parameters and observing how the transformations affected the patterns. The haptic feedback from my gloves allowed me to "feel" the texture of the fractals, making the learning experience even more immersive.

When it was time for group work, Skylar and I joined a team of students to collaboratively create our own fractal masterpiece. Using AR-enhanced tools, we combined our knowledge of mathematical functions and artistic creativity to design a breathtaking piece of virtual art.

One of my favorite moments was when we started discussing the practical applications of fractals in real life. Skylar showed me how they could be used to model natural phenomena, such as the formation of coastlines, and even to create realistic computer-generated landscapes in movies and video games.

In the past year, I have really grown to love math. The combination of interactive virtual environments, personalized guidance from Skylar, and the collaborative spirit of my fellow students made learning math enjoyable and engaging. A subject that I once considered dry was now an exciting journey of discovery. Now, I'm not only building a strong foundation in math but also gaining a new appreciation for the beauty and wonder of the mathematical world around us.

As I exited the math class, I glanced at the time and realized I had a two-hour break before my next class. I decided it was the perfect opportunity to do some shopping and grab lunch at the nearby Experitopia Mall. Skylar was excited to join me on this little adventure.

When we arrived at the mall, we were greeted by an incredible virtual space that felt like a futuristic shopping paradise, a cross between a gorgeous parkland setting that was floating through space. Holographic signs and interactive displays guided us to our destinations. Skylar, always eager to help, pulled up a map of the place and suggested the most efficient route to cover our shopping list.

Our first stop was the shoe store, where I needed to buy a new pair of running shoes. Skylar scanned my feet and suggested a few models based on my gait, foot shape, and running habits. I tried on different pairs of shoes, and when I found the pair that seemed to work best, I put on my haptic shoes and tested them on a virtual running track. They not only looked great, but I could feel the support and balance in these puppies. I felt like I was walking on air, which I guess I actually was.

Next, we headed to that trendy clothing area called Chill Fashions to find a new shirt. Skylar, with a keen eye for fashion, helped me browse through the virtual racks and select a few options that matched my style preferences. I was able to "try on" the shirts virtually, making it easy to choose the perfect one that complemented my avatar. The AI attendant was also quite helpful as she made suggestions of various accessories that I might want to consider to compliment the shirt.

With our shopping done, I completed the transactions with a simple swipe to acknowledge acceptance for the shirt and shoes in my virtual basket. I also decided to add a real pair of shoes to my virtual ones. I opted to stay just virtual with the shirt, for now, to see what kind of response it received. I could always buy the real one later with a simple expression that Experitopia had just introduced called "Make it Real!". One use of that expression and the object selected would appear at your door within two hours. It was fun to say, but you had to be careful because it was considerably more expensive to "Make it Real."

Skylar and I then ventured to the restaurant island for a well-deserved lunch. We decided on sushi and bubble tea – a delicious combination! We sat in a gorgeous Japanese-themed retreat area, complete with cherry blossoms and the soothing sound of a nearby koi pond. Upon ordering, my meal arrived at the door, as advertised, within twenty minutes.

As we enjoyed our meal, we couldn't help but marvel at the level of detail and realism in this place. Even the Koi in the pond responded when you fed them virtual breadcrumbs. Oh, and the food was fantastic. Each piece of sushi looked and tasted authentic, and the bubble tea was the perfect blend of sweet and refreshing.

After finishing our lunch, Skylar and I took a leisurely stroll through the old-growth forest and back to Metaversity One, feeling refreshed and ready to tackle our next class. Skylar and I were both looking forward to our English literature class, where we would be studying ancient playwrights from the fifteen hundreds.

As we entered the virtual classroom, we found ourselves transported to a stunningly realistic recreation of the Globe Theatre in London, England. The wooden stage, open-air setting, and lively audience created an atmosphere that truly captured the essence of the Elizabethan era.

Our professor, an expert in Renaissance literature, appeared on stage dressed as a playwright from the fifteen hundreds, complete with a feathered quill and inkwell. Today's class was focused on the works of William Shakespeare, arguably the most famous and influential playwright of all time, at least from Europe.

The professor began by providing historical context and an overview of Shakespeare's life and work. Skylar, ever the helpful Koyaboki, pulled up additional resources, images, and interactive displays that enriched the lecture and provided a deeper understanding of the subject matter.

As we delved into the analysis of Shakespeare's original version of King Lear, professional actors appeared on stage, performing scenes and monologues from the play, allowing us to see the characters and their emotions come alive before our eyes.

Skylar and I were invited to participate in a virtual roundtable discussion with other students, sharing our thoughts and interpretations of the text. The lively debate and exchange of ideas fostered a deeper appreciation for the complexities and nuances of Shakespeare's writing.

As the class progressed, we also explored the works of other playwrights from the fifteen hundreds, such as Christopher Marlowe and Ben Jonson, and were also able to witness live performances of their plays.

Toward the end of the session, we challenged ourselves with interactive quizzes and games that tested our knowledge and understanding of what we had learned.

Being here in the Globe Theatre made studying English literature a captivating and engaging journey. We left the theatre with a newfound appreciation for the brilliance of these ancient playwrights and the timeless power of their words. The fusion of this cutting-edge technology and classic literature created an unforgettable learning experience.

But that was enough learning for today. I thanked Skylar for her wonderful support, took off my glasses, and decided to chill for a bit. It was only 3 pm, and my friends and I weren't scheduled to meet until seven, so I took the time to go for a walk around the lake and hit the gym for some much-needed cardio and weights. After my workout, I summoned Skylar to help me create the coolest stir fry with all the ingredients I had in my fridge. This would be fun. It was incredible how creative we could be together.

The base of the dish consisted of fluffy jasmine rice, which provided the perfect foundation for the medley of ingredients. It featured a colorful assortment of vegetables, including thinly sliced bell peppers in red, yellow, and green, which added a sweet and crunchy element to the dish. There were also tender-crisp broccoli florets, fresh carrots cut into matchsticks, and vibrant sugar snap peas that offered a satisfying snap in each bite. To balance out the flavors, thinly sliced onions and garlic were also included, providing a savory depth to the dish.

For our protein fix, the stir-fry had succulent pieces of marinated tofu, which absorbed the flavors of the sauce and spices brilliantly. It was pan-fried to achieve a slightly crispy exterior while maintaining a soft and tender interior, making it a delightful addition to the dish. Finally, it was garnished with a sprinkling of toasted sesame seeds and chopped green onions, adding an extra layer of flavor and a pop of color. The result was a harmonious balance of flavors, textures, and colors that made for a delicious and satisfying dinner.

Skylar and I both agreed that we'd store this recipe for later when we wanted to really impress someone. After a twenty-minute power nap and a quick shower, I was ready for some fun.

I began the evening at a popular virtual hangout spot, a beautifully designed space reminiscent of a trendy rooftop lounge. The view of the city skyline was breathtaking, and the atmosphere was enhanced by a lively soundtrack of modern jazz playing in the background. When my friends Nathalie, Lisa, Tom, Doris, and Richard arrived, we decided to jump into a game called "Tossed in Space.", the exciting new massively multiplayer online game that was taking the Metaverse by storm.

The premise of the game was simple. The Earth has been destroyed, and you and your friends have been tossed into space. Hence the name of the game. It was a thrilling space adventure that had us working together to settle on a new planet. What made it fun was that you had to fend off hostile aliens and develop a thriving new world, all while competing with other parties trying to do the same.

To start the evening, we headed over to the virtual space station to choose our avatars and roles for the game. Nathalie was the skilled engineer, Tom was our fearless pilot, Lisa was our cunning strategist and head of security, and I was our resident scientist. Richard, the most experienced among us, assumed the role of Starship Captain, while Doris became our resident empath. Together, we made an excellent team, ready to face the challenges ahead.

As we embarked on our journey, our spaceship traveled through the vast expanse of space, reaching our destination: an uncharted planet in the Goldilocks zone, ripe for settlement. The game's graphics were stunning, making us feel as if we were truly exploring the cosmos.

Upon landing, we began the process of colonization, using our unique skills to establish a foothold in the alien world. Under Richard's direction, Nathalie built and maintained crucial infrastructure while Tom charted the planet's terrain to scout for resources. I conducted research on the local flora and fauna, and Lisa devised plans for our growing colony's defense and expansion. As for Doris?

She kept us all sane with regular psychological consults that helped us mitigate PTSD and the travails of regular alien attacks.

As we progressed in the game, we encountered a hostile alien species headed by an evil supervillain named Zorbax4 Theta and his first mate John. They threatened our nascent settlement, but we worked together to fend them off and protect our new home. The intense battles and high-stakes encounters kept us on the edge of our seats, making the experience even more exhilarating. In the end, we blew Zorbax4 Theta and his entire crew into smithereens, collecting the pieces and using them for fertilizer to improve local crop production. The taste of victory was sweet, and so also would be the taste of the new crops.

In between skirmishes, we continued developing our colony, drawing inspiration from the American settlers of the late sixteen hundreds. We established farms, trading posts and even developed cultural centers that showcased the unique aspects of our new world. We learned to adapt to our environment, grow as a team, and celebrate our victories.

As the night ended, our little colony flourished into a thriving, self-sufficient world. We took a moment to appreciate the fruits of our labor and admire the virtual landscape we had shaped together. The camaraderie we forged and the challenges we overcame made the experience truly unforgettable.

And We're Back

As I opened my eyes, it felt like I'd been lucid dreaming. I immediately reviewed my thoughts and felt a much better sense of the possibilities. I quickly wrote down everything I could remember so that I could share it with the rest of the team.

Visualization was a hit-or-miss process for me, but this time I felt like it worked. When it did, I always gained insights that I could never have obtained otherwise. Apparently, our most creative time is in that hypnagogic state of mind between wakefulness and sleep, so I would strive to let myself drift, but not too much.

I sent an email to the team the following day and shared my visualization with the hopes of providing a bit more context for our thinking related to potential opportunities. Most agreed that this step proved beneficial, as I noticed our focus become sharper and more deliberate.

Before long, it would become abundantly clear that the futuristic mirage of 2044 was not as distant as I had previously imagined. Several seemingly avant-garde applications such as V-Commerce, Virtual Yoga Sessions, and Immersive Virtual Universities had already begun to blossom, sprouting their roots in the fertile soil of this digital revolution. The locomotive of progress had already commenced its journey, and we found ourselves to be not merely spectators but active passengers on this exciting voyage. There was still a long journey ahead, but the treasure map was slowly materializing.

CHAPTER X

The Story Express

Dear readers, at this point, the deeper dive into the backend technical infrastructure is an optional journey, one that will invigorate some while challenging others unnecessarily. So, much like a game of snakes and ladders, you can choose to climb right back into the heart of the story. As such, we've summarized succinctly the essence of each of the three bonus chapters for those who prefer story progression while making the "Bonus Chapters" available in the Appendix for those who prefer to get their geek on.

Chapter X.1 – Getting into the Headspace

This chapter discusses the critical importance of understanding and keeping pace with technological evolution, using the downfall of Blockbuster Video as a cautionary tale. Blockbuster, once a dominant retail giant, failed to adapt to digital streaming technologies and declined rapidly after dismissing the opportunity to purchase Netflix. This is juxtaposed with Netflix's astronomical growth to a market capitalization of $200 billion. Similarly, Uber's innovation severely disrupted the taxicab industry.

We reflect on the need to identify potential areas of disruption and apply innovative models to future business ventures that emphasize the accelerated pace of technological change, presenting both higher risks and greater opportunities.

A subsequent lecture by Elias, suggests an unconventional learning environment—a VR beach classroom—to engage in a thought-provoking educational experience. This method aligns with Daniel Kahneman's research on "slow thinking" processes, which are activated in unfamiliar settings and can enhance learning.

In the VR classroom, Elias challenges the class to identify essential components of a virtual reality application, encouraging hands-on learning. The teams brainstorm in a gamified setting on virtual docks, simulating a real-world collaborative workspace. The exercise proves fruitful in understanding the complexities of VR and related technologies like Edge Computing, Blockchain, Biometric sensors, and Artificial Intelligence (AI). The narrative conveys the excitement of experiential learning and the profound implications of technological foresight and innovation in shaping the future.

Elias provides a list of essential components for creating a virtual reality application within the Metaverse, highlighting the significance of internet connectivity as its foundation. The list includes VR/AR headsets, haptic devices, development software, cloud services, content delivery networks, 5G networks, edge computing, artificial intelligence, blockchain, and IoT devices. He compares the internet's role in the Metaverse to roads in transportation and plumbing in water supply.

Providing hope to those "less youthful" teams, Elias debunks the notion that younger 'digital natives' are inherently better with technology, citing research that suggests 'personal innovativeness' is a more crucial factor for adopting new technology, regardless of age.

As a backgrounder, Elias explains the workings of the global internet, the role of ISPs, IP addresses, and the packet-switching process that ensures efficient data transmission. He then details how routers direct data, utilize protocols like BGP for path determination, and provide security features. He then clarifies computing protocols as sets of rules for communication, using TCP/IP as an example of protocols ensuring reliable data delivery over the internet and reiterates the importance of understanding these internet basics for building businesses in the Metaverse.

We then explore the evolution and components of Virtual Reality (VR) devices, focusing on the mid-2020s technology. The VR Head Mounted Device (HMD) creates a simulated 3D environment using stereoscopy to project depth, providing an immersive experience. HMDs track user head movements with sensors like accelerometers and gyroscopes and use spatial audio for a realistic sound environment. Some HMDs have haptic feedback for a tactile experience and offer controller-less interaction through hand gesture tracking. Standalone systems like the Meta Quest line of VR headsets are noted for their portability and built-in computing power.

We discuss the collaboration of components in VR headsets: sensors for movement tracking, high-resolution displays for each eye creating depth perception, lenses for image focus, 3D audio for immersive sound, controllers for interaction, and CPUs for software application control. These components communicate synchronously with cloud-based services to update avatar positions and environment interactions in real-time.

Finally, we conclude the learning session with an interactive VR exercise, reinforcing the learning about internet routers through a basketball shooting simulation, demonstrating the potential of VR to enhance education through engaging and multisensory experiences.

Chapter X.2 – Cloudy with a Chance of Software

"Cloudy with a Chance of Software" covers the importance of cloud computing in the backend operations of VR headsets and metaverse applications. Elias explains to the class that cloud computing is centralized computing resources on the internet which provide various services and that leveraging cloud-based computing is more cost-effective than hosting services on local servers. He then details specific cloud-based services vital for the metaverse, including Content Delivery Network (CDN) services for low-latency content delivery, cloud-based game engines for creating VR environments, analytics services for user data analysis, AI and machine learning services for advanced features, and Edge Computing and 5G for optimizing user experience by reducing latency.

Elias explains Blockchain technology: a decentralized ledger system that is integral to the metaverse for securing transactions and asset ownership. Blockchain's potential uses in the metaverse include creating digital assets like NFTs, decentralized marketplaces, cryptocurrency integration for transactions, smart contracts for automated agreements, and decentralized governance for community-driven decision-making. He also touches on Biometrics and IoT (Internet of Things) technologies and their applications in the metaverse for identity verification, personalization, immersive interaction, health monitoring, and creating smart environments.

Elias emphasizes the synergy between these advanced technologies—cloud computing, blockchain, biometrics, IoT—and their combined potential to revolutionize user experience within the metaverse as he segues into a more comprehensive discussion about the role of AI in metaverse businesses. He then breaks down complex Artificial Intelligence (AI) concepts into six primary categories and personifies them as superheroes to aid understanding and recall in the context of VR-metaverse applications.

Machine Learning AI: It enables computers to learn from data and make decisions or predictions without explicit programming. Machine Learning algorithms identify patterns and structures in data to infer new data. It is the most common form of AI in systems for optimizing user experiences.

Connectionist AI: Based on artificial neural networks, this AI type learns from large datasets to recognize complex patterns, including techniques like deep learning.

Symbolic AI: Also known as "Good Old-Fashioned AI," it uses logic and symbols to represent knowledge and solve problems through rule-based systems and expert systems.

Evolutionary and Swarm AI: Inspired by natural processes like evolution and collective behaviors, this AI uses algorithms that evolve over time and collective intelligence for solving optimization problems and learning within AI systems.

Affective or Emotional AI: It employs machine learning to recognize and respond to human emotions by analyzing data such as facial expressions, speech, and body language.

World Building AI Tools: This interdisciplinary effort uses various AI fields to create immersive, interactive virtual worlds, often employing procedural generation.

Elias personifies these AI categories as superheroes:

Machine Learning Man, Connector Girl, Affector, Symbolina, World Builder, and The Swarm. Each superhero represents a different aspect of AI that contributes to creating an engaging user experience in the metaverse.

We then discuss ChatGPT, an AI language model that falls under Machine Learning and Connectionist AI. Elias clarifies that despite its sophisticated responses, ChatGPT isn't sentient or self-aware; it doesn't possess genuine emotions or consciousness. It's a product of learned data patterns, not actual feelings, and doesn't directly involve the other AI categories like Symbolic or Evolutionary AI. ChatGPT functionality is likened to a collaboration between the superheroes Machine Learning Man and Connector Girl, showcasing the interconnected nature of these AI domains.

Elias emphasizes that ChatGPT, with its Natural Language Processing (NLP) capabilities, can enhance user interactions within the virtual world. ChatGPT can make virtual characters more engaging, assist chatbots, personalize experiences, and provide user support. It enables real-time communication between users in various languages, which is particularly beneficial for educational content and e-commerce within the Metaverse.

ChatGPT can also generate creative content, like descriptions, stories, and dialogues, enriching the narrative aspect of the Metaverse. Predictive analytics powered by ChatGPT can analyze user behavior to forecast trends and needs, aiding in the development of the Metaverse to align with user expectations.

The discussion shifts to quantum computing's impact on AI and the Metaverse. Elias explains that quantum computing operates on principles of quantum mechanics, using qubits that can exist in multiple states simultaneously.

This allows quantum computers to process large datasets much faster than classical computers.

Elias notes that quantum computers won't be available for personal use soon due to their stringent operational requirements, such as ultra-cold temperatures and isolation from electromagnetic interference. Instead, quantum computing will enhance cloud-based servers, indirectly improving the Metaverse experience with higher quality virtual environments, more realistic avatars, and faster response times.

He concludes the session by presenting a chart summarizing the roles of AI superheroes, suggesting that these AI tools should be considered for metaverse business proposals.

Chapter X.3 – Innovation Meets Opportunity

This section prepares the team as their submission deadline approaches. We recognize the need to integrate a VR concept with the right technology and business model, aiming for a unique and original proposal amidst stiff competition.

The final class focuses on innovation within VR applications for the Metaverse, hoping to spark the kind of epiphany that precedes great creations. Despite the excitement, we face setbacks: RoMac exits to care for his ill daughter, Frances is entangled in a difficult divorce, and financial strains are felt among the members. Despite these hurdles, we are determined to proceed with the submission.

Elias then delves into the concept of innovation, emphasizing the importance of understanding both sustaining and disruptive innovation. Disruptive innovation is particularly highlighted as it has the potential to redefine markets and industries. The session proceeds with a brainstorming activity on disruptive innovation opportunities in the education sector within the Metaverse.

We discuss the high cost and time commitment required for education, the challenges of engagement in online courses, and the inefficiencies of current educational models. We then explore how VR technology could address these issues by offering affordable, accessible, and engaging educational experiences.

Based on the insights of Elias and the prescient writings of Clayton Christensen, we were able to identify three critical questions that could inform the strategic positioning of our metaverse applications.

1. What are the 'jobs to be done' that customers are trying

to accomplish? By understanding the underlying needs and desires of customers, one can identify opportunities to create new products and services that address those needs.

2. Are there non-consumers or over-served customers in the market? Targeting segments that are either not using existing solutions or are over-served by current offerings can be fertile ground for disruptive innovation, as these customers may be more willing to adopt new, potentially lower-performing solutions with lower prices

3. Can we identify an emerging technology or business model that has the potential to disrupt existing markets? Disruptive innovations often start with lower performance compared to established products but improve over time. Identifying such technologies or business models early on can provide a competitive advantage.

In conclusion, Elias reinforces the importance of disruptive innovation in creating a successful metaverse business, and the session concludes with applause for Elias's impactful teaching. While the class sessions were over, this was not the last we'd see of Elias.

CHAPTER ELEVEN

The Submissions

Now it was up to us. The next few days were a flurry of activity and research as we worked on each of the vertical market proposals.

The earlier visualization was very helpful, and Elias' classes fortified what many of us were already feeling. We agreed to meet three days before so we could review each of the offerings before we submitted them. We also decided to enter one into each category. Even though there was intense competition, and one might argue we were defocused, it was only one page, so what did we have to lose?

We met the following Saturday before the Tuesday submission date and shared each of our vertical market one-page business plans. The one-page limit was actually defined as five hundred words or less to ensure that people weren't just cramming small text onto the page.

Given Elias's question template for identifying disruptive opportunities, we felt that each of the five submissions had sufficient merit.

On Monday night, just before midnight, we pressed the submit button on five separate one-page pitch proposals on the BDMC website. The Billion Dollar Metaverse Challenge was on.

Under the name Polar Magnates, five proposals were submitted, one for each category. They were as follows.

Submission One

Category: Education
Metaverse University – Metaversityone.com (M1)

Business Overview:
Our metaverse university will initially provide a global online Master's degree program in VR-based digital storytelling (VRDS), focused primarily on virtual reality but inclusive of augmented and mixed reality applications. We aim to provide fully immersive, interactive, and gamified learning experiences with world-class expert instructors and AI Pedagogical Agents of Learning (PALs) on a secure blockchain Learning Management System (LMS). Course content will be a mix of synchronous and asynchronous training modules affording flexibility to students to progress or "level up" at their own pace. Once we prove in the Master's VRDS program, we plan to expand offerings to additional areas of study.

Target Market:
Initially, we are targeting individuals who are interested in pursuing a Master's degree in VR-based digital storytelling. This includes recent college graduates with a background in art or computer science, working professionals looking to advance their careers, and individuals looking to develop specific skills and knowledge in VR digital storytelling.

Unique Value Proposition:
Metaversity One (M1) stands out from traditional university and online learning organizations because it offers fully immersive, interactive, and gamified learning experiences.

This allows students to progress or "level up" at their own pace. Blockchain LMS tools provide a fully secured platform, while AI learning agents accelerate the learning process. Our courses are taught by leading industry professionals and cover a range of topics related to VR, AR & MR digital storytelling, including 3D modeling, animation, narrative design, data analytics/visualization, UX, and game design. Finally, M1 course delivery will be one hundred percent virtual and ninety percent asynchronous, allowing us to scale our courses to millions of students globally and reduce the cost of the Master's VRDS program to less than $2,500 annually, with a target completion time of one year.

Revenue Streams:

We plan to generate revenue through tuition fees for our Master's program in digital storytelling in VR. Additionally, we plan to offer short-term courses and workshops to corporate customers that focus on specific topics related to VR digital storytelling. We also plan to generate revenue through partnerships with VR companies and organizations, offering services such as consulting, training, and development. Additional revenues will be added as we expand into additional fields of study.

Marketing Strategy:

Our marketing strategy will focus on targeted advertising through social media platforms, metaverse forums, and industry publications. We will also leverage partnerships with VR companies and organizations to promote our university and increase our student base. Finally, we will attend VR events to increase brand awareness

Submission Two

Category: Commerce
V Commerce Store – Experitopia.com

Business Overview:
Experitopia.com is a multi-user, fully immersive virtual shopping experience that offers apparel, shoes, art, and lifestyle products for sale in a metaverse environment. Customers may browse and model products from the comfort of their own homes using personal avatars to visualize any of the apparel, shoes, and lifestyle products and even preview what the art would look like on their virtual walls. Advanced AI curation tools will provide feedback on design, color choices, and unique offerings that augment current selections. Social environments like cafés and piazzas provide a respite from the shopping experience, while regular events like fashion shows and live entertainment further enhance the overall shopping experience. Products can be used in both virtual contexts and delivered as physical apparel to their homes.

Target Market:
Our target market is individuals who enjoy shopping for fashion and lifestyle products and are interested in exploring new and innovative shopping experiences. We believe that our virtual store will appeal to individuals who value convenience, variety, and the ability to visualize their personal avatars and art in a virtual world.

Unique Value Proposition:
Our virtual store stands out from traditional brick-and-mortar

stores and online retailers because it offers a fully immersive and interactive shopping experience that allows customers to visualize their personal avatars and art in a virtual world. The AI curation tools will provide honest and constructive feedback to improve customer aesthetics and overall satisfaction. Further, our products will be available for purchase as both physical and virtual products, and our virtual store will offer exclusive products and promotions that are not available in traditional retail stores.

Revenue Streams:

We plan to generate revenue through a variety of sources, including product sales from our virtual store, advertising, and sponsorships from fashion and lifestyle brands seeking to reach our target audience, virtual storefront rentals for brands looking to showcase their products in the Metaverse and partnerships with virtual event organizers looking to showcase products during events in the Metaverse. We also plan to offer transactional and stored value credit services as an alternative to traditional credit cards for a fee.

Marketing Strategy:

Our marketing strategy will focus on targeted advertising through social media platforms, metaverse forums, and fashion and lifestyle publications. We will also leverage partnerships with fashion and social media lifestyle influencers to promote our virtual store and increase our customer base. Additionally, we plan to attend virtual fashion and lifestyle events to showcase our products and increase brand awareness.

Submission 3

Category: Social/Community Building
The Lunch Lady Network - Lunchlady.Network

Executive Summary:
The Lunch Lady is a metaverse non-profit organization focused on solving global poverty, hunger, and wealth inequality. Our mission is to create a more equitable and sustainable world by leveraging the power of the Metaverse to promote awareness and action around these critical issues. Our iconic character, The Lunch Lady, serves as a symbol of our commitment to fight poverty and hunger in all its forms. Our programs will include educational initiatives, games, advocacy campaigns, and direct relief efforts. We will partner with local organizations on the ground to ensure that our efforts are impactful and sustainable.

Market Analysis and Target Market:
Global poverty, hunger, and wealth inequality remain major challenges facing the world today, affecting billions of people. The COVID-19 pandemic has exacerbated these problems, leading to an urgent need for innovative solutions. The Metaverse provides a unique opportunity to create a virtual space where people can come together to learn, play, collaborate, and take action to address these issues. Our target market includes individual gamers and gaming communities of all ages that are interested in wealth redistribution issues and want to take action to combat them.

Business/Revenue Model
The Lunch Lady will operate as a non-profit organization,

relying on donations, grants, and gaming revenues to fund our activities. Our primary revenue sources will be generated via an online game that allows participants to help the Lunch Lady defeat villains and build her global cafeteria both locally and globally. The Lunch Lady game will provide real-time information and data visualization of local poverty circles that need to be addressed, allowing gamers to have fun and solve problems at the same time. Players buy tokens for weapons like spatulas, pots, pans, and myriad other kitchen tools that are used in the gaming process to fight villains. Revenue is also generated through the sale of virtual merchandise, including The Lunch Lady action hero avatar and related merchandise items, with all proceeds going towards our poverty and hunger relief efforts. Donations and proceeds are provided directly to homeless people via Gift Cards and other forms of digital currency that are redeemable for food and living items in their local community.

Unique Value Proposition:
The Lunch Lady game addresses a critical issue in a manner that is unobtrusive and fun. Gamers derive enjoyment from the process yet contribute purposefully to an important cause.

Marketing Strategy:
The Lunch Lady will utilize social media, celebrity and influencer marketing, gaming forums, and virtual events to build awareness and engagement around our mission. We will also partner with other organizations focused on poverty and hunger relief to amplify our impact.

Submission 4

Category: Environment (Not for Profit)
The EnviroData Network - EnviroData.Network

Executive Summary:
Our metaverse online business, called EnviroData, is focused on providing real-time data analytics, visualizations, and dashboards related to environmental issues, such as carbon emissions, ozone levels, climate variables, water pollution, deforestation, air quality, and poverty, by region. We are dedicated to helping individuals, businesses, and governments make informed decisions to combat these issues and create a better future for our planet. In addition, we will also provide key activities, strategies, and real-time results of solutions currently in use to combat these environmental issues.

Market Analysis and Target Market:
Environmental issues are becoming increasingly critical to people around the world. Climate change, pollution, deforestation, and other environmental problems are affecting our daily lives, and many people want to take action to combat these issues. Governments, non-profit organizations, and businesses are also recognizing the importance of addressing these issues. Our target market includes individuals, businesses, governments, and non-profit organizations who are interested in environmental issues and want to take action to combat them.

Business/Revenue Model:
EnviroData will provide real-time data analytics and

visualizations related to key environmental issues. Users will be able to interact with the dashboards and explore the data in a fully immersive 3D environment. We will also provide key activities, strategies, and results being used to combat these environmental issues, along with relevant news and events related to these issues. Our revenue will be generated through subscription fees for access to our platform and donations from individuals and businesses that are similarly focused on solving critical environmental concerns.

Unique Value Proposition:
EnviroData's real-time data services tap into critical data sources through global partnerships and an open-source software development platform that allows dynamic data to be viewed in both 2D via the Internet and mobile sites but also in fully immersive 3D/VR, strengthening the power of the data visualization, storytelling, and the public's understanding of these critical issues.

Marketing Strategy:
Our marketing strategy will include social media advertising, targeted email campaigns, partnerships with environmental organizations, and celebrity/non-celebrity influencers. We will also attend environmental conferences and events to promote our platform.

Submission 5

Category: Entertainment
Metaverse Casual Games – Metagames.fun

Overview:

Metagames is a metaverse-based online entertainment portal that connects casual gamers from all around the world. The platform offers a wide variety of gaming environments and casual games like board games, cards, and other multiplayer interactive games. Players can connect directly via VR headsets, desktop VR applications, or mobile devices.

Market Analysis and Target Market

According to Newzoo, the global gaming market is expected to reach $218.7 billion in 2023, growing at a Cumulative Annual Growth Rate (CAGR) of 8.3%. The casual gaming segment is one of the fastest-growing segments in the gaming industry, expected to grow at a CAGR of 9.2% from 2020 to 2025, reaching $13.8 billion in 2025. As such, Metagames! Targets individuals who enjoy casual gaming within immersive environments, especially those who may not have access to local gaming groups or may be looking to connect with new people and different cultures around the world.

Business/Revenue Model:

Metagames will generate revenue through a combination of subscription fees, in-game purchases, and advertising. Users will be able to access the platform for free, but they will need to pay a monthly subscription fee to access premium features and content. The premium features will include access to exclusive games, tournaments, and events. In-game purchases will allow users to buy virtual goods and currency, which they can use to enhance their gaming experience. The virtual goods will include items like costumes, avatars, and special abilities. Metagames will take a percentage of each transaction. The platform will offer advertising options where advertisers will be able to target audiences based on demographics, interests, and gaming preferences.

Unique Value Proposition:

Metagames enables Multiplayer games in real-time with built-in chat and messaging for social interaction. Virtual avatars and their voices can be customized to represent players but also present visually like real humans with facial articulation and lip sync ability. Unique metaverse environments enable players to connect and play with others from around the world in culturally diverse worlds. Main competitors with similar services in the casual gaming market include platforms like BoardGameArena, Tabletopia, and Yucatan. Metagames aims to differentiate itself by offering a wider range of casual games and a more immersive and interactive experience by leveraging virtual reality and augmented reality technologies.

Marketing Strategy:

We plan to leverage social media platforms like Facebook and Twitter to reach out to our target audience and build brand awareness services and will focus on building a strong community of casual gamers. The platform will collaborate with popular gaming influencers to create exclusive content and promote the platform through their social media channels.

CHAPTER TWELVE

Round 1: The Result

According to the Just Virtual staff, there were over six hundred thousand applications, and it would take at least a month to determine the final one hundred participants, even with the use of AI evaluation agents and a huge pool of tech talent.

So, we waited and waited some more. And as we did, the media became increasingly creative. They conjured every possible result, angle, narrative, and prognostication they could muster. There were plenty of self-declared metaverse experts by now, which was astonishing since, by most media accounts, the Metaverse did not actually exist yet.

But then, after a couple of weeks, something

happened. Reality started to kick in, and life was getting back to normal. Most of us had done the math and realized that the odds of being one of the final one hundred contestants were so insignificant that it was not worth hoping for (one in almost seven thousand). Heck, there were some local lotteries that offered better odds than that.

To be truthful, our Fab Four team had sort of given up. Perhaps it was a way to manage expectations to mitigate potential disappointment. We met once about three weeks into the evaluation process at the local pub and rekindled some hope. It was nice, and even though we agreed on the likelihood, we also felt that we'd learned a great deal. Even if the "big deal" did not materialize, maybe there was something smaller that we could still do together.

According to the media, the process was nearing completion, and every team would receive a yea or nay email at some point before the end of the month. In situations like this, that usually meant that winning contestants would be informed first, leaving the others to the end.

On the eve of the thirty-first day, we still had not received an email. I continued to check all my mailboxes, junk filters, and digital trash repositories for any sign. Nothing. I decided to shut down early that night, resigned to the fact that the dream was over. Then I heard a ding from my smartphone. I normally did not do email on my smartphone, but I did have notifications on for this particular event. My heart started to race, and my breathing became shallow as I opened my MacBook Air and tapped on the email icon. Indeed, there was a message from the Just Virtual staff at The Billion Dollar Metaverse Challenge. It was simple and very direct. It read.

"Dear Team Polar Magnates,"

This was the name we'd chosen for our team, a dark tribute reference to our friend JI, who'd been mauled by a polar bear a few months earlier.

"We'd like to thank you for your submission and contribution to our contest and for your patience in awaiting the results of round one."

This was a bit too friendly, I thought. My heart was starting to sink as I read on.

"As you know, there were over six hundred thousand entries, and the elimination process took longer than expected. However, we feel confident that we've selected the best one hundred finalists for our next round. We used a double-blind review process, meaning that reviewer and author identities were hidden to eliminate any possible bias.

"There were strong ideas in every category, and teams could only proceed to the next round with one application. We noticed that your team submitted five applications, but you would only be eligible for one entry. Had you been chosen for multiple submissions, our judging team would have selected the strongest entry.

"We are pleased to inform you that the winners will be announced tomorrow morning at 10 am EST (New York) in a press release and through most global media sources. The names of the advancing teams will be presented in alphabetical order, not in any position of merit.

"Thanks again for your participation, The Just Virtual Team."

Man, these guys certainly knew how to keep you hanging. By this time, I was certain that almost every other team had now read their messages and were similarly exasperated.

I called the other team members immediately, and

we agreed to meet at the pub at 9:45 for the announcement. This was getting crazy, but win or lose, we were going to celebrate.

That night was one of the longest nights of my life. I woke up every forty-five minutes, listened to three podcasts, an audiobook, and a guided meditation where I strived to achieve hypnagogia, that state between wakefulness and sleep that induces creativity, with no luck, sadly. Finally, at 8:30 am, I got up, showered, and headed down to the pub. It was beer time.

When I arrived, Dania, Frances, and Jag were already there, seated at a high-top table in the bar next to the big-screen TV. TNN was blasting away with expert after expert pontificating and hypothesizing. It was like the lead-up to the Superbowl, and this was just round one. I'd hate to imagine how crazy things were going to be in the next two rounds.

We did our obligatory hugs, and I sat down. Our good friend Wally Billings came over to the table with a big smile.

"Today's the big day," he said excitedly. "I have a good feeling."

"I guess we'll find out, Wally. It's been quite a journey, and thanks for hooking us up with Professor Elias at the university. He was amazing. We learned so much, and we really did feel like he gave us a chance," I said.

"Yes," said Dania. "He's a different cat. He seemed to have an intuitive sense, and he took the teaching experience to the next level. I learned a ton."

"He sees the world not for what it is but for what it can be," said Wally. "That's why it's so great to work with him. It's like he comes from the future."

"Agreed," acknowledged Dania. "Cheers to you and Elias."

"You're going to need something to cheer with, though. Can I help you with that?" asked Wally.

"You can start me with a Guinness," said Jag. As Wally looked around the table, we all nodded for the Guinness as well.

"That's four Guinness coming up," said Wally.

"So, did anyone manage to get any sleep last night?" I asked as I scanned the faces of my three bleary-eyed colleagues. No verbal response, but two eye raises and a roll said it all.

While we had returned to life as usual, it was obvious that we'd somehow not let go of that one last ray of hope, like that lottery ticket that you avoid checking to keep the dream alive.

As we waited for our beers to arrive, the TNN headline caught our eye. Coming up, Katherine Hong. I really liked Katherine. While most of the tech analysts were opinionated finance people with little substance, this lady knew what she was talking about. KatyH, as she was dubbed, was not only a smart journalist but had a master's degree in Human-Computer Interface (HCI) and had worked in the field for many years. She understood technology and the user experience, and she could explain things in a way that most people could understand.

Bunk Thursday, the lead TNN anchor, was giving an update on the Metaverse Challenge and introducing her now. We watched.

"We have Katherine Hong in our studio this morning as we await the release of The Billion Dollar Metaverse Challenge finalists," Bunk continued.

"Well, Katherine, in less than an hour, we'll know the final one hundred teams in The Billion Dollar Metaverse

Challenge. Apparently, the submissions remain confidential, but the JV folks will release a short one or two-sentence description of each team's focus. What are we expecting in this top one hundred, Katherine?"

"Thanks, Bunk. So great to be here, and it certainly is exciting. There are so many potential angles and opportunities that we'll likely see, and we'll also get a sense of how broad these categories are, I suspect.

"For example, the Commerce category can include anything transactional. That means you'll see applications for many different types of retail products and concepts, real estate ideas, and travel/tourism, to name a few. All these endeavors are commercial and do offer global scalability prospects.

"The entertainment space will be all over the map and is arguably the biggest category of all, Bunk. There are just so many ways to use this technology to have fun and immerse yourself. metaverse games like Fortnite, Roblox, Minecraft, and dozens of others, are already valued as multibillion-dollar companies, albeit many within larger companies like Microsoft or Epic Games. Nonetheless, expect many innovative metaverse game concepts to challenge these early successes.

"Social environments will also be huge within the entertainment domain as well. Early social VR applications, like VR Chat, are likely already valued in the hundreds of millions and will continue to grow. Meta's own Horizon Worlds, while off to a slow start, will also continue to improve and grow further, validating this space. So, I'd expect many entrants in this social arena as well.

"So, the gaming and social entertainment opportunities are just the obvious ones, but new forms of cinema and theatre are also likely to emerge as well."

"What about the Education space, Katherine? Is there much happening there?" asked Bunk.

"Absolutely," answered Katherine. "There are hundreds of specialized VR learning applications out there already, so that market space already exists. Whether you want to learn how to fight fires, fly a plane, manage hostage situations, or even perform surgery, it is happening already.

"But I'm expecting something even bigger here. Everyone is complaining about the cost of education, student loans that ruin your life, and, quite frankly, an education system that seems more intent on preserving itself than improving the quality of the experience. So, the domain is rife for disruption. And with all the emerging edtech, this one feels obvious to me.

"Bunk, let me also say that both non-profit domains look very promising as well.

"The community-building initiatives feel like an obvious fit because, with the Metaverse, the entire world can be linked as one larger community. If we combine digital twinning and IOT technology with that global community, you have instant scalability and innovative ways of capturing real-world metrics and problems, reflecting those in the Metaverse where we can work together to solve them. So, I'm expecting lots of field-leveling initiatives in this area.

"And finally, there are so many issues with the environment and so many motivated young people that I expect a deluge of innovation in this domain. I know I've said this before, Bunk, but it can't be said enough. When it comes to the environment, the Metaverse is a big part of the solution. Imagine if twenty-five percent of our activities from the real world go virtual. Think about the impact of fewer cars on the road, less mining of precious minerals, less real building, and ultimately a mass reduction in C02 emissions. This will take much-needed pressure off the environment while still allowing the economy to grow.

"More specifically, by using AI and IOT sensing technology to replicate, twin, and simulate environmental issues within a metaverse simulation, we can understand and solve these challenges much more effectively. Solving these major environmental problems that are existential threats, serves all of humanity," Katherine emphasized.

"Katherine, you make this all sound so exciting and inevitable. But there have been some prominent businesspeople mocking the metaverse idea and suggesting that it won't ever come to fruition. Any thoughts about that?" inquired Bunk.

"Firstly, if any prominent businessperson does their research, they'll realize that it is already happening. VR applications and metaverse gaming revenues are already in the hundreds of billions, so they may be living in their own self-serving reality. If your wealth depends on selling cars, road services, buildings, or any other physical goods, then you will be impacted by the emerging Metaverse.

"Finally, I have huge respect for Naomi Grace and the people at Just Virtual. They are investing and using the global media brilliantly to seek the best new ideas and the brightest people to invest in, and they would not be doing so if they did not see a significant upside. So, to those supposed business luminaries who think they know better, I say ignore at your own peril."

"Thanks, Katherine. Always a pleasure," said Bunk, "Okay, less than forty minutes from now, the names will be released, and millions await their fate."

Just then, Wally Billing arrived at the table with a tray of four frothing Guinness. His timing was perfect.

This Guinness tasted great as we numbed the anxiety of the wait and amplified the joy of friends sharing this moment together. One beer became two, and then, the countdown.

The entire bar went silent as we all watched the alphabetic list of the top one hundred finalists and their application categories scroll down the screen. Every now and then, we'd hear intense screams of disappointment. "Ah F@$#!", "Dammit," and "Well, that's it," but no expressions of glee. Nothing.

We were Team Polar Magnates (with P, the sixteenth letter of the alphabet); we'd be just after the halfway point, I suspected. We approached the M's (halfway) and watched intently.

• Learnscape Quartet	Education
• Many Worlds Experiencers	Entertainment
• Megaverse World Builders	Entertainment
• Multiverse Madness	Entertainment
• My Little Metaverse Storekeepers	Commerce
• Network of Dreamers	Environment

Interestingly, from many of these team names, you could not really tell what business category they were related to, rather more likely a shared philosophy.

• New World Disorder	Community
• Nothing Real	Commerce
• Open for Business	Commerce
• Omega Systems	Environment

My heart started to race, and my breathing became shallow. This was it.

- Patently Oblivious — Entertainment
- People Players — Community
- Perfect Renderers — Entertainment
- Pocket Metaversians — Education

There were already four P's, so the next one had to be it, or we were done. Time stood still as I fixated on the screen. I could see my teammates in slow motion, similarly focused.

- Polar Magnates — Education

Holy F@$#!! That was us. We were in. We were in. We were in.

We looked at each other, still in slow motion but coming back to life. Dania jumped so high into the air; she made Air Jordan look like a frump. Frances had a ninety-two-inch-wide smile, and Jag had the expression you see on golfers' faces when they sink their final putt to win the championship. As for me? Total bliss. What a feeling. We'd worked hard for this, and it felt deserved.

Once Dania hit the ground, we all hugged and kissed for what seemed like an eternity. Even Wally Billings got in on the action. We hadn't won anything yet, but it felt like we'd won the Superbowl. Everyone in the bar caught the fever, too, as there was hooting and hollering all around us. We quieted down, though, to see the rest of the list out of respect for others who were awaiting their fate.

- Zero Gravitators — Entertainment
- Zookeepers — Education

- Zoro and the Sword Swallowers.   Entertainment

That was it. Done. No more elated parties at the bar. It was only us. I suggested a round for the house, which was widely accepted.

Wow! We were in. We'd beaten the odds, and today we would celebrate. To say we drank too much that night would be an understatement. I think stocks in the Guinness company (Diageo) went up ten percent that day.

CHAPTER THIRTEEN

Round 2: Three Questions

Frances, Dania, Jag, and I agreed to meet for lunch the next day. After kicking the early morning fog hat that I was wearing, I got dressed and headed back to the pub. For obvious reasons, we'd chosen to keep the positive energy flowing and made the pub our head office for the rest of the contest. They were equally excited to have us around, and Wally Billings would be our office manager and chief beer slinger.

I called RoMac on the way to bring him up to date. He was very excited for us, but his daughter had taken a turn for the worse in the past few days, so he was not going to join us for any more of the process. I wished him well and asked if there was anything that any of us could do to help the situation. He declined but did give clear instructions. "Win the damn contest, bro, then you can hire me." I agreed wholeheartedly, then bid him adieu.

I also started thinking about the next steps and what we could need to do to prepare for the second round. We had been selected in the education category, so our Metaversity One application had obviously turned some heads. As Katherine Hong had predicted, there were lots of successful applicants in the Entertainment (thirty-nine) and Commerce (twenty-nine) categories, while the Community Building (eight), Environment (eleven), and Education (thirteen) were far less successful. In fact, less than one-third of the categories were attributed to Education, Environment, and Community Building, three key pillars of any society, whereas Entertainment and Commerce soaked up over two-thirds of the top one hundred slots. It appeared that the Roman poet Juvenal was not so far off with his suggestion that "Bread and circuses" were needed to appease the masses, and the economic investment process seemed to be leaning in that direction.

The presentation process itself was straightforward, but the challenge was intense. Live, in front of millions of metaverse viewers and a half dozen JV judges, you presented your business. Metaverse audience participants and JV judges had voting power based on a 33/67 split which seemed to make sense. As an investor, putting up that much money, you would want to gather the audience's feedback, but you didn't want someone who was charming at presenting a bad idea to take a slot from a more credible team.

Each team was provided with three minutes to provide a summary pitch. Following the pitch, the JV judges would ask the team three consecutive questions, and any of the team members could answer. Once the question was presented, the team had thirty seconds to confer, then three minutes maximum to answer. None of the teams had any foreknowledge of the question content. What made the process particularly unnerving was the live scoreboard that showed the audience scores. So, after you completed your presentation, you would know rather quickly whether you were in or out of the running. The JV judges' scores remained confidential until after the final team presented.

Both audience members and judges would submit their votes, and the next teams would present until all one hundred teams were complete. The process would take roughly twenty-five hours in total and take place on the next long weekend in ten days.

All team participants were put up in a local hotel that was secured from any media access, sort of like sequestering a jury for a murder trial. While team members were able to work with their team members inside, none would have access to any of the presentations over the Metaverse or people outside. Otherwise, this could give an undue advantage to teams that would present later. Once your presentation was done, your team could leave the hotel and watch the competition with the rest of the metaverse population. Again, depending on how well you did, it could be the best or the worst thing.

Traffic was heavy that morning, but finally, I arrived at the pub. I was greeted and high-fived by several people as I made my way across the bar in search of my newly anointed celebrity lunchmates. Given that only one hundred teams globally remained, it was likely that North America would have less than fifty teams still in the running.

When I arrived at our favorite high-top table near the large-screen TV, Dania, Frances, and Jag were already there, smiling and cavorting with their new friends, trying out the new celebrity status they had just acquired. It occurred to me that this could be a problem if any of us became too enamored with our own press clippings, but for now, we would simply indulge.

"Greetings, fellow Metaversians," I said as we engaged in another joyous group hug, all still in a state of semi-disbelief. It hadn't even been twelve hours yet since we had stopped celebrating. But now it was time to get back to work.

"So, from what I've been reading, we have ten days to prepare for this next round. We need to present our three-minute business pitch like it's an Oscar speech that would make Matthew McConaughey proud and figure out what the hell the judges are going to ask," said Dania.

"Yeah, that's all," said Jag, smiling cynically.

"Well, we'd better get our sorry asses on the case right now," said Frances. "No one is going to do the work for us, so let's figure this out."

As we ate our lunch, we discussed ways of approaching the problem. We brainstormed the content of our three-minute speech and the kinds of questions that we could be asked. I wasn't the worst writer, so I agreed to do a first draft of the speech that one of us could present.

The real heavy lifting was figuring out the possible questions and answers.

Now I wasn't a lawyer, but I'd binge-watched enough legal dramas on Amazon and Netflix to know that this was like preparing for a cross-examination by an aggressive district attorney. Those lawyers worked night and day until examination day. Of course, they were billing hundreds of dollars an hour, while we were likely just losing that much. So, there was that.

While we weren't education sector experts, that was now our destiny, so we would have to figure it out quickly. Beyond just the visualization, I'd done a real crash course over the past few weeks to prepare the one-pager. I had done some teaching at various local universities over the years, but we were all going to have to immerse ourselves in this role completely if we had any chance of progressing to the next round. Nonetheless, we forged on and seemed to gain momentum as the afternoon turned into evening. We even managed to muster up a good batch of potential questions that seemed to cover much of what we might be asked.

We had come up with twenty-five questions, so we wrote each one down on the whiteboard that Sir Wally had so kindly secured for us.

In the spirit of our "Snakes and Ladders" Story Express theme, feel free to jump forward five pages if these questions feel like heavy sledding. That said, if you're an aspiring VC or fintech manager, you may want to dig in and sharpen your business savvy.

1. **Market validation**: Have you conducted any market research or surveys to gauge interest in your master's program in VR digital storytelling? Can you provide data or insights to demonstrate the demand for this type of education and the size of the potential market?

2. **Accreditation and partnerships**: What is your plan for obtaining accreditation for the Master's program, and how will this affect the timeline for launching

the program? Additionally, have you established any partnerships with VR companies or organizations or identified potential partners to collaborate with in terms of course content, internships, or job placement for graduates?

3. **Technology and infrastructure**: Can you provide more details on the technological infrastructure required to support the immersive learning experience? How do you plan to select the metaverse platform, and what hardware and software tools will be needed? What are the estimated costs associated with setting up and maintaining the required infrastructure?

4. **Team and expertise**: Who are the key members of your team, and what relevant experience do they bring to the table? How do you plan to attract top industry professionals as instructors and ensure the quality of your course offerings?

5. **Financial projections and funding**: Can you provide a detailed breakdown of your financial projections, including estimated costs, revenues, and the timeline for reaching profitability? How much funding are you seeking, and what milestones do you aim to achieve with the investment?

6. **Competitive landscape**: Who are your main competitors in the VR digital storytelling education space, and what differentiates your program from its offerings? How do you plan to stay ahead of the competition as the market evolves?

7. **Scalability and growth strategy**: How do you plan to scale your Metaverse University concept to accommodate a growing number of students and expand course offerings? What is your long-term vision for the university, and how do you plan to diversify your programs and revenue streams?

8. **Student acquisition and retention**: What strategies do you have in place to attract and retain students for your master's program? How do you plan to measure student satisfaction and the effectiveness of your courses in order to continually improve your offerings?

9. **Intellectual property and content development**: How will you protect the intellectual property associated with your courses and proprietary technology? Additionally, what is your strategy for developing high-quality course content, and do you have plans to collaborate with industry experts or utilize user-generated content?

10. **Risk assessment and contingency planning**: What do you see as the primary risks associated with your Metaverse University concept, and how do you plan to mitigate those risks? Do you have contingency plans in place in case of unforeseen challenges or changes in the market landscape?

11. **Marketing and branding**: How do you plan to create a strong brand identity for Metaverse University, and what are the key elements of your marketing strategy? How will you measure the effectiveness of your marketing

efforts and adjust your approach accordingly?

12. **Regulatory and legal considerations**: What are the potential regulatory and legal challenges you may face in offering your master's program across different countries? How do you plan to navigate these challenges to ensure compliance with international laws and regulations?

13. **Exit strategy**: What is your exit strategy for investors, and what potential exit scenarios do you foresee for your business? Are you aiming for an acquisition, merger, or public offering in the future, and if so, what is your estimated timeline for reaching this milestone?

14. **Pricing strategy**: How did you determine the pricing for your Master's program and other course offerings? What factors did you consider in setting the price, and how does it compare to competitor offerings? How do you plan to balance affordability for students with the need to generate revenue and cover operational costs?

15. **Support and resources for students**: What resources and support services will you provide to students throughout their educational journey? How do you plan to address potential issues, such as technical difficulties or learning challenges, to ensure a positive experience for all students?

16. **Adaptability to technological advancements**: How do you plan to adapt your Metaverse University offerings as technology evolves, particularly in the rapidly changing

fields of VR, AR, and MR? What strategies do you have in place to ensure your programs remain cutting-edge and relevant to the industry?

17. **Data privacy and security**: How do you plan to safeguard student data and ensure compliance with data privacy regulations? What measures will be implemented to protect both the personal information of students and the intellectual property associated with your courses?

18. **Customer feedback and continuous improvement**: How will you collect and incorporate feedback from students and industry partners to improve your offerings continuously? What mechanisms will be in place to measure the success of your programs and identify areas for enhancement?

19. **Community building and networking**: How do you plan to foster a sense of community among your students and facilitate networking opportunities, both within the Metaverse and in real life? How will these connections benefit students in terms of career advancement and collaborative opportunities?

20. **Sustainability and social impact**: What steps will you take to ensure your Metaverse University has a positive social impact and operates sustainably? How will you address potential issues related to the digital divide, accessibility, and inclusivity to ensure that a diverse range of students can benefit from your offerings?

21. **Diversity and inclusiveness in course content and team**: How do you plan to ensure that your course content, teaching methodologies, and instructor pool reflect diverse perspectives and experiences? What steps will you take to create an inclusive learning environment that is sensitive to the needs of students from various backgrounds and cultures?

22. **Language support and localization**: How do you plan to accommodate students who speak languages other than English? Will you offer courses or provide resources in multiple languages, or do you have plans to collaborate with partners who can help localize your content for different regions?

23. **Global accessibility**: What measures will you implement to ensure that your Metaverse University is accessible to students from all over the world, regardless of their location, financial resources, or technological capabilities? How will you address potential barriers to entry, such as Internet access, hardware requirements, or time zone differences?

24. **Cultural sensitivity and awareness**: How will you incorporate cultural sensitivity and awareness into your curriculum and overall university experience? What training or resources will you provide to your instructors and staff to ensure they are knowledgeable about and respectful of different cultural norms and practices?

25. **Equity and scholarships**: Do you have plans to offer scholarships, financial aid, or other forms of assistance

to students from underrepresented or disadvantaged backgrounds? How will you promote and ensure equity within your student population and provide opportunities for those who may not otherwise have access to this type of education?

Asking any of these questions would help these investors better understand our business strategy, competitive positioning, and plans for growth. Further, the additional questions related to diversity would challenge us to demonstrate our commitment to fostering an inclusive, diverse, and global learning environment for students from different backgrounds and cultures. And if we were going to be a global force, this would be critical.

By 10 pm that evening, we were completely drained and agreed we should throw in the towel and meet again at noon the following day.

And so, we did. Day after day, for the next ten days, we worked tirelessly, looking at statistics, trends, and anything related to any of the twenty-five questions we had identified. We put together high-level answers to each of the questions but agreed that we'd each be responsible for deep diving into six questions. At the same time, Dania agreed to pick up a seventh, while I agreed to finish the final script for our three-minute pitch based on the feedback I'd received from the team.

Weekend at Burnout

It was Thursday Night before the big weekend, and we were preparing to check in at the fully secured Aurora Suites Hotel. We felt that we'd done everything humanly possible to prepare for our round two presentations, so the rest would be in the hands of the Metaverse and our collective higher powers.

After the check-in, all teams were asked to meet in the main ballroom for a brief introduction and the drawing of the numbers that would identify our presentation position. It was tense. No one really wanted a number in the top or bottom twenty, as both ends of the spectrum could be problematic. In the first twenty, the metaverse voters and judges might not have a good sense of where the bar was yet, whereas the last twenty might be delivered to a fatigued audience. We had selected Dania to do the hat draw for our team, so she got in line with the rest of the hundred team designates. One by one, the speaker screamed the team names and the presentation order.

Then Dania was at the hat. As she reached in and moved her hand around, smiling like she knew what she was doing, she pulled out a small poker-like chip and handed it to the presenter, who peeled off the seal and screamed to the audience.

"Team Polar Magnates, position seventy-one," as it was simultaneously presented on a digital board that hung over the stage.

Phew! Sigh of relief. That would be fine. We'd hoped to be somewhere in the middle between the twenty and eighty slots, so that worked well. This meant that our presentation would not occur until early on day three. This would give us more time to brainstorm and work together. It might also mean more time to stress out. We'd know soon enough.

The contest was on, and it felt like we were in a sensory deprivation chamber of sorts. For two days, we reworked the questions and thought about different angles. While most of this work would not be required, as ultimately only three questions would be asked, it was a worthwhile effort invested in better understanding our grander vision.

As we strategized, we suspected that they would likely not ask specific questions related to money or people as it would be hard to analyze those key elements in such a short time. Rather, we anticipated questions related more to strategy, scaling, or concerns one might have about a business like this. More likely, the people and financial details would be part of the final round. As it turned out, we were right about that assumption. After all of us took a crack at it, the group voted that I should deliver the opening speech. Most likely, it was because I'd written the words, so it seemed to flow a bit better.

When Sunday morning rolled around, we were ready for action. Then at exactly 11:11 that morning, a very good omen, the number seventy-one flashed on the sign over our exit door, which opened and connected us to a large stage. It was not like any forum that any of us had ever experienced.

There was no audience, just a panel of six judges, and the background, though aesthetically pleasing, appeared to be a green screen that allowed our human characters to be projected on a grander stage into the Metaverse. Apparently, there were over one hundred and fifty million metaverse viewers connected in all manner of VR technology to this billion dollar contest. It was freakin' exciting.

I walked to the front of the stage and looked passionately at the imagined crowd.

The Opening Speech

"Ladies and gentlemen, esteemed colleagues, and global online audience, I stand before you today to introduce a ground-breaking concept in education that will not only revolutionize the way we learn but also shape the future of our digital reality. I present to you Metaversity One, an innovative Metaverse University designed to harness the power of VR digital storytelling to create fully immersive, interactive, and gamified learning experiences.

"At Metaversity One, we believe in breaking down the barriers of traditional education and embracing the possibilities of the Metaverse. Our mission is to provide a cutting-edge Master's program in VR digital storytelling, encompassing virtual, augmented, and mixed-reality applications. We offer unparalleled learning experiences, combining the expertise of world-class instructors with the support of AI Pedagogical Agents of Learning, all on a secure blockchain Learning Management System.

"We recognize that the world is changing rapidly, and as such, we cater to the needs of our diverse student population. Our target market includes recent college graduates with a background in art or computer science, working professionals seeking career advancement, and individuals looking to hone their skills in VR digital storytelling. With a flexible course structure, Metaversity One empowers students to progress at their own pace, embracing the concept of 'leveling up' in their educational journey.

"What sets Metaversity One apart from traditional universities and online learning organizations is our unique approach to education. We provide immersive, interactive, and gamified learning experiences where students can access courses anytime, anywhere. Our curriculum covers a wide range of topics related to VR digital storytelling, including 3D modeling, animation, narrative design, data analytics, visualization, UX, and game design.

"We understand the importance of accessibility and affordability in education. That's why we've designed our Master's VRDS program to be scalable, reaching millions of students worldwide and reducing the annual cost to less than $2,500, with a target completion time of one year.

"At Metaversity One, we're committed to generating value and forging strong partnerships within the VR industry. Our revenue streams include tuition fees, short-term courses, workshops for corporate clients, and collaborations with VR companies for consulting, training, and development services. As we continue to grow, we plan to expand our offerings to other areas of study, further broadening our reach and impact.

"Our marketing strategy reflects our forward-thinking approach. We'll focus on targeted advertising through social media platforms, metaverse forums, and industry publications while leveraging partnerships with VR companies and organizations to promote our university and increase our student base. We're also excited to attend virtual VR events, showcasing our programs and raising brand awareness.

"Ladies and gentlemen, the future of education is here, and it's called Metaversity One. We invite you to join us on this exciting journey as we unlock the true potential of the Metaverse and, together, redefine the way we learn, create, and experience our digital reality. Thank you."

There was no clapping, although my teammates were

smiling widely and sending very positive visual feedback on the presentation. The moderator motioned to the panel of judges to begin the questions. The judging plan conferred momentarily. Then one of the female judges posed the first question.

Question One

"Have you conducted any market research or surveys to gauge interest in your Master's program in VR digital storytelling? Can you provide data or insights to demonstrate the demand for this type of education and the size of the potential market?"

As we looked at each other, we all agreed that this question was in Dania's wheelhouse, so we gave her the nod. She stepped forward like the pro that she was, looking confidently at the audience that wasn't really there, and commenced the response.

Answer One

"Thank you. There are several factors that are contributing to the strong growth prospects for VR-based metaverse education: Technology advancements in VR and related technologies have made it more accessible, affordable, and user-friendly. Growing investment in the EdTech sector, with many companies exploring the potential of VR in education, has further strengthened demand while the global pandemic forced educational institutions to switch to remote learning, also contributing to a rise in the demand curve for innovative digital learning solutions.

"Based on the available data and trends in the VR

industry, it's evident that the market is growing rapidly. According to the IDC, global spending on AR and VR is expected to reach $72.8 billion by 2024, growing at a compound annual growth rate (CAGR) of fifty-four percent between 2019 and 2024. driven by the increased adoption of VR technologies across various sectors, including gaming, entertainment, education, healthcare, and manufacturing. The global VR market in education is a big part of that number and is expected to reach $12.6 billion by 2025, according to a report by Grand View Research. The same report projected a compound annual growth rate (CAGR) of 59.3% from 2020 to 2025.

"Moreover, the demand for skilled professionals in VR is also on the rise. As more industries adopt VR technologies, the need for experts in digital storytelling, 3D modeling, animation, and game design will continue to grow. Offering a master's program in VR digital storytelling could help meet this demand and tap into a growing market of students and professionals seeking to enhance their skills in this field. As a training tool, there are many advantages over traditional educational methods, such as increased engagement, personalized learning, and the ability to simulate real-world experiences otherwise not possible.

"Finally, while further and ongoing market research and surveys are crucial to validate the demand for our master's program in VR digital storytelling, existing data and industry trends suggest a very promising outlook."

Dania then bowed and stepped back with the rest of the team members. Nailed it, I thought, and while we all sent her smiles of thanks and acknowledged success. We chose to avoid the fist bump while we were on center stage.

The second judge, a younger gentleman that looked

like Wall Street trader meets triathlete, posed his question.

Question Two

"How do you plan to scale your Metaverse University concept to accommodate a growing number of students and expanded course offerings? What is your long-term vision for the university, and how do you plan to diversify your programs and revenue streams?"

Great question, I thought. The Silicon Valley mentality was "get big fast or go home." If you can't be the eight-hundred-pound gorilla, then you will be crushed at some point. As I looked at my teammates, this was considered in my domain, so they nodded, and I stepped forward.

Answer Two

"Thank you. That's a great question and something I'd want to know if I were investing in a fast-growing metaverse business. How the heck do you scale this thing?

"Our plan for scaling Metaversity One to accommodate the rapid growth of students and expanded course offerings is to leverage the power of the Metaverse itself combined with cutting-edge technology.

"By utilizing the Metaverse as our primary platform for course delivery, we can easily create virtual classrooms and learning environments that can be expanded or replicated as needed. This enables us to accommodate a rapidly growing student population without the limitations of physical infrastructure.

"We plan to aggressively deploy AI and Automation tools like Pedagogical Agents of Learning (PAL)s and other automated tools that will help us provide personalized and adaptive learning experiences and support for each student while also minimizing the need for increased faculty resources as our student base grows.

"Gamification and the use of Advanced Gaming AI Tools will provide real-time guidance, testing, and a compelling game-like experience that can be automated while maintaining a strong mix of asynchronous (on-demand) course content (ninety percent) to synchronous in-person teaching (ten percent), allowing the students to control the pace of their own progress.

"We intend to diversify our programs and revenue streams with additional course offerings. After successfully launching our Master's VRDS program, we plan to introduce additional degree programs and certifications in various fields that will enable us to broaden our audience and expand our market reach.

"We also plan to offer corporate training curricula with short-term courses, workshops, and specialized training programs focusing on specific topics related to VR and other emerging technologies. This will create new revenue streams for M1 while helping organizations upskill their workforces and remain competitive.

"Much like Amazon with AWS, a proven model, we plan on offering our metaverse learning platform as a service to other educational institutions and organizations, allowing them to implement our innovative solutions within their own programs and courses.

"In summary, by focusing on scalability and content diversification, we aim to position Metaversity One as a pioneer in metaverse education, providing students and professionals with unparalleled learning experiences and opportunities for personal and professional growth."

I stepped back. This one didn't feel as good as the pitch speech or Dania's answer, and I felt like I was meandering at the beginning, but it went okay. Two down, one to go.

The third JV judge, an elderly South Asian lady, stood up and asked.

Question Three

"How do you plan to adapt your Metaverse University offerings as technology evolves, particularly in the rapidly changing fields of VR? What strategies do you have in place to ensure your programs remain cutting-edge and relevant to the industry?"

We all looked at Frances. She was our tech expert and CTO in waiting. She stepped forward but seemed a bit nervous. Frances was super smart but did not like to speak in public, so this was going to be a challenge for her. That said, she was willing to do what it took to win. She began.

Answer Three

"Thank you for the opportunity to present today. We recognize the importance of keeping our Metaverse University offerings up to date in the rapidly changing fields of VR, AI, IoT, and Blockchain security. To ensure our programs remain cutting-edge and relevant to the industry, we plan to implement the following strategies:

"Continuous Monitoring of Industry Trends: Our team will stay informed about the latest advancements, trends, and best practices in the VR, AI, and IOT fields by regularly monitoring industry publications, attending conferences and workshops, and participating in online forums and discussions.

"Regular Course Updates: Our curriculum development team will continuously review and update our course materials to ensure they reflect our relentless pursuit of excellence. We aren't striving to meet the standard or best practice approach. We plan to be the standard. As such, this may involve incorporating new tools, techniques, or concepts as they become available, as well as updating or replacing outdated content.

"Faculty Development: We will invest in the ongoing professional development of our instructors, providing them with opportunities to expand their knowledge and skills. This may include attending industry events, participating in training workshops, or pursuing advanced certifications. By supporting our faculty's growth, we ensure they remain current in their fields and can effectively teach the latest concepts and techniques to our students.

"Embracing Innovation: We will foster a culture of innovation within our Metaverse University, encouraging faculty, staff, and students to explore new ideas and technologies that can improve our programs and learning experiences. This may involve hosting hackathons, research projects, or innovation challenges to stimulate creative thinking and problem-solving.

"Student Feedback: We will actively seek feedback from our students regarding their experiences and needs as they progress through the program. This feedback can provide valuable insights into areas where our programs may need improvement or adaptation to remain current and relevant.

"Agile Course Development: We will adopt an agile approach to course development, allowing us to respond quickly to changes in the industry and integrate new technologies and trends into our curriculum. This involves regularly evaluating and iterating on our course materials, ensuring they remain up-to-date and effective in preparing students for success.

"By implementing these strategies, we believe we can adapt to the evolving technology landscape and ensure our programs remain cutting-edge, relevant, and worth every cent."

We were done. Frances bowed and stepped back with the group. As instructed, we then acknowledged the non-existent audience and the JV judges and exited back into our suite. Round Two was over, for us anyway. Now, all we could do was watch.

We high-fived each other and hugged with a great sense of relief. It wasn't the best performance, but it was solid, and we said what we wanted to say. If they were excited about our ideas, at least we didn't sabotage ourselves. The questions were also in line with what we expected, but we had no idea how our answers compared to the rest of the competition.

We quickly packed and agreed to meet at the pub in an hour. We will find out soon.

As we stepped into the pub, we were immediately greeted with applause, handshakes, and hugs.

I could see the screen, and it looked different. Wally had hooked up a Desktop VR application and was casting it directly to the TV. We watched the performances and updates in full 3DVR on a seventy-five-inch TV. That was cool. Then after the current presentation ended, likely group seventy-six or seventy-seven, they scrolled the leaderboard.

We got our answer rather quickly on the second screen. We were fourteenth with twenty-three presentations left to go. This was arguably a good performance, but not nearly enough for big money. As the rest of the team filtered in, so also did the realization. This thing was likely over. We would have to wait for the judges at the end of the presentations in about four hours, but we'd need to be right near the top of the judges' list to have any chance.

The wait was excruciating as each performance offered a threat of pushing us further down the list. By 5 pm, three new presentations had been pushed ahead of us. We were now in the seventeenth spot. It was all over but the crying.

As we gathered around the TV, awaiting the judges' scores, my situational arrhythmia kicked in while both Frances and Dania appeared to be hyperventilating. And Jag? Were his eyes closed? I couldn't quite tell.

Mathematically, only the first fifteen positions on the judge's list mattered, but given our seventeenth place, we would need to do better than that. In fact, we needed a top-six finish on the JV judge's scorecards based on the 2:1 judge-to-audience weighting. It was possible but highly unlikely. As the screen flashed, indicating the judge's results, we grabbed each other's hands and held on for dear life like the characters in Toy Story 4, heading into the incinerator.

One by one, each position was presented on screen. As the screen turned from Position Five to Position Six, we held our breath!

Roughly two weeks before, we'd been in the same position, same bar, and likely most of the same people. We were certainly thankful for this experience and agreed that just finishing in the Top one hundred was possibly something that we could build upon in the future. I think we told each other that to manage expectations and potential disappointment. The reality. In the next few seconds, the destiny of our lives would be changed forever because a Top Ten finish would definitely have some value. The screen card flipped. Slot Six: Team Perfect Renderers. It was not us.

Our hearts sank, and I could see Dania start to tear up as the realization set in. Before we knew it, the next card flipped. Slot Seven: Team Polar Magnates.

What? Were we seventh? I quickly checked the math based on the 2:1 rating ratio, but that put us into eleventh place overall. Again and again, I checked the math, but the result remained the same. As we looked at each other, we all had come to the same conclusion, with further validation by several other interested fans at the bar.

It was over, but it couldn't be. Was this some sort of cruel joke? How could we come so far and get so close but still fail? Had one of us done something so horrible in our past life to warrant this sort of cosmic tease? No, no, no. This was not happening. We were like the team that almost won the Superbowl. We were on the verge of winning but fumbled the ball on the one-yard line with thirty seconds on the clock.

As the evening wore on, aided by copious alcohol, cannabis enhancements, and empathetic friends, our denial slowly transitioned to pain, then anger, and eventually, our new reality kicked in.

As we went home that evening, none of us were excited about waking up the next day. But we did. We had to wake up and figure out how to bury the dream and get back to whatever we were getting back to.

After a miserable morning and early afternoon, I turned on the TV and surfed over to TNN, where they were most likely hearing from every expert in the field about the top ten finalists. But that wasn't happening. In fact, there was a message streaming over the Newsroom set desk that read.

Please stand by as new information related to the Billion Dollar Metaverse Challenge has just been released. Then back to Bunk Thursday at the main desk.

"Welcome back, viewers. Thanks for your patience. This is just in. As a result of apparent improprieties, two of the teams were just disqualified, and this could potentially change the results. We don't know who will be affected yet, but oh, wait. Apparently, one of the two teams was a Top Ten finalist, while the other team was within the Top Twenty. Stay tuned. After this brief message from our sponsors, we'll have the new Top Ten list. Back in five."

I immediately tried to call Dania, Frances, and Jag to make them aware. Dania was already watching, but Frances was out with her kids, and Jag was at work. I texted Jag to watch and asked Dania to find Frances. After the commercial break, it was back to Bunk.

"Folks, in a few moments, we're going to present the new Top Ten list based on the revised scores. But before that, we now know the teams that were accused of cheating by the JV judges. Apparently, Perfect Renderers, an entertainment software company that created real-time virtual worlds, wasn't that perfect after all, and Nothing Real was also a bit of an illusion. Both were officially disqualified for inappropriate attempts to influence the judges. I think that's the code for attempted bribery, which is not surprising given the amount of money at stake. So, let's see where that brings us with the new Top Ten list."

As the list scrolled, like an April Fools' prank, this bad cosmic joke looked to be over. I wasn't sure where we would end up, but when the new Top Ten was posted, we had jumped not one but two spots. We were now in position nine. As part of the Top Ten, we had a thirty percent chance of a minimum of two hundred million dollars of funding over the next five years, and we would collectively own fifty percent of this new entity. We would still need to deliver and make that vision real, but that was the most exciting part. We would have a purpose and an opportunity to change the world. We were back in, baby. Game On! Again!

CHAPTER FOURTEEN

Round 3: Ninety Days to a New Life

You wake up one morning expecting to mourn your very existence, and then the world changes in an instant, fortunately for the better, in this case. This had been one heck of a roller coaster ride, so we would need to be careful.

Throughout this process, I always remembered the sage words my father had shared with me in my moments of sadness and defeat. "This too shall pass," he would say. What great advice. I'm pretty sure it was a philosophy he learned as a practicing member of Alcoholics Anonymous, a powerful program that changed his life and millions of others with a focus on humility and self-acceptance.

He also reminded me that in times of victory and

success, we would also need to heed those words and emphasized there was more risk of getting off track after achieving success than after failure. "When we succeed," he said, "we often pat ourselves on the back and attribute the success to something we did or a great decision we made. As a result, we can become lazy and lose that edge or drive that made us successful in the first place, and sadly, that edge is often only rediscovered through failure," he would remind me.

In sports, they used to refer to this phenomenon as the Sports Illustrated (SI) Curse. Invariably, it seemed that whenever an athlete was featured on the front cover of the magazine, the pinnacle of sports adulation, they failed to perform at the same level the following year. In hockey, when rookies performed well in their first year, quite often, they performed poorly in the subsequent year. That was referred to as the sophomore jinx. The same has also been said about the Oscars and many other highly coveted awards of excellence.

Failure, on the other hand, forces reflection and introspection. It creates a sense of urgency to dig deeper, work harder, and figure things out or risk not getting back to the mountaintop. We would need to remain vigilant, especially with the large heap of media attention that had been served our way. It was also important to recognize that we hadn't won a damn thing yet, and we could not get comfortable with what we had achieved, or we would be done. The next ninety days would be "balls to the wall", a cool aviation analogy where the pilot would push throttle levers, topped with ball shaped grips, to the instrument panel or "the wall". This meant full power or maximum effort.

Less than twenty-four hours later, we were back at

the bar. At 5 p.m., the team members met at the pub and exchanged hugs and joyous greetings of "Woohoo!" and, "Can you believe this?" It was exciting again. We finally managed to calm down but were interrupted seemingly every two minutes by well-wisher patrons and, eventually, within the hour, local media. It became apparent that our office-as-pub strategy was no longer going to work. We would need privacy and working space for the next ninety days to have any chance of competing. But tonight, as before, we would celebrate and imbibe the joy of the experience.

Over the course of the evening, through the frolic and excitement, we did manage to figure out some logistics. The local university classes had just ended, and we thought perhaps we could ask Elias to provide some space for us within his faculty over the summer. Moreover, we might even be able to hire computer science and engineering students for the summer to help us with our challenge. We quickly ran the idea by Wally, who seemed to think it would be a slam dunk. The other potential benefit was that, hopefully, Elias would be accessible and willing to help us in the home stretch. And, of course, he was. He was equally excited, with a million great ideas of his own to improve the pedagogical value of our offering.

After Wally had secured Elias' approval, we met the following morning at the VR lounge to brainstorm the daunting challenge ahead. We had $250,000 that we could spend on the entire process, which seemed like a lot, but it wasn't, especially considering how much we had to do. In the next ninety days, we would need to create a working prototype of our Metaverse University, build a rock-solid business plan, and choreograph a presentation demo that would make David Copperfield proud. We had so much to achieve in such a short period of time. Was it even possible?

Our newly acquired celebrity status was both a blessing and a curse. While the constant search for inside information was an incumbrance, the visibility had value. There was no need to seek the services that we would need. Literally overnight, there were hundreds of companies and individuals clamoring at our digital and physical doors at the university to sell us their services. Everyone wanted to be part of this thing. Many groups were even offering their software, services, and advice for free with an expectation of a longer-term service contract if we succeeded.

Within the space, Elias had also secured us an old-fashioned, square, wooden boardroom table that accommodated up to sixteen people. It was perfect. It had a large working surface that was chipped, scratched, and discolored with coffee stains and overuse. It made you feel like you were in action with "work in process" on the table. You could dig in, get your hands dirty, and get the job done. This was the opposite effect of those opulent, mahogany structures that law firms used. They were too fancy and felt like a prop that you didn't want to mess up. It was hard to get anything done. It also reminded you where much of your fee was going.

We also had whiteboards everywhere, a snack bar, Giant Tiger's top-end coffee maker, and a kettle for tea connoisseurs. We had everything we needed and were ready for action. At our first meeting, we identified and listed all the resources, both human and capital, that would be required:

Human Capital

• A UX designer to help us design our prototype

- Several software developers to code our system
- Three AI/Machine Learning specialists
- Several spatial designers to create rooms and spaces
- A graphic designer to create the aesthetic and feel
- Designers and riggers to create avatars
- A finance/business expert to create our business plan
- Production managers to manage the process
- A presentation choreographer to help us architect our masterpiece and bring out the Copperfield in all of us

Computer Hardware and Software

- Two dozen Meta Pro Headsets for testing
- A licensed version of Unreal Engine (UE) 5
- Local Edge Server: Nvidia Jetson One eVTOL
- Several Intel I9-based Programming workstations
- AWS Cloud Services (Gamelift, Cognito, Amplify, DynamoDB, S3 Bucket) and access to VIVOX or similar product for our voice services

We tabulated the cost of bringing the team and the resources together for this three-month project, and the expenses greatly exceeded $250,000, but we needed all these resources to compete.

When we put the estimates up on the board, with hardware/software costs at roughly $150K and our monthly labor costs around $100K, we would need $450K minimum to make this dog hunt. We had a $200K shortfall.

"How the heck are we going to fund all this?" I asked.

The group pondered for a bit. Then Dania had an idea.

"What if we offered advertising for some of the hardware companies? Maybe Nvidia would lend us the Jetson One for the duration of the pitch in exchange for visibility and recognition. The media exposure they would get would be huge, and we could agree to promote them as well," she suggested.

"Yeah, great idea," agreed Jag. "And Meta might also lend us a couple of dozen Meta Pro headsets for similar recognition."

"If we could pull that off, it would reduce our costs by $117K, bringing our shortfall under $100K to $83K," I said.

Frances, who had put together the original estimates for our labor costs, posited another great idea.

"Our labor estimates were based on specific individuals, but what if we used one company for all these services? For example, there is a great little company called Toonrush that does all of this. Because they design metaverse applications, they have all these skill sets under one roof. Perhaps we could negotiate a group deal with an understanding that if we were successful, they would form the core of our design team."

"If we could knock about thirty percent off our labor costs by doing this, it would bring us just under $250K," said Jag.

"The other advantage is that we would have a proven team that has worked together before, so it would also reduce the risk of personality conflicts. More certainty is always better in these short timeframes. If one person fails to deliver, it could put the whole project at risk. I say we give it a try. What have we got to lose?" I said.

Then we had to decide, more specifically, what the heck we were going to build for the final presentation. We included Elias in this process because there was no one better to help us figure out what we could possibly do to achieve maximum effect. We wanted to create something memorable but easy enough for the judges to understand. If they determined that we were too grandiose, it might not fly.

"We need some sizzle and a whole lot of steak," suggested Dania.

"Perhaps we can create a learning journey through space and time where we demonstrate what experiences we could offer in year one and then perhaps a glimpse into year five," Elias proposed.

"And maybe we could show three examples of how our system changes the nature of the experience today in ways that are otherwise not possible," I suggested.

We all agreed wholeheartedly as he outlined possible learning simulations that we could build into our overall narrative.

"Because the first program is focused on VR-based digital storytelling, these ones might work well for our opening salvo,

- **Cultural immersion simulation**: You could demonstrate a simulation that allows users to experience a different culture and customs by taking a virtual field trip to a different part of the world.
- **Science Technology Engineering Arts Math (STEAM) simulation:** The science simulation could demonstrate how gravity works, or better yet, how it can be visualized in space. Rather than experiencing a 2D Map of our solar system, we could simulate traveling across the galaxy.

"And thirdly, while the above two scenarios present compelling examples of what the students could create with our technology, perhaps something more grounded.

- **Immersive film-making simulations**: You could demonstrate how your metaverse platform could teach students how to create VR-based content, such as 360-degree films, interactive narratives, and augmented reality experiences."

"The first two are slam dunks," I said, and the rest of the team nodded in agreement. "While I like the idea of showing how to make 360 films and teach narratives, that might slow things down just a bit. What if we demonstrated the final product of what they could create?"

"Sure," agreed Elias. "What were you thinking?"

"I was thinking of a journalism simulation that would allow a student to travel to a foreign location to tell the story from that location," I began, "It would require some serious world-building, but we'd only need to build one for the demo. Maybe we build a virtual city in Ukraine to cover the war and provide a news update from there. We could also talk about how we could use digital twinning technology like IOT sensors to capture real-time information on weather, sound, and lighting based on time of day and VFX to mirror other critical variables like the state of the roads or various buildings. Our simulation could be updated in real-time based on that data, and it would be almost like being there without actually being there."

"Wow, we can really do that?" asked Jag.

I looked at Frances, and she agreed.

"Yeah, it's definitely doable, and I like the idea. I'm just not sure who is going to Ukraine to set up the remote sensors. But if we had that data, we could create real-time simulations."

I looked at Elias, and he nodded affirmatively as well.

"Okay, let me take that one away," I said. "Note to

self. Find someone willing to head to the warzone to place IOT sensing technology for the final demo." The group laughed.

"Hey, I love that we're thinking big," said Dania. "We need to literally knock their socks off. What about the two futuristic demos?"

"I had a couple of things in mind," said Elias. "We could build on the idea that Joe presented about digitally twinning a city but using it from a design perspective. We could create a complete replica of a large city that is struggling with growth and logistics issues. So, what if we built a virtual Toronto, Canada, for example? Not just for today but based on building permits and plans out twenty years. Then we simulate everything you would need to plan a city. Traffic flows, public transit, walking spaces, and crowds of people are based on projected population and demographic statistics. This simulation tool could identify problems and inform future design. What a powerful design tool to teach the students who are going to design our cities in the future."

We all agreed. Thumbs up for sure.

Elias continued, "And the second futuristic application, what about a virtual museum of the future? We think of museums today as hallowed halls where people look at artifacts from history and try to understand their stories and their historical relevance. But what if we could recreate that story? Imagine, that we were learning about post-impressionist artists. We could travel to Western Europe in the late eighteen hundreds and visit the places where the art was created and visit the actual artists. Again, there would be some world-building, but many of these spaces have remained the same for hundreds of years, so we could use photogrammetry to recreate the places easily enough, and the artists and even the crowds could be designed and simulated. We could even walk into the 'Starry Night' painting and experience what the artist was visualizing and feeling.

"Many of these things, like the Starry Night experience, are already being done today in VR, but from simulations like this, people could understand how we could recreate and literally visit any space and time to recreate the experience of being there at any moment in history.

"Would you like to attend the famous speeches of Martin Luther King in 1968? No problem. Observe what it was like to live in ancient Greece as Aristotle or Plato presented their ideas in public forums or experience what it would have been like to live in Egypt as the pyramids were being built."

So, yes, and yes, was the answer from the team. This was the future. We would be propelling people from experiences with unmotivated teachers, bad slideshow presentations, and substandard web videos to a vastly improved educational experience. This new reality would act not only as cognitive and emotional elixirs but would increase empathy and insight. So basically, we agreed that our learning experience would include five stops on the journey, including.

- Cultural immersion simulation
- STEAM experience of galaxy traveling
- VR Journalism from a simulated war zone
- Simulated City design tool
- Museum of the Future: The Art of Western Europe, Circa 1880s

These were all very powerful experiences that could make a difference in the contest, if we could execute properly. If we could help people imagine the future, they would start to connect the dots and realize how strong the economic possibilities would be.

We agreed on the plan, and over the next few days, we contacted these businesses and tried to negotiate deals. Both Meta and Nvidia agreed that this would be great visibility for their products. They agreed to three-month equipment loans and also offered up free onsite support. Both companies had a real interest in seeing us succeed as we would represent a very large customer almost immediately.

The Toonrush arrangement was even better. They counter-suggested that they could save almost sixty percent off the labor costs if we used their Campus VR platform as the base. This was the software that Elias had used in our course presentations, and that many of the universities were already using. It made sense. That way, we could focus on customization and not worry about creating new features from scratch.

They did, however, suggest that if they built these simulations as we described them, we would receive an extra bill to compensate for their costs at market value, and they would also retain a license to these experiences to compensate for the risk they were taking on. If we did not win, there would be no further costs, and they would retain the rights to the IP in perpetuity. It was a great deal for us, so we agreed.

When all was said and done, we had an extra fifty thousand dollars in our budget, and we decided to hold it as a contingency because there was a great deal of uncertainty in this process. By the end of the first week, all the people that were going to be part of the next several weeks were together in one large space. We were all in and so was Toonrush. We even added some key advisors who were but a phone call or text message away.

Toonrush, now our core dev team, had twelve people on the case and referred to themselves as "The Digital Dozen," This was a very cool group of people who had been working together for years and loved what they did. In fact, their logo said it all. While their earlier work was focused on cartoon animation, more of what they did today was focused on AI and VR, but their commitment to creating joy through their experiences remained. Lena Bender explained that the word "Toon" was placed over the smiley part of the curve, suggesting positive affect or "rush" created by the cartoon experience. The wave curve also suggested that how we feel as humans is a result of vibrational energy that is manifested by wave frequency. A bit geeky, but cool. I'm going to like working with these people, I thought.

Elias had also arranged for each team member to have a desk in the space, so we'd be within talking or soft shouting distance from each other.

The team included.

* Dania, Frances, Jag, and me

The Toonrush team

* Miguella Fujiama – UX Director
* Nadia Moretz – Writer/Director and Presentation Ninja
* Dag St. Clair – Head Writer
* Shari Shanaman – Graphic Design
* Edward Sulamen and Maddy Salto – Room Designers
* John Jackman and Mickey Mullins – Game Programmer Developers
* Garvin Joe and Amal Rafini – AI Machine Learning Specialists
* Haylin Henderson – Project Manager
* Lena Bender – Head of Production

The advisory board was there to guide us with some unique perspectives and to advise on strategic issues, so we chose a mix of gaming, innovation, strategy, finance, and academic expertise. Our advisors were.

* Elias – Engineering and Design professor and Academic Expert
* Dave Green – CEO of a global fintech company
* James Ironside – CFO of a local entertainment venture
* Alfonse Martin – Local inventor and entrepreneur
* Adam Fujiama – Professional Gamer
* Barton Cooper – Professor of Humanities and Storytelling

Then we broke up the overall leadership tasks.
While Frances worked with the development team and

Jag worked on the business plan with our financial advisor James Ironside, I focused on creating the overall experience and the final presentation.

Dania was externally focused, so any time there was a media interaction, interviews, or events that we should attend, she was our spokesperson. She loved the camera, was articulate, and looked great. Dania also worked on the Marketing and Sales strategy to plug into Jag's overall business plan.

Over the next several weeks, day in and day out, we built, tested, played, and argued. We argued about colors, textures, buttons, and processes. With all this creative energy, there were lots of diverging opinions, and we committed ourselves to an integrative method of problem resolution. In other words, no compromise but rather a commitment to digging deep to understand the "why." If we were going to build something world-changing, it wasn't supposed to be easy, so we committed to taking the path of higher resistance.

As the final presentation date grew ever closer, Nadia Moretz, our director, was pushing all of us to learn our lines and deliver them with perfection. This was particularly difficult because we were acting in imagined spaces that weren't built yet, and everyone was freaking tired.

She was super pretty, with a beautiful smile and an infectious laugh that made you want to continually induce those emotions in her. Say the wrong thing, however, and she will let you know in a second. She was a taskmaster too - firm, exact and direct; most great directors have these traits. Further, she was one hundred percent committed to the experience and insisted on the same commitment from everyone. So, the relentless pace continued.

I was okay with all of this. In fact, having not dated in

almost two years, I was developing a crush on her. I'm pretty sure she suspected as much as I was in the daily habit of bringing her coffee when I made my own, and she even reciprocated a couple of times. That said, neither one of us was going to do anything to jeopardize our project. We needed to remain focused.

What we were hoping to pull off was like the Cirque du Soleil of business presentations. We would ask the judges to attend the presentation within the Meta Pro HMDs we provided and deliver the entire performance in fully immersive VR. We had set up more than fifteen cameras in every virtual set and were doing a multi-camera live cast with camera changes every one to five seconds and cast onto YouTube and Twitch TV. This would make the live stream dynamic and compelling. And while not quite as exciting as the immersive experience, it would allow people to watch on their Macs, PCs, or mobile devices. We estimated that ¾ of a billion people in total would be watching either in Headsets from within the Metaverse, YouTube/YouTube360, or Twitch TV.

The narrative would start in a regular business boardroom as we would provide an overview of the presentation and the journey. Then we would ask people to buckle up as we would take them on a journey of a lifetime.

First to downtown Mumbai for an immersive cultural experience where we would watch some theatre and visually sample food, replete with simulated olfactory sensations; then, we would teleport to Ukraine to update everyone on the state of the war. From there, we would blast off into space and observe Earth from afar, past Venus, up to Mercury, followed by a hyperspace jump to Jupiter, around the loop, past Mars and back to Earth, where we would simulate a landing in Paris in the year 1889 to observe the making of Vincent van Gogh's Starry Night.

The team from Toonrush had done an amazing job. The simulated worlds were incredibly realistic and awe-inspiring, and the whole journey literally felt like a trip through space and time. Following the journey, we would head back to the VR boardroom and deliver our business case, with each of the partners delivering their piece. I would present the vision of our product and content experiences and how we planned to evolve them over time. Frances would deliver everything they needed to know about our technology and innovation plan, and Dania would present our vision of how we planned to market and sell our services. Finally, Jag, our CFO-to-be, would deliver the numbers.

For our final act, we would teleport everyone to the Kennedy Space Centre with a rocket ship aptly named "Metaversity One" sitting on the launch pad, ready to go. Standing on the platform in our virtual space suits, we would bid everyone adieu and enter the craft to prepare for takeoff. Ten, nine, eight, seven, six, five, four, three, two, one, and The Metaversity One would launch into space, leaving a trail of letters in the sky with "Thank You for Watching", followed by a list of credits.

It was Nadia's idea. She thought that using the rocket ship launch would be a powerful metaphor for launching a new business and would create a positive associative prime in the judge's minds. A clever idea, I thought. We would see soon enough.

It was the night before, and we felt good about the presentation. We had rehearsed our parts a dozen times, but as is almost always the case, nothing ever goes as planned.

Just when we thought we would shut it down and be

ready for the following day's presentation, Frances had a panic attack and felt she could not do her part. With all the pressure here and with her kids, Frances was stressed beyond anything she had ever experienced before, so it was understandable. It did, however, leave us in an extremely difficult position.

Each of us had over ten minutes presenting our sections, and there was no one who could deliver her talk, and even if they could, it was too late to learn everything one needed to know about the technology, then memorize and deliver the speech. This could hurt us badly, but there was nothing we could do. Frances's mental health was the most important here, so we would have to wait.

Dania spent most of the evening trying to console her, but it was no use. She was done. The more we talked about it, the more anxious she became. Not knowing what to do, we called Elias to see if he had any ideas that could help us. He was not available due to family commitments but suggested he would call back in about an hour. So, we waited.

We were desperate, but an hour later, as promised, the phone rang. It was Elias.

He suggested we ask Frances to put on the VR headset and meet him on the main launch page. So, we did, and Frances complied, willing to try anything to help herself and ultimately to help us. She was torn. She felt guilty about the panic attack but even more afraid of freaking out during the big presentation the following day and ruining our chances.

Elias asked for privacy, so we left Frances with Elias and went across the street to the pub to wait it out.

Almost three hours later, we got a call from Elias

suggesting we go back and pick up Frances.

When we arrived back at our office space, Frances was waiting for us. She was calmer than we'd seen her in weeks and seemed confident that she would be okay the following day.

The next morning, I asked Elias how he had helped Frances. He explained, "Frances was highly anxious, and that was compounded by a fear of public speaking. Based on our recent research on student anxiety, we discovered that VR-based meditation and gaming were both very effective means of reducing anxiety. So, we hung out for a bit. First, we did a guided meditation on the beach with the new Praia VR beach mediation app; then, we played Beat Saber for almost an hour. She was jumping around, laughing, and having more fun than she'd had in weeks. Then, I invited my good friend James Davis, a psychologist, to help us with her public speaking phobia. James had a special VR simulation room that he had developed for our faculty. It allowed speakers to practice and face their fears in front of a large room of NPCs. It's basically a public speaking simulator. The room could be configured in any number of different ways to provide a previsualization of the exact room for the anticipated experience. Delivering the same speech in the same environment multiple times causes those fears to become extinct. That form of repetitive exposure therapy is called cognitive-based therapy, but in VR, it is referred to as Virtual Reality Exposure Therapy (VRET). In our faculty, engineers often struggle with speaking challenges and anxiety. Our process of reducing anxiety is called VREP or Virtual Reality Experience Priming. We use experiences like gaming and meditation to help reduce anxiety levels. Now, we asked Frances to play a few games of Beat Saber before the big presentation tomorrow, but she would be okay. Oh, and by the way, you owe James a beer," he winked.

Amazing, I thought. What a powerful tool. Why didn't everybody know about this? So, with a bit of anxiety therapy (VREP) and some fear exposure therapy (VRET), Frances was like a new person.

"Well, why don't we do the same?" I asked, "We could play Beat Saber before the presentation tomorrow and get some of the same anxiety reduction benefits."

"I agree," said Elias. "It may also improve cognition."

When I told the rest of the group, they were similarly amazed.

So, the following day, we all met one hour before our scheduled presentation and played Beat Saber for almost forty minutes. We'd never been more relaxed. Admittedly we were sweating, but the whole event was being presented within avatars, and avatars do not sweat. At least not yet.

And how did Frances do at the presentation? Well, she absolutely killed. In fact, she was the best speaker of all. We all presented well that day, and at the end of the presentation, I shared an anecdote about our experience and how VR exposure and these anxiety-reduction methods had saved the day.

We didn't see any of the other presentations as all ten teams were sequestered for the weekend leading up to the final banquet on Sunday night, so we had no idea how good or bad the presentations were or how we did. We only knew that five of the ten teams were entertainment companies, two were commerce, two were educational, and one was an environmental initiative.

CHAPTER FIFTEEN

The Final Verdict

It was surreal. As Naomi started to express the words that would dictate our final destiny, time seemed to stand still, the room grew silent, and it made me think.

What a journey this had been. Six months ago, our friend Jon Isaacson and key member of the Super Six, now Fab Five, died unexpectedly at the hands of an angry polar bear. Well, perhaps not angry, but definitely hungry.

In an effort to mourn Jon's passing, we realized how dismal and uninspiring our lives had become and opted to go "all in" to compete in this crazy, long-shot contest to regain something that we'd lost. We weren't sure what it was at the time. Youth? Another chance? Or maybe just an opportunity to grab some attention and mean something to the people around us.

Nonetheless, as the contest progressed, so also did the harsh reality of life. RoMac's daughter had taken sick in the middle of our journey. She had a progressive form of MS, and RoMac had done everything to help her physically, mentally, and spiritually. Fortunately, she would be okay, and with progressive diet and lifestyle changes, she had hope for a good life. Unfortunately, RoMac was unable to remain in the contest, so our fab five became the fab four, and we soldiered on, hoping RoMac could rejoin us eventually.

Through Frances' marital woes and public speaking challenges, Dania's mental health issues, and with Jag and I pretty much broke, we still managed to get to the finish line. Of the 690K+ entries that started this amazing race, only ten of us remained, and that was something we would remember for the rest of our lives.

At this point, it really didn't matter as we'd done everything we possibly could. As I looked at Naomi, time re-engaged, and she spoke.

"There were three teams that we felt represented the best opportunity for our investors.

"Our third-place team, a group with whom we plan to invest two hundred million dollars over the next five years, is a fabulous entertainment gaming company that has created a multiplatform game concept that will simulate multiple dimensions and allow people to travel and experience these different worlds as virtual characters or yourself. Personally, I can't wait to try this game, and I hope all of you will join us on that journey.

"I present our Team Three: **The Many Worlds Experiencers!**"

The crowd errupted into exhilaration, and the victorious team, just two tables away, leaped up in jubilation. Their celebrations and genuine exuberance surpassed even the Oscars, making them appear like a mere neighborhood barbecue. Out of respect, they soon quieted down, allowing Naomi to proceed.

"The second team was equally riveting. Overwhelmed by the entertainment domain, we encountered a wealth of outstanding ideas and gaming concepts. In fact, any of the five entertainment teams merited investment. However, we opted for a different path, selecting the commerce category and the team that presented the most enthralling vision of the future we'd ever witnessed. Their futuristic retail world melded stunning aesthetics and currency integration with an ingenious concept that enabled shoppers to transform virtual products into tangible ones using the simple phrase, 'Make it Real.' We were thoroughly impressed, as it reminded us of Amazon's one-click-buy innovation years ago."

For a moment, I wondered if I was dreaming. A few months ago, as part of my future visualization, I'd seen a strikingly similar retail concept with the identical slogan, "Make it Real." Confusion clouded my thoughts, and even Frances and Dania exchanged puzzled glances. Had we overlooked this opportunity? Collecting myself, I refocused my attention on Naomi Grace.

"I present our Team Two: **Open for Business!**"

The group exploded with excitement. One girl was jumping up and down and just couldn't stop. She was overly ecstatic. It was nice to see so much joy. We clapped in support as we watched our chances slowly slip away, with two of the three slots now filled. Wouldn't it be crazy if one of the winners' key differentiators was based on the exact same slogan that I had visualized?

The group and crowd quieted down as Naomi began to speak again.

"Our choice of the first position was unanimous. All of the judges felt that these people had the idea that could change the world for the good and profitably so. Education has traditionally been a challenging sector to invest money. The risks are higher, and the rate of change is slowed by tradition, low competition, and hundreds of years of traditional ideologies that need to be shaken up."

Okay, now our hearts were racing. There were only two teams in the Education space, and we were one of them. God help us, I thought.

Just then, my cell phone buzzed. I was certain I had turned it off, but somehow it came through. It was RoMac. It read.

"Holy Sh—,! I'm with you, sending big love".

The event was VR and webcast live globally, so he was watching and would know exactly what we would be experiencing at this moment. As our future Chief Learning Officer, he would also have just as much at stake.

Naomi continued.

"What we found particularly special about this group was the grandeur of the vision, the sense of presentation, and drama. I'm a big believer in people that 'walk their talk,' and if the students of the future can experience what we did the other day, their education will be grand. This group really put on a show. For our number one investment, our team at Just Virtual is incredibly excited to blast off to wherever this team is headed with their Metaversity One platform."

Naomi looked over at the Fab Four and smiled.

"I present our Team One: **The Polar Magnates!**"

I started to cry. We all did. It was incredible.

CHAPTER SIXTEEN

The Day After

The day after the fanfare subsided. I attempted to reach out to Elias to express my gratitude. Unfortunately, he seemed to be absent during the concluding celebrations, and my attempts at contacting him proved fruitless.

Deciding to meet him face-to-face, I journeyed to the university but was met with a perplexing response from the receptionist. "There's no Dr. Elias affiliated with this institution. As far as our records are concerned, there never has been."

Bewildered and disoriented, I asked to speak to Wally, hoping there was a simple misunderstanding that he could clarify. However, the receptionist, mirroring my look of confusion, claimed that there was no record of a Wally either.

Was I losing my grasp on reality? I resorted to pinching myself, testing for the familiar sting of pain, a validation of my existence, and to my relief, everything felt normal.

I contacted Jag, Dania, RoMac, and Frances to see if they could make sense out of any of this. They were all similarly confused, and after their own research, validated my crazy revelation. We even went back to the Pub to find Wally and the owners confirmed it. While the pub was not an illusion, Wally was.

Were these characters illusions, avatars from a higher dimension, or maybe angels? We'd just navigated a life-altering event that had the potential to change the course of history, well at least "our" history, and the very people that were pivotal in empowering us were mere illusions?

Wow, it suddenly struck us like a bolt of lightning on a sunny day. These characters were virtual, at least to our understanding.

In all likelihood, the other students in our classes were also illusions or next generation NPCs created to enhance the realism of our learning experience. After all, Elias's lessons did delve into how VR classrooms could manipulate environments and characters to challenge stereotypes, reduce anxiety, boost cognition, and foster positive psychological effects. This, as it happened, was our ultimate lesson.

If we thought we had mastered virtual reality after such a momentous victory, our egos were now in check. We had just been schooled at a level beyond our comprehension. Our final lesson in VR was a poignant reminder: there is always more to learn and explore, so remain humble and inquisitive.

In hindsight, there seemed to be something uncanny each time we walked through the doors of that engineering faculty, and this may well have been related to more advanced VR research. Whether this was an advanced VR experiment like a holodeck simulation from Star Trek The Next Generation, a cosmic iteration in a higher-level game, or an unseen universal force of benevolence and grace, we would likely never know. Nonetheless, we would embrace this new reality, with gratitude and renewed humility. We were all struggling, searching, and desperately in need of a second chance to truly live. And this would be our road to redemption.

Aptly, I vividly recalled one of the verses from my favorite Blue Rodeo song; "Five Days in May".

> Sometimes the world begins
> To set you up on your feet again
> It wipes the tears from your eyes
> How will you ever know
> The way that circumstances go
> Always gonna hit you by surprise

Sitting on the steps of the university, reflecting on our final lesson, I found an unusual tranquility. These spectral guides, Elias and Wally, might not have had a physical existence, yet their influence was indelible and their lessons concrete.

While many argue that virtual reality, in any form, is simply a vice, an escape from what is real, empirical research suggests otherwise; the affective and cognitive impacts from what is real and what is virtual are similarly experienced by our brains.

I had felt their presence, their guidance, and their inspiration. They were as real to me as the steps I sat on, or the wind I felt against my skin. And that was all that mattered.

Epilogue

Technology is a crucial part of human evolution. It transcends the mere creation of products, services, and experiences; it yearns for a deeper purpose — the transformation of our very being and the resuscitation of our ailing environment.

No longer confined to the limitations of the present, our epilogue unfolds with the promise of a renaissance. As we gazed into the future, the advent of AI, VR, and a vast array of Metaverse technologies became a beacon of hope that would help us solve our world's most daunting challenges. We embraced the potential of these technologies as transformative tools and boldly conquered challenges previously considered intractable.

Yet, as the pace of progress quickened, an impending singularity loomed on the horizon. The point at which artificial general intelligence would rival and surpass human intellect appeared tantalizingly close. Experts, like Ray Kurzweil, predicted its arrival between 2029 and 2045, while others believed it to be even nearer. The same technologies that held promise could now be exploited by nefarious forces driven by greed, power, and control.

It was crucial to address these concerns head-on, for the best safeguard against misuse was knowledge and understanding. Education, awareness, critical thinking, and inclusiveness of diverse perspectives became the foundation upon which a resilient and informed society would stand.

Bonus Chapters

CHAPTER X.1

Getting into the Headspace

This next lecture was going to be important. Understanding the technology and how the technology was expected to evolve would be mission-critical. Countless companies that appeared to be dominant in a particular market space had literally died in a period of fewer than five years because they were unwilling or unable to stay abreast of technology changes. When we were younger, a company called Blockbuster Video was a retail juggernaut and "the" place to get your movies, TV shows, game cartridges, and all the wonderful culinary accouterments like popcorn and candy that we typically associate with this experience. At its peak, Blockbuster had nine-thousand stores and over fifty million members.

In the year 2000, Blockbuster had the opportunity to purchase Internet streamer Netflix for roughly fifty million dollars but balked at the high price. Over a ten-year timeframe, a company that they laughed at initially, completely disrupted their business and became the market leader. In 2010, Blockbuster filed for bankruptcy protection. By 2021, Netflix had achieved a market capitalization of nearly three hundred billion USD. Yes, that's billion with a "B" and roughly six-thousand times more than the fifty million dollar price tag for which Blockbuster could have acquired Netflix.

Most of us were also familiar with how the Uber franchise decimated the taxicab industry with a simple application that transformed the nature of urban transportation. But there were countless other stories of this type of disruptive innovation. Kodak, Polaroid, Toys R US, and a slew of large retailers and bookstore chains also fell victim to disruptive innovation. Clayton Christensen, the God of disruptive innovation, wrote several books and academic articles related to "The Innovators Dilemma", the challenges that most of these companies faced, and how they failed.

In thinking about the possible business pitches, it was clear that we would need to identify potential areas of disruption and use the Netflix innovation model to bet on a longer-term technology landscape. In doing so, we would need to use those anticipated future technology capabilities, albeit a moving target, to create a much better experience for whatever target customers we would choose. Further, the rate of change of new technology appeared to be accelerating, not slowing down. This meant more risk, but it also meant more opportunity. The prospects were exciting. I chuckled to myself as it felt completely surreal, considering where I was just a few weeks ago. Nonetheless, what a fun escape. As Elias' engineering background was focused on technology innovation, I suspected that he would cover much of this at some point over the next few lessons.

Later that week, we met at the coffee shop across from the university to discuss our thinking. I shared my thoughts on the disruptive innovation opportunities that we would need to consider, while Frances shared her thoughts on the key technologies that she felt would be most relevant within our Metaverse Challenge. We seemed to have more questions than answers, though, so the timing was perfect. We walked over to the Engineering building for our second lesson and to hopefully fill that knowledge void with Elias' insights.

When we arrived at the Virtual Reality Lab, Elias suggested that we change things up. Instead of meeting in the virtual lecture lab, he suggested we meet in the VR beach classroom. Interesting, I thought. Combining the idea of technology and nature, two concepts that were about as diametrically opposed as could be, seemed to not make sense. But then I remembered something I had read about how we think. It was a book by cognitive psychologist Daniel Kahneman called Thinking Fast and Slow. The research suggested that, while we often learn and recall more effectively within environments that are conducive or aligned with the subject matter, a concept called situated learning, there could be an equally positive learning impact by taking us out of our comfort zone and creating a more discursive or less fluent experience.

In fact, there was a whole field of study related to the

concept of perceptual fluency that seemed counterintuitive yet fascinating. As Kahneman's research would suggest, this disfluent experience should trigger our "type two" or slow thinking process, making us more thoughtful and contemplative, hence learning more. We would find out soon enough. Nothing Elias appeared to do was without purpose.

As we put on the VR headsets and arrived at the Campus VR landing page, I selected the visual icon for the beach and, in less than two seconds, was transported to a beautiful beach classroom environment. Wow, this was impressive. I knew it wasn't real, but it certainly felt real. We were ensconced within a beautiful nature scene reminiscent of a cottage you might expect near Lake Placid in upper New York State or one of the many beautiful environments in the Muskoka region of Ontario, Canada. I took my seat on a cool lime rock in the student seating gallery and readied for class.

Visuals of the Beach Teaching Environment

I could hear Dania muttering in the chair a few meters away. "Holy F—," she exclaimed, expressing her excitement at entering the beautiful beach environment while exhibiting her trucker-like verbal tendencies.

Perhaps to change the overall ethos of the presentation, or maybe for personal digital comfort, Elias' avatar was now sporting a pair of denim shorts, a white cotton shirt, and a baseball hat. He began.

"Just like any large construction or engineering project, there are several technology pieces that must come together to create a virtual reality application and the aggregate Metaverse. It's a bit like solving a complex puzzle.

"But I'm not going to tell you what those pieces are just yet; I'm going to ask you to tell me. In the spirit of the contest, we're going to play a little game. I'd like each of the teams to get together on one of those floating docks that just appeared out on the lake and come up with a list of ten items that are required."

We looked at each other and smiled. There were four docks out in the bay, one for each team. Each dock was equipped with several chairs, a table, and a screen that hung over the end of the dock. Interestingly, there was also a small motor and steer stick so we could navigate out further or come closer. Without a doubt, this was the coolest breakout room I'd ever experienced. We selected the dock closer to the mouth of the large water and, in a second, transported it across the water. The other teams chose to stay closer to the shore.

Floating Breakout Rooms

I thought to myself, it would have been even cooler if, after choosing the dock, we could have walked our avatars across the water like Jesus. At that point, Elias, always a step ahead, smiled at us and walked out across the water to make sure everyone was ready for the first exercise. Ha, so it could be done. Wow! I chuckled to myself. This was too much fun.

We brainstormed the technology required to build our first metaverse application that would someday power our world-changing company. It wasn't that easy as we were not sure how specific he wanted us to get, nor what our company was going to build. Nonetheless, we played along, and it was a good exercise to think about everything that would be required. Then with the help of the elegant virtual keyboard, we filled each of the ten slots on the screen as best we could. After fifteen minutes, our list included all of the possible VR hardware and application software, myriad Internet and cloud-based services, and some level of security technology. We were certain that we were missing many things, but it was a great thought experiment.

When all teams were done, Elias asked all teams to submit their lists, so we did. It felt like we were on the set of a family feud without all the screaming. Then Elias posted the group selections on the large screen over the lake, near the shoreline. His selection was the optimal one, but we appeared to have six-ish of the answers with mostly the right idea. That was promising. The other teams had a few less but similar selections. Nonetheless, we all failed to identify the key elements of software and network services, including Edge Computing, Blockchain, Biometric sensors, and Artificial Intelligence (AI) applications.

This was Elias' list.

1. Internet Connectivity
2. VR/AR Headsets, Haptics, gloves, and/or controllers
3. Client-Based Development Software
4. Cloud-Based Multimedia Content Services
5. Cloud-Based Content Delivery Network
6. 5G Wireless Network for Mobile Devices
7. Edge Computing Services
8. Artificial Intelligence Software and Services
9. Blockchain Software and Services
10. Biometric and other IOT Sensing Devices

This exercise provided Elias with a good sense of our current understanding so that he could focus his teaching efforts on the areas where we were weak. As we left our floating docks and repopulated the seats, Elias continued.

Internet Connectivity

"The Internet is perhaps the most important element within the evolving VR Metaverse. The Internet IS to information what roads ARE to transportation, and what plumbing IS to drinking water. The information (text, images, audio, video, etc.) that travels on these digital links is the lifeblood of education, business, entertainment, commerce, and every imaginable Internet application.

"Does anyone here know what life was like before the Internet?" Elias inquired.

Reluctantly, our team members raised our hands to acknowledge that we were the official wily veterans of the class. Perhaps that was a good thing, though. We had a baseline frame of reference that allowed us to compare the experiences before and after the Internet changed our lives. There is something transformative and enlightening about experiencing the process of change, particularly when you reflect upon it. For example, if you had to purchase something, you simply went to the store, braved the traffic and crowds, and purchased what you wanted. A shopping expedition could range from fifteen minutes to several hours, sometimes for the simplest item. Today, we have access to many times more options, and the transaction can be consummated in a few seconds. Where has all that time gone? I wondered.

Elias continued.

"If you wanted to learn or read something, you went to a library or bookstore, interacted with people, and fulfilled that need. Similarly, the school was a daily event within a physical classroom with people, real people. For anyone born prior to 1980, that was likely the reality you grew up with. While some would say that is a disadvantage to adapting to this new digital world, you could also argue that it was an advantage to have a visualization reference and concept of how successful experiences occurred. This might be an advantage in the design process for the more experienced group." he posited and continued.

"There is often a reference to 'digital natives,' youth who have never known anything but smartphones or tablets, and a suggestion that they are better with technology. Interestingly, there is new research to suggest that youth is not necessarily an advantage in dealing with rapid technological change. In fact, the research from Belgium suggests that 'personal innovativeness' is more relevant to the adoption of new technology, and that characteristic is independent of age. So, for the more experienced among us, you are on equal footing, and your base of experiences may be an asset that younger people do not share, so don't lose hope." He smiled.

If I didn't know better, I would have thought that Elias was favoring our team, but I'm certain he was simply trying to challenge outdated notions of ageism and level the playing field to empower all of us equally. Well done, I thought.

He continued.

"So, while the Internet is the lifeblood of our information economy, the experiences can vary considerably depending on what technology is specifically used. If you'll note above." A large Internet diagram appeared on the screen behind Elias.

The Global Internet

"It is important to understand the central role the Internet plays in the metaverse experience, so bear with me as we review what may seem obvious to many of you. The global Internet is a network of interconnected computers and servers around the world that communicate with each other to transmit data and information. It involves various technologies, protocols, and infrastructure components.

"Devices like your computer, smartphone, or even your VR Headset, which is really a mobile computer, connect to the Internet through an Internet Service Provider (ISP).

"The ISP provides your computing device, often referred to as a router, with an IP address, like your home address, which is a unique identifier that allows it to communicate with other devices on the Internet."

Dania threw up her hand, and Elias acknowledged her. "How does the information flow on the Internet?"

"I was just getting to that," said Elias as he threw up another diagram on the large screen.

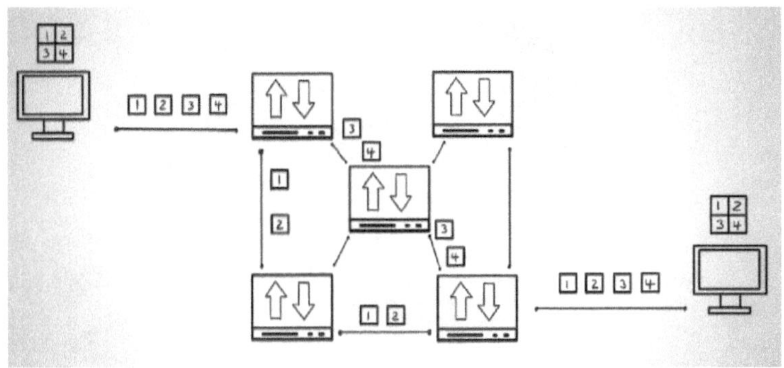

Packet Switching Diagram

"When data is sent over the Internet, it is broken into small packets of information that can be transmitted efficiently. Each packet is labeled with the destination address and other information that helps it get to its destination.

"The packets are transmitted through a series of routers, which are special devices that help route the packets to their destination. Each router determines the best path for the packet to take based on the destination IP address, kind of like a mail sorting station.

"The packets eventually arrive at their destination, where they are reassembled into the original data. This process is known as packet switching."

Dania again.

"How does the router work?"

Elias nodded and continued as the screen above changed yet again.

Internet Router

"Sure, Dania. An Internet router is a device that connects multiple devices to the Internet and routes data packets between them. It is used in homes, businesses, and other settings to provide access to the Internet. So, when your ISP sets up your Internet service, they provide you with a router. That's the little box that is connected to the wall and likely sits on a table, bookshelf, or maybe on the floor.

"The router registers the IP addresses of any device in your home and becomes the gateway to the Internet, both coming and going. Think of the router as a mail person or a switchboard operator. When data packets come in, they look at whom they are addressed to and pass them on. When data packets leave, the router sends the packets to the next router on the Internet, with the destination IP address. Getting from your computing device to the destination may involve the work of many routers that try to get the data packets to their destination using the most efficient path possible. The router uses a protocol called the Border Gateway Protocol

(BGP) to communicate with other routers on the Internet and determine the best path to take.

"Routers often provide other features as well. As central hubs of connectivity, routers may offer an array of additional features. For instance, residential routers typically incorporate Wi-Fi capabilities, facilitating seamless wireless connections for various devices. They also include ports to directly link computers via specific cards or ports present on the computer hardware. To counteract potential cybersecurity threats, many routers are equipped with security measures such as firewalls, serving as the first line of defense against hackers. Most newer devices also allow custom configurations like website or content filtering, an invaluable feature for parents aiming to regulate their children's Internet access.

"Finally, while I don't want to get bogged down in the details here, it's also important to mention a few of the critical protocols and acronyms that many of you have heard of but likely don't quite understand how they relate."

"What is a protocol?" asked Jag.

"Oh, sorry, good question," said Elias.

"A computer protocol is much like a human protocol. For example, when we see someone, we say hi and may shake their hand or exchange a kiss on the cheek, then perhaps interact in some conversation or small talk, depending on the context of the meeting.

"Similarly, in computing, a protocol defines the exchange behavior between devices. More specifically, it is a set of rules and procedures that govern the communication between two or more devices related to the format, timing, sequencing, and how it deals with errors. Error control between devices ensures that communication is reliable and efficient. These protocols are used in file transfers, email, and web browsing.

"For example, many of you have likely heard of the acronym TCP/IP and never really thought about what it means. The Internet Protocol (IP) is a protocol used for transmitting data over the Internet, while the Transmission Control Protocol (TCP) is a protocol that ensures the reliable delivery of data over the Internet. Hence, they work together to make the Internet work."

Elias looked at the audience for questions. As usual, Dania's hand was up.

"So, this is all great, but why do we need to know all of this stuff about the Internet? Isn't our focus on the Metaverse?"

Elias smiled.

"Absolutely, but as discussed earlier, this is the underlying structure of the Metaverse, and everything that exists today on the Internet is a critical building block of the Metaverse. Again, the Metaverse is really a 3D implementation of the Internet. As we get into the understanding of various Internet cloud-based services, you'll get a better sense of why this fundamental understanding is important for creating a metaverse business."

Dania acknowledged Elias for the response.

Elias continued, "Okay, now that you hopefully have a sense of how the Internet works, let's try and reinforce that a bit."

With that, Elias presented a question on the screen behind him while four basketball nets appeared in front of us on the beach that begged us to shoot the basketballs that had just appeared in our hands.

The screen read, "The purpose of an Internet router

is."

1. To direct data packets to their proper destination on the Internet
2. To direct data packets from the Internet to the local IP device
3. To provide access and a gateway for local devices to the Internet
4. All of the above

Intuitively, we all stood up, positioned the basketball in a typical free throw position, and aimed at the basket that represented our choice. I missed my first shot on basket four but managed "nothing but net" on the second, as a winning sound was emitted, indicating I had sunk the ball but also answered correctly. For the next ten minutes, we answered questions and had fun with one of the most realistic simulators that I'd ever experienced.

"You've just experienced a powerful example of how a VR application can improve the learning experience by making it more salient, fun, and memorable by using auditory, visual, and kinetic reinforcement techniques," Elias commented.

VR Devices

"Now, let's talk about VR devices. The VR devices of the mid-2020s are not your parents technology. In fact, the same capabilities of today's devices would have cost tens of thousands of dollars in academia less than twenty years ago. Many of the features would not have been possible at that time, but as is the case with technology, improvements on microprocessors, lenses, software innovations, and web-based services all contribute to improving that customer experience.

"I won't get into a specific analysis of all the products but rather a high-level overview of the key devices that are used or are anticipated to be relevant in the next few years. For this discussion, we're also assuming immersive virtual reality (IVR) as opposed to desktop VR (DVR). Desktop VR experiences can be viewed simply on a computer desktop, laptop, or mobile device.

"The IVR devices that we'll discuss are VR head-mounted devices (HMD), AR glasses, haptic suits, and gloves."

The VR Head Mounted Device (HMD)

"A VR HMD is a device that enables users to experience a simulated, immersive 3D environment. As discussed earlier, the HMD employs the science of stereoscopy, which uses a parallax effect to create the illusion of depth and immersion. It works by displaying separate, slightly offset images to each eye, creating the illusion of depth, and mimicking how humans perceive the real world. The images presented to each eye are generated by a high-resolution screen, often using lenses to adjust the focal distance and provide a wide field of view. This visual information is then combined by the brain to produce a single, cohesive perception of a three-dimensional environment.

"To create a convincing and immersive experience, VR headsets must be able to track the user's head movements and adjust the displayed images accordingly. This is achieved using a combination of sensors, such as accelerometers and gyroscopes which continuously monitor the user's head position and orientation.

"In addition to visual input, VR headsets often incorporate spatial audio, using headphones or built-in speakers, to provide realistic sound cues that help users navigate and interact within the virtual environment. Some advanced VR systems also include haptic feedback, using vibrations or other tactile sensations to simulate the sense of touch and enhance the user's immersion. Most HMDs also provide 'controller-less' software options that track hand gestures, meaning users can choose to use the controllers or simply navigate with their hands.

"To render the images and process the tracking data, VR headsets are sometimes connected to a computer or game console, which runs the VR software and generates the virtual environment. Newer systems, like the Meta Quest line of HMDs, are also wireless and standalone, incorporating all necessary computing power within the headset itself, making them more portable and user-friendly.

"By combining these various elements - visual displays, motion tracking, audio, and sometimes haptic feedback - VR headsets are able to create a convincing and engaging simulation of a virtual world, allowing users to explore and interact with digital environments in a way that feels natural and intuitive.

"Here's a quick overview of the key components to collaborate to create VR.

"**Sensors**: Most HMDs use accelerometers and gyroscopes to track the user's head and hand movements and present them visually within the virtual space. This information is shared locally and with other participants who are also present within the same virtual space.

"**Displays**: Two small, high-resolution displays (one for each eye) show different images to create the illusion of depth and 3D visuals.

"**Lenses**: The lenses in the headset help to focus and shape the images being displayed, ensuring that they appear clear and in focus to the user.

"**Audio**: 3D audio helps to create a more immersive experience by accurately reproducing sound effects in 360 degrees, often referred to as spatial audio.

"**Controller**: Handheld controllers enable the user to interact with the virtual environment to select, control, and manipulate virtual objects. The position of the controllers that represent the hands is also shared with all other users in the virtual space. As discussed earlier, most devices now offer controller-less options where visual sensors on the HMD track hand and finger movements.

"**CPU**: The Central Processing Unit (CPU) is the computer that runs the software applications and controls the various functions of the headset. The CPU often works in tandem with a companion computer called the GPU (Graphics Processing Unit) and is responsible for processing the data from the headset's sensors, rendering the 3D graphics for the displays, and handling the audio output.

"It's also important to note that all these elements work together synchronously and communicate in real-time with centralized web-based services that allow the headsets to receive other information about all other objects or avatars within the virtual space while propagating their information to all avatar participants.

"The objective of this process is to ensure that all devices in the VR environment are updated in real-time with the latest position information for all avatars. This helps to maintain a seamless and immersive experience for all users in the virtual environment.

"Let's say there are twenty avatars within a virtual environment like this classroom. In fact, I believe we have twenty people here currently. The VR application that is currently running on your headset is communicating in real-time with several cloud-based servers, including a game server, an audio server, an authentication server, and multimedia content servers that are presenting the charts, images, and objects that you are viewing now."

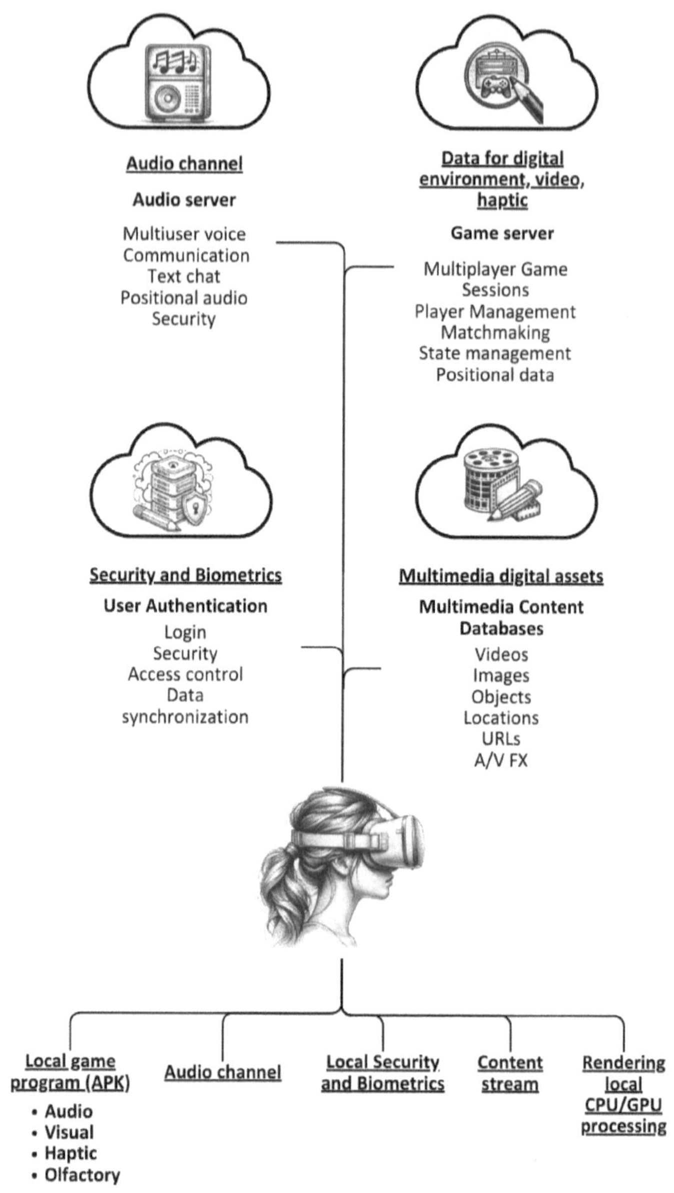

HMD Use of Cloud-Based Services

"As discussed last week in our lesson about quantifiable immersion, let's assume the headset is updating information and creating new images (one for each eye) at 120 frames per second.

"Each of those devices on your headset is sending information back to a centralized server to represent its positions in 3D space, but also receiving that same data that represents the positions of those other nineteen headsets (as avatars), as well as any other objects within the environment. Further, it must sample any changes within the environment itself, like lighting or visual effects.

"Then, with all that information, the processor 'does the math' and recreates the frames that represent the visual environment. It does this whole operation 120 times per second (every eight to ten milliseconds). This is a complex procedure, and the timing is equally critical. It's really an incredible process."

Elias surveyed the audience. "Are there any questions?"

He was right. This was an incredible technological innovation that transcended geographic space. It's hard to believe that all this information is being sampled and transmitted around the world to bring people together in a virtual space, a shared illusion, and 120 times every second. Amazing, I thought. I know our eyes and our optical cortex process data in a similar manner but only locally. As most of the group attempted to digest this information, Elias continued to reinforce the idea.

"This application transmits the same information that we perceive locally to individuals anywhere in the world, bringing people together into a common space to learn, laugh, play, socialize, or transact. While everything we experience is an illusion, the result of those experiences, the feelings, thoughts, memories, and actions are very real.

When you buy a pair of shoes from a virtual store, they manifest into a real physical product and arrive at your door.

"With a well-executed VR learning application like this one, most participants report that they feel like they were 'in a geographic space' rather than just viewing images, and that is how they will remember that experience. At one point, when reviewing previous memories, it may be difficult to differentiate real-world and virtual locations because, to our brain and emotional processes that underlie cognition, they are the same.

"Okay, so now that we have a sense of how the VR headset works, let's review Haptic devices that will work in concert with the HMD to enhance the experience and feelings of presence even more. Then you'll have earned a break," he smiled. "Okay, Haptics."

VR Haptics

"Haptics is a technology that aims to simulate tactile sensations. This process allows users to feel and interact with virtual objects in a more immersive and realistic manner. By combining visual, auditory, and haptic feedback, we can now create a deeper multimodal sensory experience that more closely mimics real-world sensations. This can further increase feelings of authenticity and presence.

"To create that tactile experience, haptic devices use actuators, sensors, and even software algorithms to generate forces and vibrations that simulate touch sensations. The two main processes used are called sensing and actuation.

"**Sensing** technology helps devices like headsets understand when and how a user touches or presses them, while **actuation** turns electrical signals into physical actions like forces, vibrations, or movements, creating what's called tactile feedback. This can be achieved through various methods, including electromagnetic forces, air pressure (pneumatics), or water pressure (hydraulics), each providing different types of touch sensations.

"There are several types of haptic devices that provide a unique way to interact with virtual environments. VR haptic gloves, as you might expect, provide tactile feedback to the user's hands and fingers while haptic suits, most often full-body wearable devices, provide tactile feedback across the entire body. These suits contain multiple actuators placed strategically to simulate various sensations, such as impacts, temperature changes, and even muscle contractions. Omnidirectional treadmills enable users to physically walk or run in a virtual environment while also providing haptic feedback. These devices can simulate ground textures and even slopes.

"VR haptics is a growing technology that will become increasingly important as the technology becomes more mainstream and specialized applications become more economically viable. Eventually, I suspect most applications will utilize some of these haptic devices as they do greatly improve the true feeling of an experience and consequently, the subjective feeling of presence."

Elias paused further, feeling the students would be well served by a break at this point.

"Okay, we'll leave it there for now. We'll see you back here in an hour, where we'll explore more about the cloud-based software services that we use to create the experience," said Elias.

Tired, overwhelmed but invigorated, I took off my headset and agreed to meet the other team members back at the coffee shop in fifteen minutes after bio breaks. We picked up our snacks and coffee and met at the table.

RoMac was the first to comment, "Guys, I don't know about this stuff. I feel like I'm a bit out of my league here. I mean, it's incredible, and I can appreciate how complex and magical this technology is, but there are millions of other people who know how all this works and how to apply it far better than I could."

He had a point, but he was missing the idea of a team, I thought.

"You're right RoMac," I said. "This is wild stuff, and it requires a solid technical understanding, but not everyone on the team needs to be the expert. Frances is our CTO in waiting. Frances, how do you feel about this stuff?" I asked.

"I'm good," said Frances. "I actually think this is very exciting, and I keep imagining all the things we could do with this technology to bring people together and create amazing experiences. Admittedly, I don't understand much about business, I've never run one myself, but that's what I can rely on the rest of you for."

"I agree," said Jag. "We don't all have to be technology experts. We do need to understand at a high level how it works, and we do need at least someone like Frances who can put all the pieces together, but our focus should be how we could use this to make money."

"Spoken like a true finance guy," I quipped.

Jag smiled and politely retorted, "We can't all be dreamers like you, Joe."

"You're right, Jag. Touché'!" I smiled, "We need to put the technology pieces in place with a business model that makes sense. I also think it's important that we remain focused on transforming the user experience. With all this amazing technology, it is imperative that we create a game-changing experience if we hope to compete."

As we ate our lunch, we discussed various ideas related to our vertical market assignment, but before we knew it, it was time for class again.

"We better get back," said Dania.

CHAPTER X.2

Cloudy with a Chance of Software

We donned our headsets and eagerly awaited the second half of the lecture. I felt like we had gained a very good sense of how the VR headset worked on the front end, but there seemed to be a whole lot of stuff going on with the backend or cloud-based servers, and I was excited to find out more. Elias began.

"Okay, so in the last section, we gained an understanding of how the HMD front-end application works, but we also realized that much of the hard work and communication is happening on the web, or 'the cloud,' as they call it. Does anyone know what 'Cloud Computing' is?"

Frances's hand went up, and Elias acknowledged.

"It's really centralized computing resources that provide various services to user applications anywhere on the Internet. Rather than everyone having a supercomputer, it's like a shared resource," responded Frances.

"Very well summarized, Frances," said Elias.

"To add to what Frances so elegantly summarized, here are a few more specifics.

"Instead of relying on local devices or servers to store and process data, users can access and use these services remotely through cloud-based service providers. Managing one's own services on their business premises can be a very expensive proposition, requiring people, power, and specialized environments.

"Instead, cloud-based computing provides all sorts of remote computing services. Popular cloud computing providers like Amazon Web Services (AWS), Microsoft Azure, and Google Cloud Platform offer a range of services, from simple storage solutions to complex machine learning and AI platforms. Because of the scale of these services, it is much more cost-effective for the average business to share these services than host their own. These services can be centralized or distributed across the web, which makes applications more reliable, scalable, secure, and accessible from anywhere on the Internet.

"For VR-based metaverse applications, there are specific cloud-based services that are required.

"I'll simply provide an overview of some of the more critical services, as you do not need to know all of this in detail. It is important, however, to know that these services are working together to create and manage the user experience. While networking, database, and real-time communication services are used, the most heavily utilized services that will underlie the Metaverse in years to come will be focused on content delivery, game engines, analytics, and AI. Here are some examples.

"**Content Delivery Network (CDN) Services**: Sorry, Canadians, this one is not about you." Elias smiles and continues, "Content Delivery Networks help deliver content, such as images, videos, and 3D assets, to users with low latency, ensuring a smooth and immersive experience. CDNs are critical to distribute content closer to the point of consumption rather than transporting every asset from a centralized location. Your Netflix movie will not be streamed from a local server but very likely from a computer that is within your local area. If your neighbor is the first to watch a hit movie, it will likely download from the main central server to a server closest to them, then will be streamed directly from that local server. Then subsequently, when you or any of your neighbors choose to stream that same movie, you will simply access the local server for the stream. It is far more efficient than every person streaming from a central source. That would bog down the Internet rather quickly. It is like what Amazon or other large retailers do when they distribute physical products to warehouses that are closer to their consumers, shortening the time and cost of local delivery.

"**Game Engines and Services**: Cloud-based game engines and services can be used to create VR environments and experiences within the metaverse application. All the rooms reside both locally, but their state is managed centrally on an Unreal Engine gaming server."

"What is a state?" asked Dania.

"Hmm, okay. I should have explained that earlier. Basically, it is a set of variables that describes what an object, environment, or avatar is doing at any moment or 'state' in time. That could include an on/off state of audio or muting that can be invoked by touching a microphone button, a user's position in 3D space, or any other condition that describes a situation in time. As we discussed earlier, all this information, which is really 'state' information, is sent and distributed to all other HMDs through a centralized server. Managing everyone's 'state' is one of the services the game servers perform. Think of it as 'managing the state of things.' Does that help?" asked Elias.

"Yes, for sure. Thanks." acknowledged Dania.

"Okay, moving on." Elias continued.

"**Analytics Services**: Some of you may have already used Google Analytics. This is, as aptly named, an analytics service. These services help collect and analyze user data to gain insights and optimize the metaverse application. This information tells us where the users were and what they were doing at any point in time and will then aggregate that information for larger groups to provide interesting insights. These analytics can be used to improve the overall experience or identify opportunities for marketing or selling.

"**AI and Machine Learning Services**: These services can enhance the metaverse application with features like natural language processing, image recognition, embedded human-like chatbots, and recommendation systems. Many of you have heard of ChatGPT or Bard, but there are many other AI product applications that are used today. We'll get into more detail shortly about the type of AI applications that are most relevant to us.

"**Edge Computing and 5G Wireless**: Networking technologies are critical to how VR-based metaverse applications are deployed. Content delivery networks

(CDN) bring the frequently consumed content to regional areas, whereas Edge Computing and 5G extend the reach of CDNs and optimize that last mile of the user experience.

"Edge computing is a distributed computing architecture that brings computer power closer to the end-user application. It relies on various types of devices and nodes, including Internet of Things (IoT) devices, sensors, routers, switches, and specialized servers. These devices and nodes are equipped with the necessary processing, storage, and networking capabilities to handle data processing tasks locally. The aim is to reduce latency, save bandwidth, and improve the overall performance of applications by processing data locally.

"This is not to suggest that centralized data servers do not work, but applications like VR-based metaverse applications require massive computer power. The need to build high-quality 3D worlds and characters in real-time benefits considerably from computing power that is closer to the end-user. The higher resolution and reduced latency will increase immersion and improve the feeling of presence.

"Do any of you recall from last week what presence is?" Elias asked.

RoMac put up his hand. This was a first.

"It's the feeling of 'being there,' right?" he responded.

"Excellent," said Elias, "And that feeling of 'being there' helps us suspend disbelief and engage more effectively within that virtual world, whether for learning, playing, or even buying something.

"To improve that sense of presence, I suspect that within the next five to ten years, most homes and businesses will have mini supercomputers (like a small box) that perform this edge computing task, dramatically improving the metaverse experience and feeling of presence.

"5G is also a technology that offers a similar benefit but more directly to mobile computing devices like HMDs that may be utilized in more public areas. Many of you have heard about 5G in the media and how it's a dangerous technology that is going to appropriate our cognitive processes and lead us all into a state of permanent dementia. Hopefully, I can help demystify it here.

"5G refers to the fifth generation of wireless communication technology designed to meet the growing demands for high-speed data, low latency, and massive connectivity. It uses key innovations and architectural changes to deliver improved performance and new capabilities.

"Without getting too much into the weeds here, the important thing to note is the 5G networks allow us to increase data rates, create more dense networks, and more efficiently use the radio spectrum resources. 5G is also designed to work effectively with edge computing resources to create a more efficient, flexible, and high-capacity network that can support the growing demands of data-intensive applications like the Metaverse."

"And drive us insane!" shouted Dania.

Elias smiled.

"Not unless you're already headed there!"

The crowd chuckled. Elias continued.

"Seriously, there is no evidence that 5G is any worse than any other wireless technology. And while many feel that our proximity to technology does affect us negatively, it is mostly conjecture and opinion. So, at this point, I would say no."

Elias waited momentarily for general acknowledgment that Dania was okay with her concern, then proceeded.

"Now, while network efficiency is critical to the metaverse experience, the security and integrity of the information are equally important and understanding blockchain technology is central to that challenge."

Blockchain Technology

"Does anyone know what Blockchain technology is and how it works?" asked Elias.

"It's a cryptocurrency like Bitcoin, isn't it?" came a voice from the front.

"Anyone else?" asked Elias. The room was quiet, so he continued.

"Blockchain is a technology that is often confused or associated with cryptocurrencies and NFTs. And while it often underpins those applications, it is something more fundamental. A blockchain is a decentralized, distributed ledger system that enables secure and transparent transactions without the need for a central authority."

"So, it's like an accounting system?" asked Jag.

"Yes, in fact, it is, but a very secure system of accounting," said Elias.

"It consists of a digital chain of blocks, each containing a set of transactions. These blocks are cryptographically linked, making it difficult to alter any individual block's data without affecting the entire chain. The block-chaining process uses several steps. Here's how it works.

"When a transaction occurs, it is broadcast to a

network of nodes (computers) that validate the transaction based on predefined rules (e.g., checking if the sender has enough funds). Once validated, the transaction is grouped with other transactions into a new block. This block also contains a reference to the previous block in the chain through a cryptographic hash."

"What is a cryptographic hash?" asked one of the students in the front row.

"Okay, fair question," said Elias, "A cryptographic hash is like a special digital fingerprint for data. It's a way to turn any amount of information, like a sentence or a whole book, into a short, unique series of numbers and letters. Each input has a unique hash, and even a tiny change gives a completely different hash. It's a one-way process, meaning you can't get the original information from the hash. This makes it great for verifying data hasn't been tampered with, like in secure online transactions."

"And a hash is like a mathematical function?" inquired Jag.

"Exactly," said Elias, "Here's an example. Let's say we have a basic hash function that operates on a string of English text by assigning each letter a value (A=1, B=2, C=3, ..., Z=26), adding up those values, and then taking the remainder when divided by ten. If we take the input 'DOG', it would be calculated as follows:

$$D = 4$$
$$O = 15$$
$$G = 7$$

"Adding those up, we get twenty-six. Taking twenty-six mod ten (the remainder when twenty-six is divided by ten) gives us six. So, the hash of 'DOG' under this simple hash function would be six. In real applications, hash functions are significantly more complicated and produce more complex outputs, often represented as hexadecimal strings.

"For instance, in SHA-256 (a commonly used cryptographic hash function), the hash of 'DOG' is:

"06dcd4bfdd2c77f0041c8e6dce9ecd68b8bb2c76ee417adfb5c2a4898125f8d7.

"Does this make sense to everyone?" Elias inquired as he surveyed the crowd receiving nods of acceptance. He proceeded.

"Okay, let's get back to understanding the blockchain process.

"To add the new block to the chain, a process called 'mining' or 'consensus' takes place. Miners (or nodes) compete and are paid to solve a complex mathematical puzzle using the new block's data. The first miner to solve the puzzle adds the block to the chain and broadcasts it to the network. When a new block is added, the other nodes in the network validate it by checking the block's data and the correctness of its hash. If the majority of nodes agree on the block's validity, it becomes a permanent part of the chain.

"Due to the cryptographic linkage between blocks, it is considered immutable. Any attempt to alter the data in a block would require recalculating the hashes for all subsequent blocks, which is computationally infeasible and very difficult to hack. The screen illustrates the process."

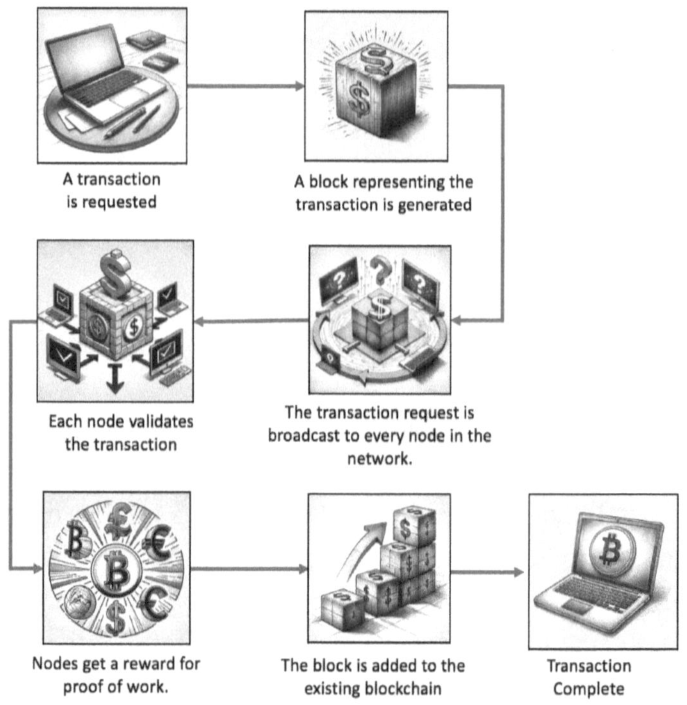

The Blockchain Process

"How is that relevant to the Metaverse?" asked Jag.

"Ah, it is very relevant to the Metaverse, and one might argue that the Metaverse is the killer app for deploying blockchain technology," offered Elias.

"Because the Metaverse is a virtual manifestation, it must create the authenticity of the world and the assets that will remain consistent to all users over time. Therefore, it requires something foundational and immutable that is far more secure than most other technologies, and blockchain technology is the ideal instrument. Here are a few ways that blockchains can be utilized in the Metaverse:

"**Digital Assets and Ownership**: Blockchains can be used to create unique digital assets, such as virtual land, items, or characters, represented as non-fungible tokens (NFTs). These assets can be bought, sold, or traded within the Metaverse, and their ownership is securely recorded on the blockchain, ensuring transparency, and preventing fraud."

"I've heard a lot about these in the media, but what is an NFT?" asked Jag.

"Yes, many people are confused about this in the marketplace," said Elias.

"An NFT is a digital asset that is a Non-Fungible Token (NFT), that cannot be transacted like a currency that is 'fungible' or interchangeable like Bitcoin or the American dollar.

"Rather, each NFT asset is unique, secured with blockchain technology, and translatable based on a unique market value. Many of you probably remember hearing about people paying tens of thousands of dollars for a unique digital picture of a bored ape or a lazy lion.

"Well, those NFTs were considered unique digital assets that were going to increase in value someday, much like the value of a famous painting by Van Gogh or other great artists. Sadly, history has shown that in a short time, almost all those assets have lost most of their value."

"Why do you think that is?" asked Dania again.

"Well, like any asset, it increases in value due to scarcity and long-term demand. The reason why Van Gogh's paintings have escalated in value, aside from their incredible aesthetic value, is because there are a limited number of authentic works. Further, Van Gogh has been increasingly recognized and promoted as one of the greatest artists of all time. So, people will pay a premium to own the genuine article."

"But are there not artists today that could become the next Van Gogh? And would their NFTs not be worth something someday?" challenged Dania.

"Yes," Elias acknowledged, "and there are some digital assets that have retained their value. They may be associated with currently famous artists or unique individuals that can create true scarcity of demand. The challenge is that ninety-nine percent of the NFTs today are driven simply by a group of individuals that are creating digital pictures that are neither unique nor truly scarce relative to real demand that can change in an instant. Hence, when someone has a choice to make, 'Do I keep my three-hundred-thousand-dollar JPEG of an ape or pay the mortgage?' Increasingly, the mortgage will get the nod. And ultimately, it will drive the value of those non-scarce assets toward zero.

"Most people would love to show off an original authentic piece of art hanging in their hallway to their friends but would shudder at the thought of a three-hundred-thousand-dollar ape picture, now worth nothing, hanging on the same wall. They would be considered foolish. So, when owners of these NFTs start to sell, everyone heads for the door. So far, that has been the history of most NFTs."

I suspected that Dania's persistent questioning method might have been getting under Elias' skin just a bit. She had some good questions, but I suspected she was trying to assuage her concerns about a bad investment or two that she may have made in an NFT get-rich-quick scheme. Nonetheless, he handled the questions well and provided us with a good understanding of NFTs and blockchains.

Elias continued, "Now, unless anyone has any more questions, let's get back to looking at other metaverse applications for blockchain.

"**Decentralized Marketplace**: Blockchain enables the creation of decentralized marketplaces within the Metaverse, allowing users to trade digital assets without the need for a central authority like a bank. This promotes fair and transparent transactions, as well as reduces fees and barriers to entry.

"**Cryptocurrency Integration**: Cryptocurrencies like Bitcoin, Ethereum, or native metaverse tokens can be used for transactions within the virtual world. This enables seamless, secure, and borderless payments for digital assets, services, or experiences.

"**Smart Contracts**: Smart contracts are self-executing contracts with the terms of the agreement directly written into code. They automatically execute when predefined conditions are met. Within the Metaverse, smart contracts can be used for various purposes, such as facilitating transactions, managing digital asset ownership, or automating virtual events and experiences.

"**Decentralized Governance**: Blockchains can enable decentralized governance systems within the Metaverse, allowing users to participate in decision-making processes related to the virtual world's rules, policies, or updates. This fosters a more democratic and community-driven approach to managing the Metaverse. It could also easily be used to manage the voting in a democratic election process.

"**Provenance and Authentication**: The transparent and immutable nature of blockchains allows for the tracking and verification of digital assets' history, ensuring their authenticity and provenance. This can be particularly useful for verifying the origin of rare or valuable assets within the Metaverse.

"**Digital Identity**: Blockchain can be used to create secure and decentralized digital identity solutions within the Metaverse, allowing users to manage and control their personal information and online presence. This can enhance privacy, security, and trust in virtual environments.

"**Interoperability**: Blockchain technology can enable interoperability between different metaverse platforms or applications, allowing users to transfer their digital assets, identities, or experiences across virtual worlds seamlessly.

"So, as you can see, there are many applications where blockchain technology can be utilized to make the Metaverse more secure, efficient, and democratic.

"All good with blockchains?" asked Elias.

"Now, I'd like to take a look at an area of technology that is rapidly evolving and is increasingly becoming part of VR-based metaverse applications. Biometrics, Biological Signals, and Internet of Things (IoT) Devices."

"**Biometrics and IOT**," Elias began. "Firstly, can anyone tell me what biometrics are?"

Dania responded, "It's the process of measuring your bodily functions like your heart rate, blood pressure, breathing, and other important health indicators. And you can do it with your smartwatch."

"That's part of it, Dania. Thank you for that. Measuring your bodily processes is considered biometric monitoring," said Elias. "The biometrics that Dania mentioned are also referred to as physiological or biological signals. They are continuous but can vary over time due to various factors such as stress, physical activity, and health conditions. To add to Dania's explanation, biometrics also includes many other things.

"Biometrics, in general, refers to the measurement

and analysis of an individual's unique physiological or behavioral characteristics. There are two main types of biometrics.

"Physiological biometrics are based on the physical traits of an individual, such as fingerprint, palm, facial, iris, or retina recognition. It also includes DNA analysis. These biometrics are unique to each individual and, as such, can be used for any sort of activity that requires one hundred percent user identification or authentication. Tracking our bodily functions, as in Dania's examples, is also considered physiological biometrics.

"Behavioral Biometrics, on the other hand, is based on the unique patterns of behavior exhibited by an individual, like the recognition of signature, voice, keystroke, or gait.

"In the real world, both of these biometric types can be used for many applications, including access control, border security, and mobile device authentication. They offer a higher level of security and convenience compared to traditional authentication methods, such as passwords or ID cards. They can be used similarly in the Metaverse.

"What about IoT? Anyone?"

RoMac, more engaged than I'd seen him in a while, threw up his hand, and Elias motioned to him.

"I know about that," said RoMac. "Those are the sensors that monitor stuff in our environments and communicate over the Internet. It includes cameras, motion sensors, thermostats, and all sorts of things. In fact, my brother-in-law runs a company that makes and manages these devices for businesses, and he's doing very well."

"I don't doubt he is," said Elias. "That is an area of tremendous growth and very relevant to our VR metaverse applications.

"More generally, though, the Internet of Things (IoT) refers to the interconnected network of physical devices that may include vehicles, buildings, objects embedded with sensors, and even software programs. These devices and programs collect, exchange, and process data over the Internet.

"IoT is based on the idea of connecting almost everything to the network, and it can revolutionize the world with real-time information about almost every aspect of life. These devices can communicate with cloud platforms or each other allowing for remote monitoring, control, and automation of a myriad of tasks and processes.

"Here are several example applications quite relevant to metaverse environments:

"**Identity Verification and Authentication**: Biometrics, such as fingerprint, facial, or iris recognition, can be used to verify user's identities when they enter the Metaverse. This ensures that each user is unique and authentic, enhancing security and privacy. The same authentication techniques can also be used for secure transactions within the Metaverse.

"**Personalization**: IoT devices, such as wearables or smart home devices, can collect data on user preferences, habits, and activities that can be used to create personalized metaverse experiences tailored to each user's interests and needs. For example, a user's preferred music, lighting, or virtual decorations could be incorporated into their metaverse environment.

"**Immersive Interaction**: IoT devices and biometric sensors can enable more natural and immersive interactions within the Metaverse. For instance, virtual reality (VR) headsets, haptic gloves, and motion tracking sensors can capture user's movements, gestures, and expressions, translating them into corresponding actions in the virtual world. This allows users to feel more connected and engaged with their metaverse surroundings.

"**Health Monitoring and Well-being**: Biometric sensors and IoT devices can monitor user's vital signs, such as heart rate, body temperature, and stress levels, while they interact with the Metaverse. This information can be used to adapt to the virtual environment or provide feedback to users, promoting a healthier and more enjoyable experience. For example, if a user becomes stressed during a metaverse activity, the environment could automatically adjust to help them relax. This could be achieved by reducing sound, light, or even changing elements within the environment.

"**Accessibility**:   Biometric sensors and IoT can improve accessibility within the Metaverse, enabling users with disabilities to interact better with the virtual environment. For instance, voice recognition and eye-tracking technologies can allow users with limited mobility to control their virtual avatars or navigate the Metaverse more easily.

"**Smart Environments**: IoT devices can be used to create smart, interconnected virtual environments within the Metaverse. User's smart devices can communicate with virtual objects and systems, automating certain tasks or providing real-time information, such as weather updates, notifications, or personalized recommendations.

"**Data Analytics and Insights**: Data collected from biometrics and IoT devices can be analyzed to gain insights into user behavior, preferences, and trends within the Metaverse. These insights can inform the design and development of new features, applications, and virtual experiences, driving innovation and growth within the metaverse ecosystem.

"**Industrial IoT (IIoT)**: IoT technologies can be integrated into manufacturing, logistics, and supply chain operations, improving efficiency, safety, and productivity. Similarly, IIoT could be easily utilized within a metaverse application, particularly as a tool to visualize and inform commerce or logistics activity.

"**Healthcare**: IoT devices like remote patient monitoring systems, smart pill dispensers, and wearable health sensors can enhance patient care, reduce costs, and improve health outcomes. The health of systems, avatars, and virtual metaverse life forms could also benefit from these remote sensing and management systems, dispensing health resources based on time of day or usage/traffic levels.

"This is all very exciting, and while IoT has the potential to revolutionize various aspects of daily life, as you can imagine, it also raises concerns related to privacy, security, and data ownership. So, you will need to consider these concerns if you are combining the use of these devices within your metaverse businesses.

"In summary, biometrics and Internet of Things (IoT) devices can play a crucial role in enhancing the metaverse experience, and they can also provide more immersive, secure, and personalized interactions.

"Are there any questions about biometrics or IOT technology?" Elias waited and then proceeded. "Okay, now my favorite part of this lesson. Let's look at how AI technology can be used in our VR metaverse businesses."

Artificial Intelligence

"Before we start, please understand that this is subjective and my fun way of remembering many of the most important AI resources that are available to us in our VR-metaverse applications. It's also important to understand that what we discuss here is simply a subset of every form of human intelligence, and numerous forms of AI, that will eventually be utilized within your metaverse businesses.

"For simplicity, I've summarized the key areas of AI into six main category concepts that will likely be most important in building your metaverse business.

- Machine Learning AI
- Connectionist AI
- Symbolic AI
- Evolutionary and Swarm AI
- Affective or Emotional AI
- World Building AI Tools

"While some would argue that machine learning, world-building, and even Affective AI are really components of Connectionist AI, they tend to intersect and are used in many different categories, so I have broken them out as their own categories. You would not be expected to know about all these types of artificial intelligence as each one represents a large domain of science on its own. Nonetheless, here is a brief summary of these approaches to AI.

"**Machine Learning (ML)**: Machine Learning enables computers to learn from data and make predictions or decisions without explicit programming. ML algorithms identify patterns, relationships, and structures in data and use them to make inferences on new, unseen data. Machine Learning is perhaps the most common form of AI activity and is used in conjunction with most systems that you will use. As you will see, this is why the data you derive from the user experiences is so critically important. It is mathematically and statistically analyzed to create classifications and predictions to optimize any user experience.

"**Connectionist AI**: Connectionist AI is based on artificial neural networks, inspired by the structure and function of biological neural networks like our human brain. Connectionist AI focuses on learning complex patterns and representations from large datasets and includes techniques such as deep learning. These artificial neural networks attempt to simulate the processes of the human brain and, in concert with Machine Learning algorithms, strive to enhance and refine most systems that you will develop.

"**Symbolic AI**: Symbolic AI is known as 'Good Old-Fashioned AI' (GOFAI), an approach that uses formal logic and symbolic manipulation to represent knowledge, reason, and solve problems. Symbolic AI includes methods such as rule-based systems, expert systems, knowledge representation, and reasoning. They often rely on explicitly defined rules, facts, and relationships to draw conclusions and make decisions. Based on many of the programs and approaches from the twentieth century, many of these systems remain in effect today. Driven by expert recommendations and rules that diagnose and recommend medical treatments, legal advice, or optimization techniques for supply chains continue to perform well.

"**Swarm and Evolutionary AI**: This category encompasses AI techniques that are inspired by natural processes, such as evolution and collective behavior. It includes evolutionary algorithms, which are optimization techniques that evolve solutions over time (e.g., genetic algorithms, genetic programming), and swarm intelligence, which studies the collective behavior of decentralized, self-organized systems (e.g., ant colony optimization, particle swarm optimization). These approaches are often used for solving complex optimization problems or for learning and adaptation in AI systems. This AI will be increasingly important in metaverse worlds because they are critical to managing the organic growth and characteristics of both player and non-player characters (NPC). Understanding how bees swarm, birds fly, or ants colonize are valuable models to help us build those metaverse worlds and evolve these algorithms. Swarm and Evolutionary AI will be a factor anywhere there is nature or where large groups meet in the Metaverse.

"**Affective AI**: Affective AI, or Emotional AI, often leverages machine learning techniques, particularly deep learning, to recognize, understand, and respond to human emotions. It involves processing and analyzing data from various sources, such as facial expressions, speech patterns, text, body language, and physiological signals, to infer emotional states and adapt AI system behavior accordingly. Affective AI is becoming very important as the emotional experience of the user is the prime intent of any experience, so being able to understand emotional states and optionally, finding ways to regulate and help users improve their feelings is a key focus of User Experience (UX) design. These algorithms can be used in educational metaverse applications to reduce user anxiety and optimize their performance.

"**AI World Building and Creation Tools**: The development of metaverse world-building AI tools is an interdisciplinary effort, requiring collaboration across various AI fields and expertise to create immersive, interactive, and coherent virtual worlds. These techniques may include Procedural Generation (PG) and myriad other techniques to automatically generate virtual environments. World Building AI technology is incredibly important because we are at the precipice of the biggest building boom in history. The building of the Metaverse, where millions of diverse worlds that most humans will inhabit for some portion of their day, is beginning. So, understanding the value of these tools is paramount.

"As mentioned earlier, I've also chosen to focus on each of these AI categories for a good reason; they represent the AI that you will most likely require and use in your metaverse business. So, with that said, I'd like to provide you with something to help you understand and remember these complex ideas. I present you with our AI superheroes. These characters work together to create the most compelling user experience and ultimately to help your businesses succeed."

Elias moved his spot from the front of the beach to the side giving way for what was to come.

"I give you, Machine Learning Man, Connector Girl, Affector, Symbolina, World Builder, and The Swarm!"

As he introduced each character, the first five superhero characters materialized as they were introduced and took a bow. Finally, a buzz and swarm of about ten thousand bee-like characters circled the area above the water and then reassembled as an attractive lady next to the other five heroes on the beach. Then she bowed, and the crowd of avatars clapped enthusiastically.

Now, I've seen one too many Marvel movies, but I had to admit, this idea caught my attention. What an entrance. Yet another memorable experience to help us reinforce these concepts. Well done, Elias, I thought. I was taking note of how he was using the medium to facilitate the learning process.

The AI Superheroes (Left to Right)

Machine Man, Connector Girl, Affector, Symbolina,
World Builder, The Swarm

He continued. "One way to think about these cloud-based AI services is as a group of superheroes, residing in the heavens, or clouds if you will, helping to create and deliver the metaverse experience," said Elias.

One by one, the characters introduced themselves and provided a brief overview of what they were responsible for.

Machine Learning Man

"Hi there, nice to meet you all. I'm Machine Learning Man."

He was confident and dressed in the finest superhero fashion. He was Captain America but with math symbols on his chest.

"I play a crucial role in making metaverse applications by building algorithms and models that help me to learn and improve from experience. I also work closely with most of my other AI colleagues. Everyone seems to want a piece of me these days because I'm good at math and absolutely love to learn. My mom thinks I should get a real job, but my friends love me for who I am. Here are a few types of learning that really get me excited.

"**Supervised Learning**: I learn from examples with correct answers, like a student learning from a teacher. This allows me to solve similar problems by finding patterns and connections in those examples.

"**Unsupervised Learning**: I explore data to find patterns or groupings without specific goals or answers. This part is fun because I have more autonomy to explore, though it takes me a bit longer, and I can be a bit unpredictable at times.

"**Reinforcement Learning**: I learn by making decisions and getting rewards or penalties, aiming to get the most rewards over time, like the carrot and stick thing. My goal is to find the optimal strategy that maximizes my rewards over time. That means more carrots for me. For example, when I play chess, if a move eventually leads to me getting a 'checkmate' against my opponent, this will generate a reward, and that particular move will be weighted higher in priority for subsequent games. On the other hand, if a move leads to me being placed in check, this would be a negative reward (or penalty), reducing the weighting or importance of that move or course of action for future games. Over time, by playing many games and experiencing different actions and outcomes (winning, losing, drawing), I will learn a strategy that increases my chances of winning.

"**Transfer Learning**: I use what I learned in one area to do better in a related area, especially when there's little data for the new task. This can help me answer questions, understand emotions, and more. For example, if I'm good at understanding natural languages, maybe I can parlay that into a career as an expert that answers questions. Maybe I can get onto Jeopardy someday.

"I can also help personalize your experience in the Metaverse. I use my algorithms to analyze your behavior and preferences and tailor the virtual world and its elements to you, and you, and you and you," He points at several avatars in the crowd. "The truth is, I use a whole bunch of other learning and mathematical techniques, but that's way too much to talk about now. You can ask me about it over a coffee sometime."

Finally, in the spirit of a real superhero, Machine Learning Man offered one final bit of advice to the crowd.

"Remember, kids, take your vitamins, and learn your math. It will make you healthy and successful." He then did a slight bow and stepped back to allow the next hero to present.

Connector Girl

Connector Girl stepped forward. She looked confident, clad as a contemporary superhero with a skin-tight suit that you'd likely see on a Marvel character like Black Widow.

"Hi there, I'm Connector Girl. My job involves a lot of things, but I'm mainly focused on artificial neural networks. I work very closely with Machine Learning Man. And yes, we have been in a relationship for some time. So, let's get that out of the way right up front before it becomes an issue.

"I play a pivotal role by enabling various aspects of virtual experience development. Here are examples of what I do.

"I use smart tools to create lifelike images and animations, making the virtual world look better. I help characters and chatbots talk and interact better with people, working well with Machine Learning Man, and I teach computer characters to act in smart and fun ways, making them more enjoyable for users. Finally, I use Real-time Analytics, with Machine Learning Man's help, to analyze lots of data and quickly improve performance, experiences, and resources in the virtual world. In summary, I work with Machine Learning Man and World Builder to make the virtual world look real and custom-fit to your liking."

She bowed and stepped back, making way for Affector.

Affector

Affector stepped forward, wearing a multicolored body suit that appeared to be changing color constantly.

"Hi, I'm Affector. What did you say? I thought I heard you say something."

Affector stared at the audience of avatars for a few seconds, then continued.

"Sorry, I can be a bit sensitive. I'm trying to calibrate my emotional sensing tools, and they still need some tuning.

"So, yeah, as I was saying, I am Affector. I use emotion recognition tools that analyze facial expressions, speech patterns, text, body language, and physiological signals to infer user's emotional states, helping to make all of us more empathetic. For those of you who don't like all those fancy words, I read faces, voices, words, and movements to understand how we're all feeling, making everyone more caring.

"Oh yeah, I also do stuff to improve your mental health, which may be one of my more important roles. Using tools to detect your emotions, I can even help you regulate those feelings, that is, if you'll let me. I guess I'm a bit like Freud that way, but a whole lot cheaper.

"To put it more simply, I figure out how users feel by looking at what they do and say in the virtual world. Ultimately, I help to create a deeper sense of immersion and emotional connection within the Metaverse."

Symbolina

Symbolina was a bit shorter than the others, and her hero suit looked more like something from the 1970s. She had the cape, the belt, and a bad set of tights. She still had a bit of a swagger, but I sensed just a tad of cynicism, like she'd been passed over for a big role.

"Hi, I'm Symbolina. I used to spend more time with Connector Girl until Machine Learning Man came riding in on his white horse. Now, he's all that and, ah, you know what I mean. And me? Some people think I'm 'old fashioned,' but I like to think of it as 'rich in experience.' And yeah, I still do matter, and I can do a great deal to help your metaverse work. Here are some of the things I do.

"I use formal logic and symbolic manipulation to facilitate various aspects of virtual experience development. For example, I use rule-based systems to define the logic, physics, and interactions governing the virtual world, enabling consistent and predictable behavior across various elements within the Metaverse. More simply, I create virtual experiences that ensure everything in the virtual world behaves consistently and as expected. Just like Aristotle, I help you make sense of your virtual world.

"By providing a clear map of the virtual world's items, features, and connections, I can help you and even virtual characters think, plan, and make better choices. I still use expert systems, though. In that way, I can offer domain-specific guidance or recommendations within the Metaverse with valuable advice in areas like the virtual economy, gaming, or education. Hey, experts are still experts, right? So, yeah, that's what I do."

World Builder

Unlike the other superheroes, World Builder didn't have a fancy suit, but rather overalls and a tool belt. She was much more nondescript. She slowly stepped forward and looked out at the crowd with a slight awkwardness, struggling to make eye contact.

"Okay, so I'm World Builder. I'm not much of a speaker because I'm usually busy doing stuff. I mean, someone's got to build this Metaverse, right? Oh, yeah, you may notice that I do some things that the other heroes do as well. The difference is I get them done.

"Basically, I try to streamline the development of virtual environments, objects, and characters. I create these virtual worlds with less work by following rules and patterns. I use smart systems to make things look real and make content faster. I help characters and chatbots talk like humans for better interactions. I understand what's happening visually to make things more realistic and enjoyable. I use tools to make creating and improving the virtual world easier and faster, working with my team to make the perfect Metaverse."

The Swarm

Finally, The Swarm. Not one to shy away from drama, The Swarm disassembled and performed several squadron-like jet maneuvers in the sky over the lake, then reassembled in position, again to boisterous crowd applause.

"Thank you. I'm The Swarm. I use tools inspired by nature to make the virtual world better in many ways, like creating environments, improving character actions, and managing resources. I also use techniques based on group behavior to make characters more lifelike and interesting. I ensure the online space runs smoothly for everyone and work with other AI helpers to solve problems and make the virtual world more interactive. I also help find the best paths and solutions in complex situations."

As The Swarm finished, the rest of the group bowed and, in unison, pointed to the sky.

"See you in the Metaverse!" they exclaimed in chorus.

And with that, united, our superheroes bid us adieu and flew off over the lake.

As we watched our superheroes disappear into the sky, Elias sensed that we'd had our fill of intellectual stimulation for the day. He summarized and concluded.

"The role of AI is critical in creating, managing, and evolving the Metaverse. Machine learning (math and statistics), neural networks (models of our brain), affective algorithms, nature simulations, common sense logic, and good old-fashioned expert guidance work together to help metaverse designers build authentic virtual worlds and characters that are realistic, believable, and emotionally engaging.

"Further, you can use these superheroes to help you remember what AI can do to help you build your metaverse businesses as each of these characters represents something critical to the Metaverse.

"Any questions before we call it a day?"

Dania, of course, had her hand raised, and Elias acknowledged, "Dania?"

"What about ChatGPT? What kind of AI is that?" Dania asked.

"Okay, that's a very relevant question, Dania," Elias continued. "ChatGPT is an AI language model that can understand and generate human-like text. It works by learning from lots of text examples and finding patterns that allow it to predict the most likely words or phrases to follow in order to create meaningful responses. It relies on interconnected nodes or artificial neurons to process information inspired by how the human brain works."

"So how would ChatGPT relate to those six AI categories you provided?" asked Dania.

"ChatGPT encompasses aspects of various AI categories, but it fits most squarely within Machine Learning AI and Connectionist AI," Elias replied.

"Is ChatGPT sentient or self-aware? It seems to be," said Dania.

"It does seem that way, doesn't it?" acknowledged Elias. "While ChatGPT does not have a capacity for genuine emotion and thus isn't an instance of Affective or Emotional AI, it has been trained on diverse datasets and can generate text that simulates emotional responses. However, these responses are based on learned patterns and not actual feelings.

"Regarding the rest of the categories - Symbolic AI, Swarm AI, and World Building Tools - they do not directly apply to ChatGPT. It doesn't use symbolic reasoning, it doesn't evolve strategies based on population dynamics or collective behavior, nor is it specifically designed to create expansive digital environments.

"Specifically, ChatGPT uses a type of AI called a Transformer-based language model based on deep learning techniques and uses layers of neural networks to understand and generate text. Getting back to our AI Superheroes, it is a form of Connectionist and Machine Learning AI, so I guess you could say ChatGPT is a coproduction of Machine Learning Man and Connector Girl."

"I know Dania's next question," inserted RoMac. "How is ChatGPT going to help us with our metaverse applications?"

Elias laughed and agreed, "Yes, I expected that."

"In the Metaverse, ChatGPT can be relevant by helping create more engaging interactions with virtual characters, assisting chatbots, personalizing experiences, and providing support or guidance for users within the virtual world.

"Using Natural Language Processing (NLP), you can facilitate natural language interactions between users, both real and virtual, within the Metaverse. This can also allow users to communicate with each other in real time in their preferred language. This is a very important feature for educational and transactional commerce activity. By eliminating language barriers, sales can be improved, and more can be learned.

"It is also very creative and can be used to generate text, such as descriptions, stories, and dialogue to enhance the Metaverse's immersive storytelling capabilities. This can enable users to create more engaging experiences within the Metaverse.

"Predictive Analytics - ChatGPT can be used to analyze user behavior within the Metaverse and make predictions about future trends and user needs. This can help inform decision-making around metaverse development and ensure that the Metaverse is evolving to meet user needs and expectations.

"I'm quite certain there is a great deal more, but that gives us just a glimpse of the possibilities within the Metaverse when our AI superheroes and their offspring (ChatGPT) get to work."

Elias surveyed the crowd, "Any more questions?"

"What about Quantum Computing?" asked Jag. "Will that affect AI and the Metaverse?"

"Yes, it will. Absolutely!" responded Elias. "The cloud-based centralized servers will be made thousands of times more powerful when quantum computing is fully realized in the next decade or so. This extra processing power will make the whole digital experience better, faster, more intelligent, and far more resolute. Let me first help everyone understand what it is and how it will affect the current technology.

"Quantum Computing is a type of computation that leverages quantum mechanics principles to process information. For those of you not familiar with quantum mechanics, it is a branch of physics that describes the behavior of particles at the smallest scales, like atoms and subatomic particles. It introduces concepts such as superposition, where particles can be in multiple states simultaneously, and entanglement, where particles are interconnected regardless of distance.

"Unlike classical computers that use bits (zeroes or ones), quantum computers use quantum bits or 'qubits', which can be both zero and one simultaneously. Qubits, through superposition, can represent multiple states at once, unlike binary bits that represent either zero or one. This allows quantum computers to process vast amounts of data simultaneously, potentially solving certain complex problems much faster than classical computers."

"I've heard that we have as much computing power in our iPhone as what NASA required to launch a man into space. Does that mean I can have a quantum computer on my desk, or in my phone someday?" asked Dania.

"Likely not any time in the near future," said Elias.

"Quantum computers require extremely controlled conditions to function. To maintain qubits in a quantum state, they're typically kept at temperatures close to absolute zero and isolated from all forms of electromagnetic interference. These requirements make current quantum computing technology too large and impractical for typical desk or home use. Most likely, these quantum supercomputers will reside within carefully controlled computing environments that connect directly to other 'cloud-based' computers.

"To the end-user, this increased processing power will not be clearly evident. Rather, it will be manifested as higher quality virtual environments, more realistic and intelligent avatars, faster response times, lower latency, and a much more authentic immersive experience."

Elias surveyed the crowd one more time, "Any more questions?"

"Okay, for your reference, here is a chart that summarizes the roles of our AI superheroes. You may want to think about using some of these tools when you are conceiving what is possible for your metaverse business proposal. And that's a wrap for today. We'll see you next week for our final session."

The AI Superheroes of Your Metaverse					
Machine Learning Man	**Connector Girl**	**Symbolina**	**Affector**	**World Builder**	**The Swarm**
Uses Math and Statistics to classify and predict things	Specializes in Neural Networks of all kinds. Simulates the human brain.	Works with symbols and logic	Emotion Recognition Tools	Procedural Generation	Use natural evolution and nature based algorithms
Supervised Learning	Realistic Visuals with specialized neural networks (GANS and VAEs)	Knowledge representation used for reasoning, planning, and decision making	Adaptive Environments	Generative Models like GANs and VAEs to create realistic visuals	Infrastructure Management and optimization
Unsupervised Learning	Dynamic Interactions with Natural Language Processing	Inference and reasoning based on predefined rules	Personalization	Automation and Optimization	Crowd simulations methods
Reinforcement Learning	Adaptive Behaviors	Domain specific guidance	Sentiment Analysis	Computer Vision for physics, lighting, and interaction	Special Particle Effects
Transfer Learning	Realtime Analytics	Narrow AI used in legal, medical, supply chains, and other specializations	Mental Health	Natural Language Processing	Collaboration Techniques to enhance dynamics and interactivity
Works well with World Builder and Connector Girl	Works well with Machine Learning Man and World Builder	Good old fashioned AI based on Expert systems, logic, and predefined rules	Improves immersion and optimizes emotional connection with metaverse	Tools to build the virtual worlds, objects, and characters	Creates more natural, authentic, and believable simulations

CHAPTER X.3

Innovation meets Opportunity

I felt like we'd learned a ton in the past two weeks, but with the submission deadline looming, we needed to connect the dots between the VR-based metaverse idea, the technology, and the business model that was going to define our future. We all had some rough ideas, but considering the depth of competition, our submissions would need to be unique, original, and very well thought out. And we'd need to get lucky.

The final class was meant to focus on innovation and immersive VR applications within the Metaverse. Hopefully, this would allow us to "connect the dots" and have that epiphany that many great artists and creators have before they make something great. So far, it had been a whirlwind of technology insights, virtual worlds, and confusion, but apparently, things were darkest before the dawn. I wondered if things worked the same way in the Metaverse. Nonetheless, I convinced myself that the best was yet to come and moved forward.

Sadly though, things had taken a bit of a bad turn for our team. RoMac, who seemed to be gathering momentum and interest, now had to bow out. Unfortunately, his daughter had become seriously ill, and he had to tend to her. They weren't sure what it was, but she was having trouble walking, and she could barely get out of bed. RoMac, the world's best dad, was going to be there day and night until his daughter was well. What else could he do? We respected him immensely for this, but it was a blow to the team. He was the only one with real teaching experience, so our education category took a hit.

And that wasn't all. Frances's divorce from her ex was getting a bit contentious, and she wasn't sure how much time she could give going forward. I was also starting to stretch thin on finances, and although Dania didn't say anything, she also appeared to be struggling. Nonetheless, we forged on and committed, at least, to the first round of submission.

We met at 1 pm at the coffee shop before the final session with Elias. There were just four of us now. We discussed our progress, or lack of, and reminded ourselves that the submission process would be over in a week. After that, life could return to normal unless the unthinkable happened and we somehow made it to the second round.

As we entered the computer lab, Elias threw another curveball at us. Today, the presentations were going to be performed in person. While we had become accustomed to immersive VR, he suggested we mix it up and invited us to meet in the small theatre classroom next door.

We took our seats, and Elias assumed the presentation position at the front of the theatre.

"Welcome to the final session, my friends. I suggested we do this class in person because there is clear evidence that people tend to focus better within situations that are less familiar, so going back to reality breaks your emerging comfort zone," Elias said.

Of course, I recalled the idea just last week of how discursive experiences could trigger that type two critical thinking, so this tactic fit right in. Get someone out of their comfort zone, and they are more attentive. Elias didn't leave anything to chance. He was always changing things up to improve engagement.

He continued.

"I think it's important for you to contrast the pros and cons of the experience within an immersive medium versus the traditional medium as you pull together your proposals for next week.

"Today, we're going to focus on two things.

- Understanding innovation, particularly disruptive innovation
- Determining the critical questions for disruptive innovation and identifying opportunities within the Metaverse

"In the end, we hope to identify a few ideas that you might want to consider for your proposal next week.

"Now, some might consider this class on innovation somewhat superfluous and unnecessary. They may think, 'I understand innovation, I've witnessed Netflix and Uber take over industries. What else do I need to know?' Well, I'm hoping to show you that there are some very specific innovation questions and ideas that you should consider if you hope to build a globally disruptive metaverse company, so please bear with me.

"So, what is innovation?" he asked us.

Dania threw up her hand, and Elias immediately motioned to her.

"Innovation is doing something different, better, or unique. It uses creativity and a different lens to solve an old problem."

"Yes, that definitely covers most of it, Dania," said Elias. "Those things are all true, but let's generalize a bit more.

"I propose that innovation is a process of developing and implementing new ideas, methods, products, or services that improve upon an existing solution. Usually, there is something novel about the concept or idea that is central to the change.

"Is innovation just about technology?" he queried, waited for a moment, then continued. "No. Innovation can happen in many domains; business processes, how organizations are structured, social practices, or even how you manage your culinary lifestyle.

"The refrigerator, for example, changed how we kept our food cold but also the whole process of how we purchased food, cooked, and consumed it. Being able to store food for longer periods in our homes allowed us to maintain small inventories of available food, reducing the trips to the store and freeing up more time to cook and perform other activities. It also reduced food spoilage and allowed us to cook more creatively. If a critical ingredient could be refrigerated, it could be used frequently, adding taste to your meals and improving the overall quality of the food experience."

I was a bit of an innovation junkie myself and had read many of Clayton Christensen's books a few years ago. In fact, I shared some of his ideas with my teammates the previous month when we were brainstorming for our submission. This lecture, however, would dig deeper and fortify our understanding.

Elias continued, "Clayton Christensen was considered one of the foremost thinkers in the field of innovation, and he refers to two different types of innovation: sustaining innovation and disruptive innovation.

"Sustaining innovation focuses on making small improvements to existing products, services, or processes, enhancing their performance or efficiency without fundamentally changing their nature. Incremental innovation often involves refining or optimizing what already exists to create additional value.

"Disruptive innovation, on the other hand, refers to the introduction of new products, services, or business models that initially target overlooked or underserved market segments but eventually displace established market leaders as they improve and gain wider adoption."

"Can you give an example of an incremental innovation and a disruptive innovation?" asked Dania.

"Yes," said Elias. "I guess the simplest example is the mouse trap. An incremental or sustaining innovation would be the process of making the mouse trap more efficient, perhaps faster, or less prone to failure. A disruptive innovation would be a different way of catching mice, or better yet, a different approach to dealing with the problems that mice create. Perhaps the use of sonar could drive the mice away from your valuable items of clothing and rid the general environment of their presence. Same issue but a different way of solving the problem."

Dania pushed, "But what about a real product that we use every day?"

Elias countered, "Okay. If you would like an example with real products, I would say that Toyota's introduction of Hybrid engine technology in the early 2000s combining electrical and combustion engines was an incremental or sustaining improvement on the process of how a car worked. As such, many other car manufacturers followed the process, and the technology became a feature in many other vehicles as well.

"The car still operated in very much the same manner, albeit much more efficiently and less expensively, but it was an improvement on the existing process of generating energy for the drivetrain that would turn the wheels, which in turn would bring you to your desired destination. Similarly, I would argue that electric cars are also a sustaining innovation over traditional hybrid technology, eliminating the need for gas altogether but essentially providing transport in a very similar manner. As such, many companies are now adopting this approach to improve their vehicles, not just Tesla.

"I would, however, suggest that the use of analytics and data visualization on automobile dashboards was a disruptive innovation. This changed the nature of the driving experience by providing relevant information to the driver, like location maps, status indicators, entertainment systems, and a visualization of what was happening at any given time in the automobile. It also changed the process of navigating from a manual process of looking at paper maps and asking strangers for help to an automated set of instructions that directed you to your destination.

"While this technology was used by many cars in the early twenty-first century, it was further improved and perfected by smartphone applications like Google Maps that could connect to your automobile dashboard and sound system to provide more reliable information. This was another sustaining innovation over the less flexible, poorer-quality dashboard navigation systems.

"Before we go too far in our discussions, let me first summarize the difference between sustaining and disruptive innovations. Then for the remainder of the lecture, we will focus on disruptive innovation. Does anyone know why?"

I fielded that question. It was a no-brainer.

"Because if someone is going to give you five hundred million dollars, you sure as heck better disrupt something and change the world in a big way. Otherwise, what's the point?"

Elias smiled. "Well said. And now the summary.

"Characteristics of Sustaining Innovation:

- Focus on incremental improvements or enhancements to existing products, services, or processes without fundamentally altering their nature or market dynamics.
- Innovations aim to maintain or increase the performance, efficiency, or value of current offerings, catering to the needs and expectations of an established customer base.
- Do not disrupt existing markets or technologies but rather help companies maintain their competitive edge and market share.
- Incumbent firms are generally well-equipped to handle sustaining innovations as they align with existing business models, organizational structures, and

customer demands.

- Examples of sustaining innovations include regular software updates, smartphone iterations with improved features, or the development of more fuel-efficient engines for cars.

"Characteristics of Disruptive Innovation:

- These innovations often start with a smaller market share and appeal to a niche audience, but they eventually improve over time and gain wider adoption.
- As disruptive innovations mature, they have the potential to displace established market leaders, technologies, or business models, fundamentally transforming industries or creating entirely new ones.
- Usually pose a significant challenge to incumbent firms, as they often require a shift in mindset, organizational structure, or business strategy to adapt and compete effectively.
- Examples of disruptive innovations include digital photography, which disrupted the film-based photography industry, Uber, and streaming services like Netflix, which disrupted the traditional cable and DVD rental businesses.

"Disruptive innovations have the potential to transform markets and displace established players, whereas sustaining innovations focus on maintaining or improving existing offerings without fundamentally changing the market landscape.

"This image presents a simpler way to understand the differences.

Sustaining vs. Disruptive Innovation

"The two classic examples of disruptive innovation that most of us remember in the past twenty years are Uber and Netflix. In both cases, the early services were targeted at 'nonconsumption,' niche markets that were not users of comparable services.

"Uber initially targeted younger people who could not afford to take cabs but would be willing to pay a bit more than public transit. They were also more likely to use apps on their smartphones and were not as picky as wealthier businesspeople. As Uber effectively 'cut their teeth' on this market, it perfected and refined the services, so much so that it became a powerful service for the public, offering a lower cost, better information, and far better access to transportation services. In less than ten years, they obliterated the local cab industries, and had these taxi services not been supported and protected by city officials, they would likely not exist today.

"Similarly, early Netflix users were very cost conscious and preferred to use public mail to access movies, games, and TV shows. Then, as Netflix launched their streaming service in 2007, a vastly inferior offering in terms of selection and overall user experience to retail services like Blockbuster and cable television networks, they were considered a joke and not taken seriously. As they improved their streaming services, movie inventories, and overall user experience, they slowly built momentum that eventually killed both the video retailers and most cable TV networks. And yes, both exist today, but they are a fraction of what they once were. Today, streaming service providers like Netflix and Amazon have global reach and scale that no broadcasters, encumbered by local regulations in their respective countries, could compete with.

"In both cases, these were new markets that were unpredictable and not well understood. They were dramatically disrupted by game-changing technology (Uber app and IP Streaming) and new business models that dramatically reduced the costs of service.

"Now, as discussed earlier, we are going to focus on disruptive innovation opportunities. So, where would we start? Anyone?" Elias scanned the room.

"Determining what questions to ask?" I offered.

He nodded acknowledgment and began.

"**The Critical Questions**: For those who have read Christensen's work, you'll note that he provides a disruptive innovation framework but not a specific set of questions. So, based on his theories, I was able to identify three critical questions that one might ask when seeking disruptive innovation opportunities for an emerging start-up business.

1. What are the 'jobs to be done' that customers are trying to accomplish? By understanding the underlying needs and desires of customers, one can identify opportunities to create new products or services that better address those needs.

2. Are there non-consumers or over-served customers in the market? Targeting segments that are either not using existing solutions or are over-served by current offerings can be fertile ground for disruptive innovation, as these customers may be more willing to adopt new, potentially lower-performing solutions with lower prices.

3. Can we identify an emerging technology or business model that has the potential to disrupt existing markets? Disruptive innovations often start with lower performance compared to established products but improve over time. Identifying such technologies or business models early on can provide a competitive advantage.

"Now, I was thinking we might brainstorm one of the market segments of the Metaverse Challenge: Education, Entertainment, Commerce, Environment, or Social/ Community Building. Any preferences?"

"Why don't we start with Education?" I suggested. Now that RoMac was out, I had agreed to pick up his pitch proposal research for the education segment, so this would definitely help me.

"Okay," said Elias. "What are the 'jobs to be done' that consumers are trying to accomplish?" Elias scanned the class.

"People want to get an education so they can get a job or improve their current jobs," said the young lady in the front row.

"Agreed," said Elias. "And why can't they do this? What is their problem or challenge? Please, let's just free-flow the discussion. You don't need to raise your hand."

The group started to throw out ideas.

Frances, a mom with limited finances and kids still in school, took aim at the elephant in the room first.

"Every decent job these days seems to require an education that is very expensive, leaving young people, or their parents, with major student debt when they are done."

"Yeah, I'm still paying off debts from twenty years ago," said Dania, "and most of the kids today will likely never be able to fully repay their debts. They'll be in lender prison forever."

The younger students in the front nodded and concurred completely, with one surfer-looking fellow adding, "I know I'll never own a house now, but I'd like to at least be free of debt at some point."

"For me, it's the time taken from our jobs. It's all very time-consuming and almost impossible to combine with a job, especially for those a bit older with family responsibilities," added Jag.

"And getting there is a total pain. I took a course last year, and I think I spent more time commuting than learning," added Dania.

"My issue is the content," I said. "Most of what I see today are bad slideshows, with way too many words on a page, just speaker points for profs, and lots of web videos. There is very little money invested in the content experience."

Another young student from the front looked at Elias and exclaimed. "Now, this does not include you, sir, but there are not that many good teachers left to inspire us and create memorable lessons."

Elias humbly acknowledged with a half-smile.

"Well, what about online degrees?" asked Elias. "They've become popular."

"Online courses are okay, but people are sick of video

chats. The experience is boring and doesn't allow you to really connect with people," said Jag.

"Yeah, and everyone has their camera off. It just seems like they're busy doing something else. No one is engaged," echoed the surfer dude.

Elias then summarized the feedback from the first question.

"So, people want to get an education and improve their jobs, but there are many problems with the process.

- Too expensive
- Too time-consuming both for the commute and the content
- Bad teachers
- Low engagement
- Boring, uninspiring content

"Did I capture the key points?" asked Elias.

The crowd nodded in agreement.

"Okay, so let's move to the second question. Are there non-consumers or over-served customers in the market?" asked Elias.

"Absolutely," said Jag. "I have several relatives that want to go back to school but can't afford to. They are immigrants, and some of them are working two jobs just to live."

"My brother is in his last year of high school, and while considering going to university, he's worried about leaving school with hundreds of thousands of dollars in student loans, so he may not go. And he's super smart. Unfortunately, my parents don't have all that money, and even with some scholarship and tuition support, he still needs to pay for living for several years," said the student in the second row.

"Yeah, my mom wants to go back to school to get her degree because if she does, she can get promoted and make more money, but she just can't afford to," added another student.

"My daughter actually dropped out of college this year because she claimed, 'it sucked,' and she may be right. This was a reputable university, and we were paying a lot of money, too," said Frances, then added, "Interestingly, her friend was studying business but felt that many of the courses were just filler, and she could probably do all the relevant stuff in half the time. She's still there but not very happy about needing four years to get a degree that could be done in two."

"Okay," said Elias, "we can answer our second question. While these situations are anecdotal and would require much more research, many of these examples are clearly a case of affordability. Now, while we don't have specific numbers, a recent report by the Institute for Higher Education Policy in the United States found that more than seventy percent of survey respondents believed they would have a better chance of attending college if they had more financial resources. That's a pretty telling statistic.

"I also thought the example about Frances's daughter's friend expressing that much of her program was filler was interesting. That suggests that there was fat in the process, and she is being over-served."

Elias paused for a moment and paced across the front of the room before he began.

"Now, question three. Can we identify an emerging technology or business model that has the potential to disrupt existing markets?

"That one is a bit of a no-brainer for all of us because the mere existence of the Metaverse Challenge strongly posits that Virtual Reality and the Metaverse are that disruptive technology. But more specifically, what kinds of things can a VR-based Education Metaverse do to address the challenges of affordability, accessibility, quality, and student engagement?"

"You could create a VR-based school that people could attend from a headset or even their desktop computer and make it available to anyone around the world," suggested Dania. "That would increase the scale and make it much less expensive."

"Absolutely," agreed Elias.

"We could gamify the whole experience allowing students to level up at their own pace and complete their degree in two years, could we not?" I inquired.

"I don't see why not," affirmed Elias.

Frances was also getting into it, "If you gamify the course, then perhaps you could create more asynchronous content, like online courses do, and that would mean you could use fewer teachers, only the best ones," she said.

"What excites me about this whole process is what we could do with the content experience," I added. "I love the AI Superheroes. I'll never forget those guys. And the ability to change environments to suit the course content and conjure visual FXs at will to illustrate an idea or concept, well, that's game-changing stuff. It takes the experience to a whole new level."

Elias smiled widely and acknowledged with a nod. He was grateful that we'd noticed and appreciated his teaching methods. I think I'd learned as much from his pedagogical approach as from the whole technology piece.

Elias concluded, "I'm hoping you all have what you need to move forward and address the submission next week. You have a good understanding of the VR-based Metaverse, the technology that makes it all work, and the disruptive innovation process.

"While we addressed only one example, if you apply those three questions and take the time to research the challenges within those domains, I'm sure you'll find many opportunities. Now, it is your job to apply all that you have learned. I wish you all the best."

Without a moment's hesitation, the class rose and offered Elias a standing ovation that went on for over a minute. He graciously accepted, offered a nod, and left the room.

References

Page 39

- Heilig, Morton L. "Sensorama simulator." *US PAT. 3,050,870* (1962).

Page 55

- Whissel, K. (2016). Parallax effects: Epistemology, affect and digital 3D cinema. Journal of Visual Culture, 15(2), 233-249.

Page 62

- Steffen, J. H., Gaskin, J. E., Meservy, T. O., Jenkins, J. L., & Wolman, I. (2019). Framework of affordances for virtual reality and augmented reality. *Journal of Management Information Systems*, *36*(3), 683-729.

- Gibson, James J. «The theory of affordances.» Hilldale, USA 1.2 (1977): 67-82.

Page 65

- Yee, N., & Bailenson, J. (2007). The Proteus effect: The effect of transformed self-representation on behavior. *Human communication research*, *33*(3), 271-290.

- Banakou, D., Kishore, S., & Slater, M. (2018). Virtually being Einstein results in an improvement in cognitive task performance and a decrease in age bias. *Frontiers in psychology*, *9*, 917.

Page 66

- Hawes, D., & Arya, A. (2021, March). VR-based student priming to reduce anxiety and increase cognitive bandwidth. In *2021 IEEE Virtual Reality and 3D User Interfaces (VR)* (pp. 245-254). IEEE.

- Banakou, D., Hanumanthu, P. D., & Slater, M. (2016). Virtual embodiment of white people in a black virtual body leads to a sustained reduction in their implicit racial bias. *Frontiers in human neuroscience*, 601.

- Banakou, D., Beacco, A., Neyret, S., Blasco-Oliver, M., Seinfeld, S., & Slater, M. (2020). Virtual body ownership and its consequences for implicit racial bias are dependent on social context. *Royal Society open science*, 7(12), 201848.

- Xu, K., Nosek, B., & Greenwald, A. (2014). Psychology data from the race implicit association test on the project implicit demo website. *Journal of open psychology data*, 2(1).

- Zajonc, Robert B. "Attitudinal effects of mere exposure." *Journal of personality and social psychology* 9.2p2 (1968): 1.

Page 73

- Cline, E. (2011). *Ready player one*. Ballantine Books.

Page 76

- Kurzweil, R. (2014). *The singularity is near* (pp. 393-406). Palgrave Macmillan UK.

Page 80

- Förster, J., Liberman, N., & Friedman, R. S. (2007). Seven principles of goal activation: A systematic approach to distinguishing goal priming from priming of non-goal constructs. *Personality and social psychology review, 11*(3), 211-233.

Page 82

- Kahneman, Daniel. Thinking, Fast and Slow. New York: Farrar, Straus and Giroux, 2011

- Bargh, John A., Mark Chen, and Lara Burrows. "Automaticity of social behavior: Direct effects of trait construct and stereotype activation on action." *Journal of personality and social psychology* 71.2 (1996): 230.

Page 83

- Mussweiler, T. (2006). Doing is for thinking! Stereotype activation by stereotypic movements. *Psychological Science, 17*(1), 17-21.

- Strack, Fritz, Leonard L. Martin, and Sabine Stepper. "Inhibiting and facilitating conditions of the human smile: a nonobtrusive test of the facial feedback hypothesis." *Journal of personality and social psychology* 54.5 (1988): 768.

Page 84

- North, Adrian C., David J. Hargreaves, and

Jennifer McKendrick. "The influence of in-store music on wine selections." *Journal of Applied psychology* 84.2 (1999): 271.

Page 85

- Capaldi, Colin A., Raelyne L. Dopko, and John M. Zelenski. "The relationship between nature connectedness and happiness: A meta-analysis." *Frontiers in psychology* (2014): 976.

- Ulrich, Roger S. "View through a window may influence recovery from surgery." *science* 224.4647 (1984): 420-421.

- Isen, Alice M., Kimberly A. Daubman, and Gary P. Nowicki. "Positive affect facilitates creative problem solving." *Journal of personality and social psychology* 52.6 (1987): 1122.

Page 86

- Bhagwatwar, A., Massey, A., & Dennis, A. R. (2013, January). Creative virtual environments: Effect of supraliminal priming on team brainstorming. In *2013 46th Hawaii international conference on system sciences* (pp. 215-224). IEEE.

- Hawes, D., & Arya, A. (2021, March). VR-based student priming to reduce anxiety and increase cognitive bandwidth. In *2021 IEEE Virtual Reality and 3D User Interfaces (VR)* (pp. 245-254). IEEE.

Page 88

- Lave, J., & Wenger, E. (1991). *Situated learning: Legitimate peripheral participation.* Cambridge university press.

- Hawes, D., & Arya, A. (2022, May). Comparing Student-Based Context Priming in Immersive and Desktop Virtual Reality Environments to Increase Academic Performance. In *2022 8th International Conference of the Immersive Learning Research Network (iLRN)* (pp. 1-7). IEEE.

Page 90

- Blair, I. V. (2002a). The Malleability of Automatic Stereotypes and Prejudice. *Personality and Social Psychology Review, 6*(3), 242–261.

- Dijksterhuis, A., & Van Knippenberg, A. (1998). The relation between perception and behavior, or how to win a game of trivial pursuit. *Journal of personality and social psychology, 74*(4), 865.

- Régner*, Isabelle, Jennifer R. Steele**, and Pascal Huguet*. "Stereotype threat in children: Past and present." *Revue internationale de psychologie sociale* 27.3 (2014): 5-12.

- Rudman, L. A., Ashmore, R. D., & Gary, M. L. (2001a). "Unlearning" automatic biases: The malleability of implicit prejudice and stereotypes. *Journal of Personality and Social Psychology, 81*(5), 856–868.

- Sassenberg, K., & Moskowitz, G. B. (2005a). Don't stereotype, think different! Overcoming automatic stereotype activation by mindset priming. *Journal of Experimental Social Psychology, 41*(5), 506–514.

- Steele, C. M., & Aronson, J. (1995). Stereotype threat and the intellectual test performance of African Americans. *Journal of personality and social psychology*, 69(5), 797.

Page 93

- Stephenson, N. (2003). *Snow crash: A novel.* Spectra.

Page 95

- Gibson, W. y IP address 192.168. 10.4 on 2023/02/21. Editorial Board, 19.

Page 112

- Kim, Y., Baylor, A. L., & PALS Group. (2006). Pedagogical agents as learning companions: The role of agent competency and type of interaction. *Educational technology research and development*, *54*, 223-243.

Page 134

- Christensen, C. M. (2013). *The innovator's dilemma: when new technologies cause great firms to fail.* Harvard Business Review Press.

Page 217

- Kurzweil, R. (2014). *The singularity is near* (pp. 393-406). Palgrave Macmillan UK.

Page 219

- Christensen, C. M. (2013). *The innovator's dilemma: when new technologies cause great firms to fail*. Harvard Business Review Press.

Page 221

- Oppenheimer, D. M. (2008). The secret life of fluency. *Trends in cognitive sciences*, *12*(6), 237-241.

- Alter, A. L., & Oppenheimer, D. M. (2009). Uniting the tribes of fluency to form a metacognitive nation. *Personality and social psychology review*, *13*(3), 219-235.

- Hawes, D., & Arya, A. (2022, May). VR-based Context Priming to Increase Student Engagement and Academic Performance. In *2022 8th International Conference of the Immersive Learning Research Network (iLRN)* (pp. 1-8). IEEE.

Page 226

- Boel, C., Rotsaert, T., Valcke, M., Rosseel, Y., Struyf, D., & Schellens, T. (2023). Are teachers ready to immerse? Acceptance of mobile immersive virtual reality in secondary education teachers. *Research in Learning Technology*, *31*.

Page 287

- Christensen, C., Raynor, M. E., & McDonald, R. (2013). *Disruptive innovation*. Brighton, MA, USA: Harvard Business Review.

Glossary of Acronyms

- 2D – Two Dimensional
- 3D – Three Dimensional
- 5K – Resolution of five thousand pixels or 5120x1440
- AI – Artificial Intelligence
- APK – Android Package
- AR – Augmented Reality
- AWS – Amazon Web Services
- BDMC – Billion Dollar Metaverse Challenge
- BGP – Border Gateway Protocol
- CDMA – Code Division Multiple Access
- CDN – Content Delivery Network
- ChatGPT – Chat Generative Pre-Training Transformer
- CPU – Central Processing Unit
- CV – Computer Vision
- CVG – Casual Video Games
- DVR – Desktop Virtual Reality
- EPROM – Erasable Programmable Read Only Memory
- FDMA – Frequency Division Multiple Access
- FoV – Field of View
- G-Force – Gravitational Force
- GAN – Generative Adversarial Network
- Ghz – Gigahertz
- GPU – Graphics Processing Unit
- GTX video card – Nvidia product (Giga Texel eXtreme)
- HMD – Head Mounted Device
- IIOT – Industrial Internet of Things

- IoT – Internet of Things
- IP – Internet Protocol
- IVA – Intelligent Virtual Agent
- IVR – Immersive Virtual Reality
- JV – Just Virtual
- JVIF – Just Virtual Innovation Fund
- Koyaboki – Learned Friend in African Hausa Language
- LTE – Long Term Evolution
- M1 – Metaversity One
- Massive MIMO – Massive Multiple Input Multiple Output
- MIMO – Multiple Input Multiple Output
- MIT – Massachusetts Institute of Technology
- ML – Machine Learning
- MR – Mixed Reality
- NFT – Non Fungible Token
- NIVR – Non-immersive Virtual Reality
- NLP – Natural Language Processing
- NPC – Non Player Character
- P = D + I + C + E – Presence = Design + Immersive + Capability + Experience
- PAL – Pedagogical Agent of Learning
- PG – Procedural Generation
- RTX video card – Nvidia product (Ray Tracing Texel eXtreme)
- SC-FDMA – Single Carrier Frequency Division Multiple Access
- SFX – Special Effects
- STEM – Science Technology Engineering Math

- STEAM – Science Technology Engineering Arts Math
- TCP/IP – Transmission Control Protocol/Internet Protocol
- TNN – Technology News Network
- UE – Unreal Engine
- UI – User Interface
- UX – User Experience
- UX/UI – User Experience/User Interface
- V-Commerce – Virtual Commerce
- VAE – Variational Autoencoder
- VR – Virtual Reality
- VRDS – Virtual Reality Digital Storytelling
- VREP – Virtual Reality Exposure Therapy
- VRET – Virtual Reality Experience Priming
- WiFi – Wireless Fidelity
- www.campusvr.net – Virtual University Campus Software
- XR – eXtended Reality

<h1 style="text-align:center">Glossary of Terms</h1>

Affordance - The qualities or properties of an object that determine how it could possibly be used. In design, it's how a user knows to interact with an interface.

Amazon Web Services (AWS) - AWS is Amazon's extensive cloud platform offering a suite of services ranging from computing power, database storage, content delivery, and others. It allows businesses to scale and grow by providing the resources needed to design sophisticated applications with increased flexibility, scalability, and reliability.

Artificial Intelligence (AI) - AI refers to computer systems capable of mimicking human intelligence processes, such as learning, problem-solving, and decision-making. These systems can swiftly process vast amounts of data, improving automation, data analysis, and decision-making. The applications of AI span various sectors like healthcare, where it's used for diagnosis predictions, to entertainment, where it can recommend content based on user preferences.

Augmented Reality (AR) - AR is a technology that layers digital enhancements atop the real world, making them interactively real-time. Through devices like AR glasses or smartphones, users can see and sometimes interact with digital overlays. Industries like gaming benefit from AR by providing gamers with real-world interaction, while retail businesses can offer virtual try-ons for customers.

Authentication - The process of verifying the identity of a person or device.

Avatar - A digital representation of a user in a virtual or online environment. It can range from simple text-based icons to three-dimensional, animated characters.

Billion Dollar Metaverse Challenge (BDMC) - The BDMC is a fictional contest within the Just Virtual narrative, to search for, and fund, the top three metaverse business ideas with one billion dollars over a five year period.

Biometrics - Biological measurements or characteristics that can be used for identification, like fingerprints or retina scans.

Blockchain - A system of recording information in a way that makes it difficult or impossible to change, cheat, or hack, most recognized for supporting cryptocurrencies.

Border Gateway Protocol (BGP) - BGP is a standardized gateway protocol that directs packets of data across the internet. By determining the optimal route for each data packet, based on the shortest path, BGP ensures the smooth functioning of the internet, managing how packets are routed across various autonomous systems.

Casual Video Games (CVG) - CVGs are designed for a general audience rather than hardcore gamers. These games are characterized by simple rules, short sessions, and require less commitment compared to more complex video games. Popular on mobile platforms and social networking sites, they're accessible and appeal to diverse age groups.

Central Processing Unit (CPU) - The CPU is the primary component of a computer that performs most processing. It reads and executes software instructions, handles data storage and retrieval, ensuring that tasks occur in order and that operations proceed smoothly. CPUs are integral to tasks from basic word processing to complex scientific simulations.

Chat Generative Pre-Training Transformer (ChatGPT) - ChatGPT is an advanced conversational AI model developed by OpenAI. It's designed for natural, human-like interactions across various topics. Drawing from vast amounts of text data, it can generate narratives, answer questions, and even simulate human-like conversations. ChatGPT doesn't "understand" content in the same way humans do. The responses are based on patterns in data it was trained on. If the training data contains biases, the model can inadvertently reproduce or amplify those biases. It can also produce incorrect answers, especially when presented with unfamiliar or misleading input.

Code Division Multiple Access (CDMA) - CDMA is a digital cellular standard that uses spread-spectrum technology. This means multiple calls can be transmitted simultaneously on the same frequency band. Its unique coding for each call enhances privacy and reduces interference, making communications more efficient.

Computer Vision (CV) - Computer Vision involves enabling machines to interpret and make decisions based on visual data, much like humans interpret what they see. It's a field within AI and has applications ranging from facial recognition systems to autonomous vehicles. By processing and analyzing images and videos, CV systems can recognize patterns, detect objects, and even predict behaviors.

Content Delivery Network (CDN) - A CDN is a system of distributed servers that work together to deliver web content to users based on their geographic locations. CDNs stores cached versions of static content in multiple locations. When a user requests this content, it is served from the nearest server, reducing the time it takes to fetch data and significantly reducing the amount of data an origin server must provide, cutting bandwidth costs. This localization reduces latency, webpage load times, improves website performance, and can handle large spikes in web traffic.

Cryptocurrency - A digital or virtual form of currency secured by cryptography, making it nearly impossible to counterfeit.

Desktop Virtual Reality (DVR) - DVR refers to virtual reality experiences that are delivered through desktop setups, usually without the immersion of a head-mounted display. Users interact with the 3D virtual environment using traditional input devices like mouse and keyboard, offering a less immersive experience than full-scale VR but more accessible.

Disruptive Innovation - A breakthrough product or service that creates a new market and value network, disrupting existing markets and displacing established leaders.

Edge Computing - A distributed computing paradigm that brings computation and data storage closer to data sources, like IoT devices, reducing latency.

Embodiment - The sense of having and being in a body. In virtual environments, it refers to feeling as if a virtual body is one's own.

Erasable Programmable Read Only Memory (EPROM) - EPROM is a type of memory chip that can be reprogrammed after being erased by exposure to ultraviolet light. Its significance lies in its non-volatility; the data remains even when power is switched off. EPROM chips were used widely in the past for firmware updates before being replaced by EEPROMs which can be electrically erased.

eXtended Reality (XR) - XR is an umbrella term encapsulating AR, VR, MR, and any future reality technologies. It merges the physical and virtual worlds to create a fully immersive experience where physical and digital objects co-exist and interact in real-time.

Field of View (FoV) - In graphics and imaging, FoV indicates the extent of the observable environment or visual field that you can see without moving your head. In virtual reality, FoV is critical as it determines how much of the virtual environment the user can see. A broader FoV contributes to a more immersive experience. When we say the Oculus Quest 2 has an FoV of 90 to 100 degrees, it refers to the angular extent of the virtual world that the user can see when wearing the headset. This angle reflects how much of their vision the VR environment occupies.

Five K Resolution (5K) - Resolution of five thousand pixels or 5120x1440: A display resolution that measures approximately

5120 pixels horizontally and 1440 pixels vertically, resulting in a total of over 7.3 million pixels. It offers a higher level of detail and clarity than traditional HD resolutions. This specification is common in high-end monitors and screens, catering to professionals in video editing, photography, and graphic design for its enhanced clarity and detail.

Frequency Division Multiple Access (FDMA) - A method of sharing a broadcasting channel through dividing it into multiple distinct frequency bands.

Generative Adversarial Network (GAN) - GANs are a class of machine learning systems where two neural networks, the generator and discriminator, compete in a game-like setting. They're used in generating new data that can be almost indistinguishable from genuine data, like creating lifelike images from random noise.

Goldilocks Zone - Refers to the habitable zone around a star where conditions might be just right for life as we know it.

Graphics Processing Unit (GPU) - A GPU is a specialized electronic circuit designed to accelerate image rendering to output on a display. It manages complex computations faster than CPUs for tasks like 3D graphics rendering, making them essential for gaming, design, and more recently, certain AI operations.

Gravitational Force (G-Force) - A measurement of acceleration felt as weight, typically used to describe the force exerted on a body due to the effect of gravity or sudden acceleration/deceleration.

Gustatory - The gustatory system functions through taste buds (receptor cells) located primarily on the tongue. These receptor cells are sensitive to the basic taste modalities: sweet, salty, sour, bitter, and umami (a savory taste). With advancements in technology, there are efforts to replicate or stimulate the gustatory sensations in virtual reality or digital environments, though it remains a challenging frontier.

Haptics - The science of touch sensation in interfaces. In digital technology, it's about providing tactile feedback to users, often via vibrations or force feedback.

Head Mounted Device (HMD) - HMD is a display device worn on the head or as part of a helmet that has a small screen in front of one or both eyes. It's used in VR to provide users with immersive visual experiences and in AR to overlay digital content on the real world.

Heads Up Display (HUD) - An interface displaying key information in a user's line of sight, usually in games or AR applications, without the need to look away.

Holographic - Relating to holograms, three-dimensional images formed by the interference of light beams.

Immersion - The feeling of being completely engrossed or absorbed into a particular environment, especially in reference to digital or virtual spaces.

Immersive Virtual Reality (IVR) - A VR environment that seeks to fully immerse the user, making them feel as though they are truly "inside" the digital space.

Industrial Internet of Things (IIOT) - IIOT, a subset of IoT, refers to interconnected sensors, instruments, and other devices networked with computers in the industrial sector. It includes technologies for smart manufacturing and smart grids, optimizing operations, reducing costs, and improving worker safety.

Intelligent Virtual Agent (IVA) - Digital representatives that interact with users, often employing AI to simulate conversation or tasks.

Interactivity - The ability of a system to interact with its user or with other systems.

Internet of Things (IoT) - IoT encompasses a network of physical devices embedded with sensors and software, interconnected through the Internet Protocol. These devices, ranging from home appliances to vehicles, can collect and exchange data, making our environments smarter and more responsive.

Internet Protocol (IP) - IP is a set of rules governing the format of data sent over the internet or local networks. Every device on a network has an IP address, enabling data packets to be routed and delivered to their intended destinations.

Latency - The delay or time taken for data to travel from its source to its destination. In virtual environments, it refers to the delay between an action (like moving a joystick) and the response (seeing movement on screen).

LIDAR - A method of measuring distances by illuminating a target with laser light and measuring the reflection, commonly used in autonomous vehicles.

Long Term Evolution (LTE) - LTE is a standard for wireless broadband communication, commonly associated with mobile devices and data terminals. It provides faster data rates and reduced latency compared to older generations, improving mobile internet access quality.

Machine Learning (ML) - ML is a subset of AI, involves algorithms allowing computers to learn from and make decisions based on data. Rather than being explicitly programmed to perform a task, the machine learns from patterns in the data, improving over time as it's exposed to more data.

Massive Multiple Input Multiple Output (Massive MIMO) - Massive MIMO is an advanced wireless technology that uses many antennas at a base station to serve many users simultaneously, improving data transmission efficiency and reliability. By doing so, it boosts the capacity of a wireless connection without requiring more spectrum.

Metaverse - A collection of themed and interconnected virtual experiences that may use virtual reality, augmented reality, or mixed reality, underpinned, and connected via the Internet.

Mixed Reality (MR) - MR blends real-world and digital elements. Unlike VR, which immerses the user completely in a virtual environment, or AR, which overlays digital elements on the real world, MR lets digital and physical objects co-exist and interact in real-time.

Multiple Input Multiple Output (MIMO) - MIMO technology uses multiple antennas at both the transmitter and receiver ends. By exploiting the spatial domain, MIMO systems improve link reliability and increase communication speeds, vital for modern high-speed systems like 5G.

Natural Language Processing (NLP) - A branch of AI, NLP enables machines to understand, interpret, and generate human language. This technology underpins chatbots, machine translation, and voice recognition systems, bridging the gap between human communication and computer understanding.

Non-Fungible Token (NFT) - NFTs are unique digital tokens representing ownership of a specific item or piece of content on the blockchain. Unlike cryptocurrencies such as Bitcoin, where each token is identical (or fungible), each NFT has distinct information or attributes that make it unique.

Non-immersive Virtual Reality (NIVR) - NIVR offers a computer-generated environment that can be explored and interacted with by a person but doesn't fully immerse the user. It's experienced through a desktop monitor rather than immersive equipment like a VR headset.

Non-Player Character (NPC) - In gaming, an NPC is any character that's not controlled by a human player. NPCs can be allies, bystanders, or adversaries, providing depth and interactivity to the game's narrative.

Olfactory - The intricate sensory system responsible for detecting and identifying odors. Located within the nasal cavity, these specialized receptor neurons recognize specific odor molecules inhaled from the environment and can evoke powerful memories or feelings. There have been endeavors, albeit unsuccessful, to integrate the sense of smell into virtual and augmented reality environments with the goal of enhancing realism and presence.

Parallax - The apparent change in position of an object when viewed from different angles. Used in graphics to give depth cues.

Pedagogical Agent of Learning (PAL) - Animated agents in learning environments designed to facilitate and guide learners through content.

Presence - The psychological feeling or sense that one is truly "inside" a virtual environment. It's the illusion that the virtual experience is real, often sought after in VR development.

Presence = Design + Immersive + Capability + Experience (P = D + I + C + E) - This formula captures the elements contributing to a person's sense of presence in a virtual environment. Each component - design, immersion, capability, and experience - plays a role in how "real" or "present" someone feels within a virtual space.

Priming - A psychological technique wherein exposure to one stimulus influences a response to a subsequent stimulus, without conscious guidance.

Procedural Generation (PG) - In gaming and graphics, PG refers to content generated algorithmically rather than manually. This allows for vast, varied, and unpredictable game environments. Games like "Minecraft" use PG to create unique terrains and worlds.

Proprioception - The body's ability to sense its position, motion, and equilibrium. In VR, technologies aim to simulate this to enhance immersion.

Provenance - The origin or source of something. In blockchain, it's often used to track the history or origin of an item transparently.

Science, Technology, Engineering, Arts, Mathematics (STEAM) - STEAM is an educational approach that goes beyond STEM (Science, Technology, Engineering, and Mathematics) by integrating the Arts. The philosophy behind STEAM recognizes that creativity and technical knowledge aren't separate realms but intersecting domains that enhance each other. This comprehensive framework emphasizes the need for students to be both creative designers and logical problem solvers, preparing them for a world where disciplines continuously overlap.

Science, Technology, Engineering, Math (STEM) – STEM is an interdisciplinary educational approach that integrates four primary disciplines: Science, Technology, Engineering, and Mathematics. STEM emphasizes real-world applications and hands-on experiences to foster problem-solving, critical thinking, and collaboration skills. Beyond academic pursuits, STEM also seeks to inspire creativity and cultivate curiosity, preparing students for a rapidly evolving world.

Single Carrier Frequency Division Multiple Access (SC-FDMA) - A digital modulation scheme used in wireless communications, notable for its power efficiency.

Special Effects (SFX) - Artificially created or enhanced sounds or visuals used to create an illusion or enhance storytelling in movies, TV, or other media.

Stereoscopic - A technique for creating the illusion of depth in an image or set of images, often used in VR or 3D movies.

Sustaining Innovation - Innovations that help established companies improve existing products and operations to better serve their current customers.

Three Dimensional (3D) - Pertains to images or designs that incorporate three dimensions: width, height, and depth. This depth allows for a more realistic representation, giving viewers or users a sense of volume and spatial presence. 3D graphics are commonly found in modern video games, movies, and computer-aided design (CAD) software.

Transmission Control Protocol/Internet Protocol (TCP/IP) - TCP/IP is a suite of communication protocols used to interconnect network devices on the internet. TCP ensures data integrity while IP handles addressing and routing, ensuring that data packets are sent and received accurately.

Two Dimensional (2D) - Refers to graphics or designs that have two dimensions: width and height. These are flat images that lack depth, commonly seen in traditional drawings, photographs, and some older video games. Though they represent objects or scenes, they don't give the illusion of depth or volume like their 3D counterparts.

Unreal Engine (UE) - UE is a powerful game engine developed by Epic Games. Apart from video games, it's used in simulations, architectural visualization, and film production, thanks to its high-fidelity graphics and physics simulations.

User Experience (UX) - UX pertains to the overall feeling and experience a user has when using a product or system. It considers the product's usability, accessibility, and the pleasure users will get out of interacting with it.

User Interface (UI) - UI is the space where interactions between humans and machines occur. Its goal is effective operation and control of the machine from the user's end while providing feedback that aids the operators' decision-making.

Variational Autoencoder (VAE) - A sophisticated AI model, primarily used in the realm of deep learning. VAEs belong to a class of generative models that can produce new data that closely resembles the input data they've been trained on. The unique aspect of a VAE is its ability to not just generate data, but to also encode and decode data in a structured manner. The "variational" part comes from the use of variational inference techniques, which enable the model to make probabilistic decisions during the encoding process, making it versatile and powerful.

Vestibular - Relating to the inner ear system responsible for balance and spatial orientation. The vestibular system detects changes in motion and head position, helping us maintain our equilibrium. In virtual reality and other digital experiences, mismatches between what we see (visual input) and what the vestibular system detects can lead to motion sickness. Addressing this synchronization is crucial for creating comfortable VR experiences.

Virtual Commerce (V-Commerce) - The buying and selling of goods and services using virtual reality platforms or environments.

Virtual Reality (VR) - VR is a computer-generated simulation of a three-dimensional (3D) environment using various technologies (e.g., VR headsets or multi-projected setups) to create a user experience that feels real. The goal of a VR experience is to make is feel so real that your brain interprets the virtual reality as your current reality and will treat all environment cues as if they are real. Interactions in these environments can feel as real as those in the physical world, used in gaming, training, and therapeutic applications.

Virtual Reality Digital Storytelling (VRDS) - The practice of using virtual reality to convey narratives or stories, offering a more immersive experience for the viewer.

Virtual Reality Experience Priming (VRET) - Preparing an individual for a real-life event by simulating experiences in virtual reality.

Virtual Reality Exposure Therapy (VREP) - A therapeutic technique using VR to expose patients to sources of distress or trauma in a controlled environment.

Wireless Fidelity (Wi-Fi) - Wi-Fi is a wireless networking technology that uses radio waves to provide high-speed internet connections. It allows electronic devices to exchange data or connect to the internet without the need for wired connections.

Index

Symbols

A

B

C

Field of View (FoV) 30, 56
FoV 30, 31, 34, 56, 57, 302
Framework 7, 17, 288
French 84

G

German 83, 84
German Bierkeller music 84
G-forces 75
Google 16, 68, 246, 248, 285
GPU 33, 236, 302
Gustatory 29, 38, 39, 40

H

Haptic 36, 240
Hardware 56, 191
Harry Potter 69, 72
Healthcare 262
Health Monitoring 261
HMD 61, 234, 236, 238, 240, 245, 302
Holographic 113, 115, 117

I

Identity Verification 260
IIoT 262
immersion 29, 34, 39, 40, 41, 42, 51, 54, 61, 63, 64, 66, 70, 74, 93, 193, 196, 234, 235, 238, 249, 271
Immersive Interaction 260
implicit racial bias 65, 296
innovation 7, 15, 20, 21, 75, 95, 103, 155, 181, 199, 202, 209, 220, 221, 239, 262, 279, 281, 282, 283, 284, 285, 287, 288, 289, 294, 301
Interactivity 40, 67, 92
Interaural 36
Internet 13, 21, 73, 94, 97, 102, 146, 170, 220, 224, 225, 226, 227, 228, 229, 230, 231, 232, 233, 246, 247, 249, 258, 259, 260, 262, 302, 303, 304
Internet of Things 21, 73, 249, 258, 260, 262, 302, 303
Interoperability 258
IoT 21, 73, 180, 249, 258, 259, 260, 261, 262, 303
IP 94, 197, 228, 229, 230, 232, 233, 288, 300, 303, 304
IVR 61, 234, 303

J

JV 3, 154, 162, 163, 180, 182, 183, 185, 303

About the Author

Dan is a writer, producer, academic researcher, and technology entrepreneur. His portfolio encompasses an array of creative and technical works: he has developed and produced twelve television series, nine films, over fifty games, and pioneered applications in Artificial Intelligence and Virtual Reality. Notably, he co-created "Chilly Beach," making waves as one of North America's first web properties to transition to network TV (CBC 2003). He is currently CEO and Founder of Just Virtual (justvirtual.com) a technology design studio that creates AI, VR, and Metaverse applications for education and V-commerce businesses. Dan has previously founded and sold two Internet companies.

Dan's work marries the worlds of technology, design, and academic research. As an adjunct research professor in the School of Information Technology at Carleton University, he explores the use of advanced technologies to optimize perspective change, cognition, and help reduce cultural biases within immersive learning environments. His scholarly contributions include several IEEE publications focused on cognitive priming effects within virtual reality. Dan also teaches courses related to game design, digital storytelling, and managing creative companies at Carleton and Toronto Metropolitan University and has been delivering university courses in fully immersive VR since 2021.

He holds a Bachelor of Management Science and Honours, Management and Information Systems (MIS) from the University of Ottawa, Master of Digital Experience Innovation from the University of Waterloo, and Ph.D. in Information Technology from Carleton University.

This book brings together his passion for technology innovation, learning, and digital storytelling. You can find out more about the topic from his weekly metaverse podcast at justvirtual.com.

Dan's IMDB https://www.imdb.com/name/nm1457516/